A pictorial guide to
HOME IMPROVEMENTS

AURA BOOKS

Editor: Mary Lambert
Designer: Chris Walker

This edition published by
Aura Book Distribution Limited
2 Derby Road
Greenford, Middlesex

Produced by
Marshall Cavendish Books Limited
58 Old Compton Street
London W1V 5PA

ISBN 0 86307 268 2

Printed and bound by New Interlitho SpA, Italy

Introduction

More and more people today are extending and improving their own homes, either through necessity or for pleasure. Now you too can enhance your property while adding to its value with *A Pictorial Guide to Home Improvements*. And it needn't cost the earth; we suggest hundreds of exciting but economical ways to make your home more beautiful.

Give your living room a completely fresh appearance with an exciting colour scheme and matching accessories. We show you how to make the most of your creative skills too, by building your own furniture; from an elegant sideboard, to a child's rocking chair. Make your bedroom a stylish place to relax, with a cosy studio bed or simple sofa, and complementary cushions and rugs. A neglected bathroom can easily be made luxurious by a few simple additions. *A Pictorial Guide to Home Improvements* even makes redesigning your kitchen uncomplicated and enjoyable, from drawing the plans, right through to the finish.

And don't stop there — transform your garden too. A play area, a patio or a garden pond, all these projects are easy and straightforward. If you need more space, there's no need to move house, as we show you the safe way to extend your property by building additional rooms, or converting the loft and other under-used areas. Each project is illustrated with full colour photographs and comprehensive step-by-step diagrams, so with a little imagination, and plenty of enthusiasm, you can have the house and garden of your dreams.

Contents

Planning your home interior

Bathrooms and kitchens

Children's rooms and play areas

Making your own furniture

Conversions and extensions

Improving your garden

Index

PLANNING YOUR HOME INTERIOR

Basic interior design

Pulling together all the various elements in a decorative scheme is not difficult to accomplish. And using continuity of pattern and colour to co-ordinate your entire home can achieve some really effective results

We all want our homes to be attractive, pleasant places to be in and at the same time reflective of our personality. And yet it is obviously clear that while some homes are instantly welcoming and full of atmosphere, others seem cold and friendless.

If you really think about it and analyse the rooms that you feel happiest in, you will probably find that they all have one thing in common—continuity and a sense of harmony. This is not difficult or expensive to achieve and can be accomplished in many different ways.

Any professional decorator will get to know his client's needs before he even considers an interior design for

Above: *Very effective co-ordinating schemes can be achieved by building a multitude of different patterns around a simple colour scheme*

their home. And if you want to create harmony and co-ordination in your home, this is a good place to start.

Consider carefully the way you live. Whether you are on your own, newly married, with children or pets should to a large extent dictate your choice of decor. Be realistic with yourself—there is no point in hankering after white carpets if you have no chance of keeping them clean. Or in choosing an expensive silk fabric wallpaper if you have young children around.

You might also take into consideration the extent to which you are 'house proud', or the amount of time you have to keep it clean, as some furnishings and materials are easier to maintain than others. For example, fitted carpets, PVC and laminate surfaces, slip-off chair covers are all well worth considering if you have a full-time job as well as the home to take care of.

Most people grow up with very definite ideas on how they would like their home to look. And it often comes as a shock when their plans do not turn out quite as they expected. Many people tend to buy conventional furnishings they live to regret or hardly use simply because they thought it would look right.

Putting your ideas down on paper first can save considerable heartache after the event. Make a floor plan of all the rooms in your home then cut out paper shapes for all the furniture you wish to use. Move them around in each room until you feel entirely happy with the setting.

It is a good idea to make a list of all your priorities. including hobbies and recreations, and bear them in mind when planning your furniture. If you prefer evenings around the fire watching television or playing cards, for instance, it might be a good idea to have a large coffee table which you can use for the occasional informal evening meal.

Introducing harmony
Whether you live in a rented flat, a town house or country cottage, the same rules for introducing harmony apply. Always bear them in mind whatever your style of decoration.

Every room needs a centre of interest to which the eye is drawn. It might be a fireplace or pretty latticed window which is already there. Or you may need to create one yourself.

An unusual window could be accentuated, dadoes or cornices picked out. Or you might have an interesting architectural feature such as an arched alcove or unusual decorative moulding which could be highlighted. Even boxy rooms have a symmetry that can be improved on.

The real art lies in keeping your feature part of an overall theme.

Try to think of furniture arrangements in relation to the shape of the room. If you can get the layout of the room to work, you are half way to overall harmony.

If you have an attractive fireplace with either a log-burning stove or open fire choose a seating arrangement which will enhance it. Twin two-seater sofas might be more useful than a conventional three-piece suite, with perhaps a long coffee table in between. One or two second-hand or antique chairs could be included for economy and visual interest.

Few of us have the funds to buy exactly what we want all at once—and perhaps it is just as well. All homes look and feel better for a mixture of old and new. You need to live with furnishings and decor in order to get the balance right.

Deciding which corner would be better filled with a circular pedestal table or triangular display unit will be that much easier when you have a true feeling for the room.

You will probably find your ideas change as you start adding to your furniture and accessories. And the end result might be totally different to what you originally envisaged.

When you are satisfied that the design for the room is right—including plans to buy things over the course of a year or two—you can start to consider colour and character.

Many people would never consider second-hand furniture and want everything new. In this case it is better to invest in good quality soft furnishings rather than buying cheap designs which are likely to fall to pieces before long. But if you are unable to buy everything you want straight away, you can turn to other means of giving your home character.

Choosing colour

Colour and pattern play a tremendously important part in our lives and those you choose should feel comfortable as well as decorating the home.

Wallpapers, fabrics and paint all go towards achieving a co-ordinated look and the subtleties with which you can use them are almost endless.

Strangely, the colours we choose for clothes are not necessarily those we like to live with. A good example is white—ever popular for decorating but over-demanding for everyday clothing.

Brown has the quality of serenity and blends well, both with natural woods and materials and neutral shades like silver, black and gold. It is ideal for a study, antique-filled living room or anywhere a neutral back-drop is required, but needs to be

Syndication International Ltd

Above: *Matching curtains and bedspread will look even more stylish with co-ordinated border trim and curtain tie-backs*
Right: *A simple pattern in different colourways can be used to enliven an alcove cupboard. Use wallpaper on drawer fronts and shelves and the basic colour to highlight—you may even find some china to match!*

sparked off with pinks, reds and creams if it is not to seem too dull.

One of the easiest of colours to plan a room around—and to use for camouflage—is blue, in all its many hues. Also tranquil and relaxing, it offers far more variety than brown and mixes well with just about every other colour.

Many of the good things of nature are green—trees, plants, vegetables, fruit—and when introduced into a room, this immediately brings it to life. Green, probably more than any other colour, lends itself well to co-ordination.

Yellow is a colour that either attracts or repels you; but it can be amazingly stimulating when used to

Sanderson

introduce a touch of sunshine to an otherwise dark room. Graduations of yellow can be very successful together, say one shade of paint for walls, another for woodwork and a third for the ceiling.

Red is the boldest colour of all and unless it is used as an accent colour, should be spread over a total area.

The secret of co-ordinating colours well is to keep things simple and to know what effect you want to achieve before you start. The fewer colours you use, the more effective the end result will be. Build up variety with different tones and hues.

Cool pastels create a feeling of spaciousness while vibrant colours tend to make walls stand out. Use darker colours in a large room for cosiness and in a small one for dramatic effect.

Pattern and design

When you have decided what effect you want to create and have chosen the colours you want to live with, your next decision will be to pattern.

Modern wallpapers are increasingly versatile, designed for mixing and matching with great flexibility. For example you can buy patterned wallpaper with two or three mini-print designs related to it, and with plain paper and paint colours also keyed-in.

The idea is to use the main pattern on three or four walls with the mini print in an alcove, the side walls of a fireplace, or in an adjacent room. Or vice versa.

Then there are co-ordinating friezes and borders, which you can use with either paint or wallpaper and matching or co-ordinating curtains. This concept used to be confined to the luxury end of the market, but is now available in every price range.

There are literally thousands of wallpaper designs available and many people find it impossible to visualize them in their own homes. Some books have coloured room settings which help to show a pattern in depth, but it is always a good idea to take along fabric samples of existing furnishings for a colour match. It is surprisingly easy to get a colour you are trying to remember completely wrong.

Mini prints are increasingly popular because they are undemanding and easy to relate to. Yet a large scale, dramatic design can do miracles for the right room and needs fewer pictures and ornamentation. If you like the idea of an unusually dramatic design but have a few doubts, buy one roll and pin it up in the room for a period of time. Quite often, the more you have of a bold pattern, the more it seems to merge into the background.

You can use large repeat designs in both large and small areas. Take a bold design up a two-storey hallway for instance, and into a cloakroom in a quieter contrast to the living room.

Mini prints used in small rooms on all four walls and on the ceiling create a cosy effect. Having them everywhere in quantity, colour-keyed to each room, creates greater continuity throughout.

But take care not to swamp a room with the same design; aim instead for a build-up of slightly different types of pattern.

Leading wallpaper and fabric producers aim at collections which blend together so that not one, but half-a-

dozen or more patterns can be used without seeming overpowering.

This co-ordinating theme can be applied to anything from fabric, wallpaper and ceramic tiles to lampshades, tablecloths and roller blinds. The secret is to mix designs in no more than one or two colours, or even to use the same design in its different colourways.

Mix and match ideas

When first introducing pattern into a room, decide what is to be the pattern focal point—sofas, walls, curtains, carpeting, a collection of paintings or ornaments are all suitable.

In the living room, for instance, take the sofa or chairs as a starting point and cover them in a blue and green floral print. Then, using furnishing or dress fabric remnants in paler and darker blues and greens, make cushions and curtains to match. Add a border of plain blue or green petersham to the curtains and make matching tie-backs. The walls could be painted magnolia, or very pale turquoise with a border or central dado painted in plain blue or green to match the curtain border.

To further accentuate the blue-green theme, make a circular tablecloth out of the same, or a co-ordinating fabric with placemats to match. Add a border and use the same fabric or colour for a picture frame.

Collect blue ornaments and group them together—even a row of blue paper-backed books can look good in the right position. Introduce other colours as accents, rather than main colours so that the room does not become too stylized.

You might inherit a patterned carpet, perhaps in a rented flat or from a relative, which you would not necessarily have chosen yourself. But if you decorate around it, rather than against it, the design will seem less dominant. Use loose covers in plain materials for chairs and paint, rather than wallpaper, on the walls. Also, invest in greenery and pleasing objects: concentration of one colour on a side table or shelves will attract more attention away from the floor.

Be clever with pattern—some designs can be cut into friezes for bordering a hatchway to a dining room or framing up a door. A home-made cornice at about 300mm below ceiling level makes plain walls more interesting. Wallpapering above a central dado and gloss paint below can define a rather dull room by drawing the eye to its borders.

The bed is probably the largest

Michael Boys/Susan Griggs

Above: *A novel way to introduce co-ordination and harmony into an otherwise neutral room is with a variety of matching coloured cushions*

single item in the bedroom and a good starting point for your colour and pattern theme.

There is an enormous range of designs for both duvets and bedspreads and a variety of plain colours. The valance, bottom sheet and pillow cases can all be mixed and matched.

Use co-ordinating paper on the walls and ceiling for a very pretty effect and perhaps even add matching curtains. **If the window has a private aspect, keep the curtains permanently tied back at either side and use a co-**ordinating roller blind at night.

Kitchens and bathrooms take well to pattern, particularly if they are small or irregular in size. Floral designs in particular can disguise corners out of true, awkward areas around appliances and uncomfortably high ceilings.

Many wallpaper ranges now have matching or co-ordinating tiles which can be stuck around the bath or wash-basin or used to frame a work surface or window.

Finally, remember that using co-ordinating effects for the home can be a lot of fun. Always aim at harmony rather than shock effects and keep to a one- or two-colour theme for best results.

The modern look

To some people the modern look seems stark and bare, but if it is done well it is a stunning style of decoration. Simple, uncluttered lines, neutral or bold colours and plain or geometric patterned fabrics are the key points

Below: *The soft, neutral colours of the walls and carpet plus a simple glass coffee table between the leather seating combine to achieve a relaxing, uncluttered look in this modern-style living room*

Among the many different styles of furnishing and decorating a home, one of the easiest and most labour-saving schemes is the modern look. Although many people might find the modern style stark and bare, its furniture and furnishings are easy to clean and the neutral colours often used are relaxing to the eye.

The modern style calls for a spacious look with no unnecessary furniture—each piece being carefully chosen to fulfill a particular purpose. The over-all effect should be one of uncluttered, streamlined efficiency with simple shapes and no unnecessary ornament. There should be a predominance of straight lines and flat surfaces, although some curves—perhaps a moulded plastic chair—may be introduced for dramatic effect.

Colour schemes are usually light, with plenty of white. Simple, emulsion-painted walls in neutral shades such as white, cream and grey will achieve the right look. Pattern should be added with extreme caution.

On the whole, the modern style favours geometric designs rather than florals and tends to use boldly pronounced pattern concentrated into one area, rather than having it scattered around the room.

Generally speaking, patterned wall papers are not in keeping with the modern style of decoration. However, it is possible to introduce texture by using a fabric wallcovering such as hessian or wool.

In a large room it is possible to make one wall a feature of the room by covering it—or even part of it—in a natural material such as wood cladding, cork, or brick. In older houses you may be able to strip away plaster to reveal attractive brickwork underneath. This can either be cleaned off to its natural colouring or painted in white or cream.

Floorcoverings too should be in pale tones wherever practical and if you want a patterned carpet, it is best to choose a neat, all-over geometric design. Again, you can introduce texture by using plain twist piles or

Jessica Strang

Above: *A quarry tile platform, covered with window seat cushions, creates an unusual, but practical feature. The geometric print of the cushions has been chosen to tone perfectly with the curtains*
Left: *Furniture, in different shades of green, is set off well by white walls which are decorated simply with large, square picture frames*

Rivista Deli Arremento

as they are very skilful. For example, a plastic laminate imitation of marble, or a PVC leather look is perfectly acceptable providing the effect is realistic.

Otherwise, choose natural materials such as wool, cotton, leather, cork, stone and all kinds of wood so long as the natural grain is not concealed by heavy polish or stains. Man-made materials might include metals such as steel, often with a shiny chrome finish, aluminium, glass and all kinds of plastics moulded into exciting and unusual shapes.

Ideally, furniture should be low and streamlined. Modern seating has abandoned the three-piece suite in favour of compact units grouped in an L or U shape to suit the room. Modern look furniture is often flexible, and sometimes serves a dual role—for instance seating doubling as a bed; tables and beds comprising storage space; adjustable shelves and furniture units which can combine into different sizes and arrangements.

Solid foam sofas and chairs which can convert to a bed in seconds are inexpensive and ideal for a modern setting. Otherwise, look for comfortable yet stylish seating in textured coverings like tweedy or knobbly

long shaggy piles. A cork or wood floor also provides a good background for a modern setting.

Another good alternative where the floorboards are in fairly good condition is to sand and seal them. You can then add a modern Scandinavian wool rya rug, or a flat weave kelim or oriental rug with a geometric design to introduce warmth and colour.

In a dining room or hallway where the floor is likely to receive a lot of wear, and collect more dirt, plain vinyl tiles or sheeting is probably the best choice.

A spacious effect, which is such an important aspect of the modern style, can often be heightened with a clever

use of mirrors—on walls, doors or celings. They can give an impression of doubling the space within a room.

Another, more radical, alternative for achieving a spacious effect is to remove all, or part, of a wall to open up your house. A popular modern arrangement is to combine kitchen, dining room and living room into one big living area. However, it is best to take expert advice before making any structural alterations.

Modern-style furniture
For furniture and furnishings the modern style can quite happily mix both natural and man-made materials and is not averse to imitations, so long

Above: *A bedroom which would be suitable for a teenager needing plenty of storage space. Bold colours are an important feature of the room*

fabrics, smooth weaves in wool, corduroy or linen union—or for a more expensive look, in leather. Avoid shiny materials like velvets or figured brocades and choose plain rather than patterned fabrics unless they are of a geometric design. Again, wherever practical, choose pale colours such as oatmeal or peat.

Small, low tables with wood, marble, glass or perspex tops in wood or steel frames are ideal for books, magazines and the occasional TV snack meal. Table and chair legs are often replaced by pedestals to give a more elegant look that is also easier to clean.

Streamlined storage

Storage furniture should be as unobtrusive as possible and it is a good idea to concentrate all the storage requirements of a room on to one wall.

Wall storage units can be bought or made to your own design to fit along side each other and fill up any given space. Various compartments and drawers provide space for anything from cutlery, china and glassware to television, hi-fi and records.

Sometimes it is possible to give older more ornate pieces of furniture a modern feel simply by painting them to merge in with their background.

Bedroom fittings

In the bedroom, too, streamlined fittings have taken over from the more

Left: *A room which makes the most of natural daylight through the windows and the roof. A plant and two pictures prove quite sufficient adornment*

Below: *To avoid a stark look in this dining room, different tones of beige have been combined to create a warm, welcoming atmosphere*

Jessica Strang

conventional wardrobe, dressing table and chest of drawers. Now, even the beds are low and streamlined and often incorporate storage drawers below. Some types even have elaborate headboards incorporating all manner of modern electronics, including a telephone, hi-fi system, television and radio, door entry phone and so on.

Again, furniture may be finished in medium to pale colour woods such as teak, pine, ash or beech, though more sophisticated, luxurious, modern pieces may be made of richly-figured rosewood. Otherwise a simple finish of white melamine, plain and unadorned,

is perfectly suitable in most cases.

Windows are an important part of the modern style and elaborate curtain treatments which may block off natural light from the room should be avoided at all costs.

Multi-paned windows look very attractive for some styles, but for a modern look they should be replaced by a single sheet of glass. Pelmets are not in keeping with a modern scheme —unless they are specially designed to suit the room and windows—and curtains are best left loose without elaborate swags or tie backs. Use plain white track and simple gathered or pinch pleated heading for curtains.

Choose only bold, striking, geometric or abstract designs for bedroom curtains or stick to plain fabrics which can be trimmed with a decorative border or a single row of braid, mitred at the corners for a tailored effect.

The modern trend is to leave windows unscreened during the day, though plain, heavy nets or 'sheers' or

Left: *A modern look kitchen which exemplifies the principle of clean, simple lines—giving a feeling of space and organization*
Below: *In this modern bedroom a platform has been covered with plain carpeting—a design which looks best in a good-sized room*

loosely woven linens or acrylics can be used to provide a degree of privacy. To screen the room by night, either draw the curtain across the window or use roller blinds, featuring a bold, modern design. On a large window it is often better to have two or three individual roller blinds than one large, cumbersome one. Venetian blinds and vertical blinds, particularly in white or silver, also suit the modern style.

Lighting is sophisticated and subtle and should be designed to enhance the room, emphasizing the effect of the lighting rather than the fittings themselves. Spotlights mounted on tracks for greater flexibility are popular, both for general lighting and for highlighting pictures or objects.

Remember that the modern style is clean and uncluttered, and decorative extras should be kept to a minimum. It is better to have one large, impressive picture or print than a cluster of small ones. Similarly, avoid collections of ornaments, using instead just one or two striking pieces of china, treasured porcelain, or sculpture.

Greenery always fits well into modern interiors—particularly large, leafy plants which create a dramatic effect in the room. Cheese plants, aspidistras and rubber plants are the perennial favourites, but smaller green and variegated plants can look equally good when highlighting furniture.

Camera Press

The oriental look

Despite the obvious differences between western and eastern architecture, it is still possible to create an oriental style of decor in your home. Whether you want a total look or just an oriental flavour, the results can be quite stunning

Above: Natural colours and selected accessories combine well to give this bedroom an oriental flavour. Discreetly patterned wallpaper tones perfectly with the carpet and provides a perfect setting for the decorative bamboo bedside table and unusual cane lounger

The essence of an oriental look is perfect simplicity. The idea is to provide a haven of tranquillity and harmony, where nothing jars the mind or the senses. Colours are soft pastels or natural shades, lines are low and smooth, and surfaces are uncluttered – almost to the point of starkness. Ornaments and pictures are few and each one is carefully chosen as perfect and complete in itself, yet integrated completely in the whole effect.

Oriental furniture and furnishings imported from the Far East are sold in various specialist shops and large department stores, and this increasing availability has brought many of these beautiful, exotic and craftsman-made items within a price range that most people can afford.

Of course some items, such as Chinese carpets or Japanese lacquerwork, are still very expensive but it is worth bearing in mind that these are often items of real and lasting beauty which might almost be regarded as investments.

Because of the vast architectural differences between western and oriental houses it is probably impractical to attempt to create a totally authentic look throughout the home. The interior paper walls of Japanese houses, for instance, hardly lend themselves to the western way of life – especially in colder climates.

Right: *A formal arrangement using an interesting combination of shapes and textures. White lamps and teapot contrast well with wooden objects*

Below: *A simple collection of oriental fans, trays and containers makes an attractive display for a mantelshelf and would look equally good on a table*

Michael Nicholson/EWA

Camera Press

Walls and windows

The oriental look relies on subtlety and restraint, so avoid those heavily patterned western-designed 'Chinese' wallpapers featuring pagodas and dragons. Choose instead more subtle western papers, perhaps with a woven cane design—although not authentic, they are much more suited to the desired effect.

Painting the walls white is a cheap and easy way of making them appear less obtrusive and certainly provides an excellent background for displaying Japanese woodcuts or Thai temple rubbings. However a much more exciting treatment would be to hang silkcloth—a luxurious fabric made of fine threads of dyed silk laminated on to coloured backing paper. It is expensive and requires care in hanging, but the final effect is really stunning.

A less expensive alternative also in keeping with the oriental style would be grasscloth, hand-dyed grasses or reeds, laminated on to paper backing. This is available in a wide range of natural colours and a variety of textures.

You might even consider the bold approach of painting some, or even all, of the woodwork with black, crimson or cinnamon gloss paint to give an appearance of 'lacquerwork'. Apply several thin coats for a really hard shine. If carefully thought out and properly applied, this treatment can create amazing effects.

Curtains are distinctly western in style and even 'oriental' patterned ones are best avoided. Blinds are the best choice for creating an oriental feel and you can buy extremely pretty, authentic hand-

Above: *A cleverly achieved Japanese-style bedroom with a 'futon'—a conventional mattress could be used instead—on a slatted wooden platform*

Below: *An imaginative open-plan living area favouring a combination of straw, bamboo and raffia. Exotic paper kites add a touch of colour to the effect*

painted blinds from specialist shops and some large department stores. Alternatively, plain bamboo or split cane blinds are fairly cheap and achieve just the right effect.

Floors

Hand-woven Chinese rugs are exceptionally soft and beautifully patterned but even the smallest ones are extremely expensive. However, an equally authentic and considerably cheaper floor covering would be one of the types of grass or rush matting. This would look particularly effective with grasscloth-covered walls.

Split reed mats are available in a variety of patterns and have a delicate, slightly shiny texture. Unfortunately, they are not very hardwearing, so are probably best used in conjunction with stripped and lacquered floorboards and positioned away from areas of heavy use.

Coir and rush matting, while slightly less authentic, are still appropriate to the overall effect and very much more durable. They can be used as a complete covering or as individual small rugs. They are available in a wide range of weaves and patterns in a selection of natural colours.

Furniture

Obtaining suitable furniture is the easiest part of creating an oriental effect. There is a wide variety of bamboo and cane furniture available and both genuine and 'fake' lacquerwork can also be readily obtained.

Bamboo armchairs and sofas can be found in an immense range of designs and are relatively inexpensive. Usually, plump, loose cushions are added to provide greater comfort. Bedroom furniture, including wardrobes, dressing tables and bedside cabinets are also made in both bamboo and cane as are dining tables and chairs. Bookshelves and display units are also available, and while such items would not necessarily feature in a real oriental house, they do have an exotic eastern flavour.

Rattan is also widely used for occasional tables of all shapes and sizes, often with chairs to match. This lends itself well to an oriental style.

Fine examples of Japanese lacquerwork can be very expensive. Many layers of lacquer are painstakingly built up and dried under carefully controlled conditions to achieve the finished effect. The background colour is black and designs in red, gold and other colours may be very elaborate. Of course not all lacquerwork commands astronomical prices but because of the skill and time involved in its production it is almost always expensive. However, 'fake' lacquer is remarkably effective and attractive.

Traditional items for such treatment were small tables, screens and multi-drawer cabinets, though chairs and sofas with lacquered frames are also available.

For an oriental style bedroom, you might consider buying a Japanese 'futon' – a thin sleeping mattress which can be rolled up during the day. Only about 80mm thick, they can be extremely comfortable and are particularly good for backache sufferers. They are made of cotton and stuffed with cotton wadding

Right: *Plain and simple yet far from boring, a low level dining arrangement in red and black certainly sets the scene for entertaining Japanese-style*

Transworld Feature Syndicate

Michael Boys/Susan Griggs

Michael Nicholson/EWA

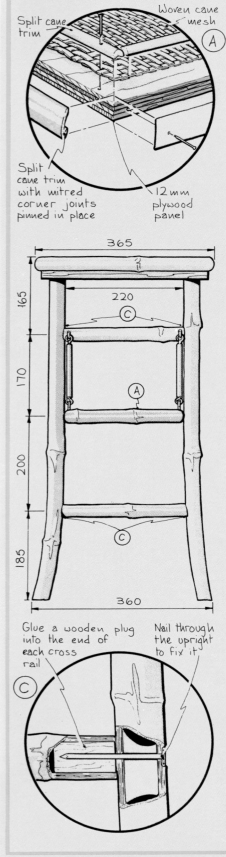

secured with silk tassels. The traditional Japanese style is to spread the futon out on a specially constructed wooden sleeping platform raised above draughts. But you can either use the futon directly on the floor or on top of a hard-based bed.

Screens are a feature in oriental houses and an inexpensive and easy way of achieving an eastern flavour. Bamboo and cane screens are made in a wide variety of sizes and patterns and would look especially attractive in a bedroom. Lacquer screens and carved wooden screens are more elaborate, so they are better suited to a living room.

You can make your own 'oriental' screen quite easily by painting a suitable frame with black gloss paint then attaching 'Chinese' fabric to it with upholstery studs.

Accessories

Clever use of accessories is the secret of creating an oriental effect and there is no need to spend a great deal of money to achieve an authentic look. Paper lampshades, both plain and patterned, are cheap and easily obtained. So too are decorative Japanese three-dimensional paper wall hangings, such as colourful fish and peacocks. A collection of pretty paper fans is equally suitable.

Above: *A comfortable dining area with just a hint of the Far East. Split cane blinds are perfect on the windows and help to create the right atmosphere*

Scroll paintings and wood-block prints are uniquely eastern and are original works of art. Of course, those by famous artists cost quite a lot of money, but delightful pictures and prints by lesser known artists are very reasonably priced. Temple rubbings are unusual and make attractive wall decorations. These are made on fine paper in red, blue or black, using the same technique as that for brass rubbings.

Not everyone can afford jade ornaments and vases but carved soapstone is very similar in appearance and costs much less. A collection of images and figures in this softer and less precious mineral provides an equally delightful showpiece for an oriental flavour.

Porcelain and bone china is relatively cheap and as well as the more common teapots, tea bowls, rice bowls and spoons, there are attractive plates, jugs, vases and jars which also make excellent oriental accessories. They range from traditional patterns to ornate, abstract designs and also include the well known blue and white 'willow' pattern.

An oriental-style table

Hang the trays on 150mm lengths of dowel or thin cane with screw eyes and hooks in each end

Woven cane mesh

12mm plywood panel

Split cane edging pinned in place

Fix the back by nailing through

520

Plywood top covered with woven mesh

110

Fixing blocks 310mm long from 75x16 mm

410

230

Uprights and cross rails from approximately 30mm diameter cane

Heat the cane in order to make it pliable enough to bend out at the base as shown

385

185

480

All parts except for the three trays are made from bamboo cane of about 30mm diameter. Cane is a variable material, so all dimensions are approximate. The trays are made from plywood covered with cane mesh and edged with split cane

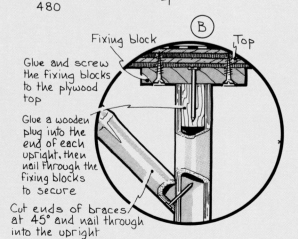

B

Fixing block

Top

Glue and screw the fixing blocks to the plywood top

Glue a wooden plug into the end of each upright, then nail through the fixing blocks to secure

Cut ends of braces at 45° and nail through into the upright

Ray Duns

This small cane table is the perfect complement to an oriental-style room, but it would blend in well with many other furnishing schemes.

Make it using readily available bamboo cane from hardware stores or garden centres. You will also need some small pieces of plywood and some woven cane mesh, which is obtainable from specialist cane suppliers.

Most of the construction is quite straightforward, following the working drawings. Before starting this project, make sure you wet the bamboo cane to facilitate easy handling.

Start by making the two ladder-style end frames. Note that where you need to join into the end of cane, you must insert a glued wooden plug to provide grip. Pre-drill the outer nail holes to avoid splitting the cane.

When the end frames are complete, fix each to a softwood crossbar. Fix to the top, adding diagonal braces and a bottom rail.

Complete the top by covering with woven cane mesh and edging with split cane, then make up two similar panels for the side trays. These simply hang from the main structure, on nails at the back and on diagonal front stays.

Dining rooms

Whether your dining room is large or small or simply an area within the living room or kitchen, by choosing the right furnishings and decorative scheme you can create a mood and atmosphere entirely conducive to eating

Elizabeth Whiting

Modern open-plan living tends to dispense with the notion of a separate dining room in favour of eating areas either in the kitchen or living room. Nevertheless, when there is space available, most families still opt for the old-fashioned idea of a separate room for dining.

In many houses, however, there simply is not space for a separate dining room. But with careful attention to decoration, lighting and furniture you can create a sense of division even in an open-plan living room.

Of course, some cooks prefer a combined kitchen/dining area for the convenience of having everything to hand for both cooking and serving.

But even though the dining room is perfect for all occasions, most families still prefer to have more casual meals in the kitchen—leaving the dining room unused for a considerable

amount of time. So, when planning the room and choosing furniture, it is worth bearing in mind that the room can be used for all kinds of other activities besides eating. For instance, if there is room for a comfortable armchair, it might provide the ideal surroundings for reading and relaxing.

Basic planning

The dining room needs as much careful planning as any other room in the house. Tables that are too small for instance, with cramped space for pulling back chairs, and inadequate surfaces for serving, all add up to unnecessary meal time frustrations.

Try and arrange for an unobstructed passage between kitchen and dining room for bringing in food. A serving hatch is very useful but should be big enough to take your largest dishes and tall wine bottles.

Another alternative is a serving trolley. Sturdy wooden versions can often be picked up at secondhand shops, and can be given a coat of bright paint and a top of ceramic tiles or plastic laminate. Otherwise there are more expensive modern designs in wood or metals, including sophisticated electrical versions with heated compartments to keep food warm for each course of the meal. Less elaborate electric hotplates are also handy for keeping one or two dishes hot.

Square tables tend to be rather wasteful of space. For instance, a table for four persons needs to be about 900mm square. In the same space, a round table of 900mm diameter could accommodate five persons, provided it was supported by a central pedestal leg. A rectangular table, about 1500mm × 900mm provides enough space for six people.

old oak table. Such unusual combinations take a bit of decorating nerve, but do create exciting effects.

An attractive arrangement for an oblong table is to have two chairs without arms at either side, and 'carvers' (chairs with arms) at each end. But be sure the carvers tuck in neatly below the table top when they are not being used.

Dining chairs are often subjected to rough treatment, being pulled back and forth, and tilted on their back legs. In the long run, it pays to buy well-made chairs in solid wood—even if it means spending more money than you intended.

Look for stretcher rails between the chair legs—these add to the strength of the construction—and inspect the joints to see that they are well made.

Chairs are also available in moulded plastics which often prove functional, durable and elegant in use. Where space is tight you can also buy chairs that stack or fold flat. Some even come with a rack that will stow two or four chairs away, folded flat.

Benches are sold as an alternative to chairs with some tables, especially pine styles, and are particularly use-

Below: *Glass topped dining tables provide a modern look—and can be covered with a tablecloth for a more traditional approach*

Each person sitting around a table needs about 600mm of space all together and about 500mm from the table edge to the back of the chair—though you need up to 700mm to allow room to draw back the chair in order to get in and out. It is best to experiment yourself to find the amount of space you feel happiest with both for sitting at table and getting in and out.

Make sure that there is comfortable knee room underneath the table. Again, test this for yourself and be particularly careful when matching old chairs to a modern table.

Choosing dining furniture
You can buy dining furniture as a set or you can make up your own combinations, making sure that table and chairs work comfortably together. Visually, some of the most stunning results come from an extreme contrast in styles.

For instance, heavily carved antique upholstered chairs can look most impressive teamed with a modern table in chrome with glass top. Modern cantilevered chairs with steel frames and leather or cane seats look very good contrasted with a heavy,

Elizabeth Whiting

ful in the kitchen. In the same space a bench seats more people than chairs. In very small rooms, a table in the corner, with a built-in upholstered bench running around two or three sides can save a great deal of space. However, this does have the disadvantage that everyone must get in at the same time and anyone wanting to get out disturbs others seated on the same bench.

Where space is limited, it is a good idea to choose one of the rectangular or square tables which may be extended to take extra people.

Other suitable space-saving alternatives are those which fold flat against the wall or the drop-leaf styles which fold down to take up very little space. Otherwise there is always the popular traditional gate-leg style—but make sure that it is well-made and perfectly stable.

Materials for tabletops vary widely but choose those which have a minimum of cracks and crevices likely to trap crumbs, dirt, and spilt liquids. Always find out about cleaning and maintenance and follow the maker's recommendations carefully. Most modern furniture is protected with synthetic lacquers and needs no polishing.

Veneered woods are commonly used for reproduction styles to produce attractive combinations of grainings, though many modern teak or rosewood tables are also likely to be veneered. The core material is usually chipboard which is perfectly satisfactory provided the furniture is made by a reputable manufacturer.

The edges are the most vulnerable part of a table, and as veneered strip edgings are liable to chipping or peeling, it is wisest to buy a table with an edging of solid wood.

Solid wood is still one of the most popular forms of tabletop—if it gets badly marked it is a simple job to sand out the scratch and re-finish. Solid wood tops are widely available in pine, and, less commonly, in mahogany. It is often possible to find a secondhand solid oak table which can be stripped, stained and varnished to produce a first class table.

Older country-style tables in stripped pine also look very attractive though the planks that make up the tabletop often 'open out' during the stripping and drying process to leave ugly, dirt-collecting gaps. These must be glued and cramped before the table goes into permanent use.

Plastic laminates can now be found which imitate a whole host of other materials including woods, marbles, hessians, leather and grasscloths. Although a functional, easily cleaned choice for family meals, it lacks a little in atmosphere for those special or functional occasions.

Glass is very elegant and glamorous, particularly the smoked versions. However, some people find it disconcerting being able to see through the top to the table legs and floor! Glass for tabletops should be at least 6mm thick, and it is important to choose safety glass which does not break into jagged fragments in the unfortunate event of an accident. Glass tops are commonly available set into metal frames or cane surrounds.

In the meantime, however, if you are stuck with an ugly tabletop, remember that a decorative tablecloth can work wonders in creating a more formal or more intimate setting.

A sideboard is the traditional way of providing dining room storage and many styles are available to match tables and chairs. However, if you are short of space, a floor-to-ceiling arrangement of wall storage furniture will provide more storage than a traditional sideboard, in the same amount of floor space. If the budget is tight, this can simply consist of open shelving.

Many people like to build up a set of 'best' tableware—silver-plated cutlery, cut glass and bone china—for the dining room with a second set kept in the kitchen for everyday use. Ideally your wall storage should provide cupboards to protect better quality china and glass with drawers for silver. Store the heavier items such as serving dishes below waist level and use shallow shelves up to eye level for glasses. Shelves higher than this are best kept for display items only.

It is useful to incorporate into your storage arrangement a surface for serving food which can also hold extra dishes when entertaining. An electric point conveniently placed will enable you to use the surface for small appliances such as a coffee percolator, toaster, hot plates.

Floorcoverings

It is essential that floorings are durable and easy to clean. Although there is not likely to be a lot of through traffic (except in combined living/dining areas) flooring should never-

Elizabeth Whiting

Left: *A dining room/study is easy to arrange if you keep the decor classic and simple*

theless be tough enough to stand up to the constant scraping of chair legs.

Carpets should be of a fairly hard-wearing quality but also provide a soft, warm and welcoming surface that deadens noise. A good choice would be a twist pile and, of course, patterning of any kind will help disguise inevitable spills and stains. Avoid ridged cords which trap dried-on food, or long piles which can be awkward to clean and likely to flatten under table and chair legs.

Carpet tiles are a good choice as they can be individually lifted for cleaning, and can also be moved around to shift areas of wear. A large rug underneath table and chairs looks attractive and will protect flooring at its most vulnerable point.

Synthetic fibres such as acrylic, nylons and polypropylenes are well suited for dining rooms. Some such carpets are now manufactured with a stain-resistant treatment which is ideally suited to dining rooms. Provided some spills are wiped up within 24 hours, there is no staining.

Smooth floorings are easy to sweep clean, resist staining well and can usually be damp-mopped. But they lack the soft appeal of carpet. Cork tiles are a good choice, being warm, resilient and the most noise-deadening of all smooth floors. The most

suitable tiles are those which have a coating of polyurethane lacquer or a clear vinyl 'wear-layer'.

Vinyls provide a wide choice of patterned effects which can, if carefully chosen, look most sophisticated. Cushioned vinyls, sold in sheet form, are now available in wide widths up to 4m to provide a seam-free finish for larger rooms. However, although quiet in use and easy to clean, they may suffer indentation marks from spiky chair legs. Vinyl tiles can be laid in designs that echo room shapes and furniture arrangements, but must be well laid on an absolutely smooth sub-floor in order to withstand constant scraping from chairs.

Decorating

If you have a separate dining room, this could be your chance to plan an effect that is a little bit out of the ordinary and suited to special occasions. Plain painted walls can look stunning if you choose a deep rich colour and perhaps add a wallpaper border and some tasteful pictures.

Or take a bolder approach and choose a patterned wallcovering or one of the many new rich textured effects for more dramatic results. With the many co-ordinated ranges of paper now produced, it is even possible to match tableware to your wallcovering.

Above: *Experiment with unusual chairs and tables in the dining room. They can be a significant part of the decor*

Remember that pale blues and greys have a chilly effect, especially when viewed by artificial tungsten light. Study the decor in your favourite restaurants—these are generally chosen with great care to create the most pleasant background for eating. Colours are most often selected from the warm side of the spectrum—rich reds, browns, oranges, pinks, tans or yellows. Deeper blues and bright greens, however, can also provide a stunning background for a dining room.

Lighting too should be chosen with care. It is most important that people seated around the table should not be disturbed by the glare from any unshaded bulbs. Pendant lamps hung low over the table are always effective. It is a simple job to extend a flex from an existing ceiling point and secure it from a hook in the ceiling over the dining table.

The best lights of all for the dining room are the rise and fall type fittings which can be lowered for an intimate atmosphere, and then pulled up to give overall general lighting. A table lamp, or wall-mounted spotlamp can provide light for serving by.

Make a 'Lazy Susan'

Make this attractive and practical centrepiece for your dining table. All you need are a few offcuts of plywood and some steel balls to make a revolving condiment set with candles.

You will also need a cruet set and some storage jars which match each other in size and style. Measure their bases to give you a cutting guide for their housings.

Cut all the discs from 12mm or 6mm plywood using a coping saw. Cut the central holes using the saw, or a hole saw in an electric drill. Cut a disc from plastic laminate, then assemble the parts in the order shown.

Before you screw the two parts together, add a ring of ball bearings which you can buy from hardware stores or bearing suppliers. If these need more clearance, sand the top of the plywood. Finish off by sanding the surface and painting or staining.

Ray Duns

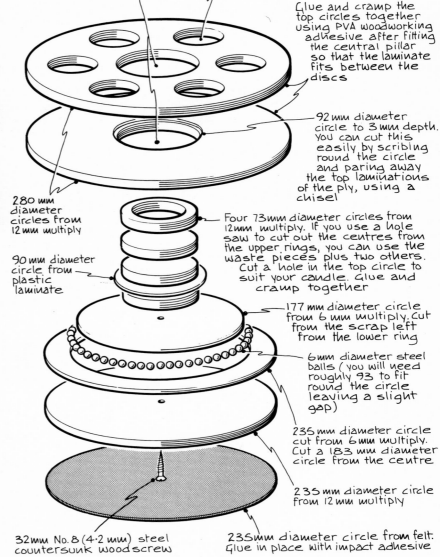

75mm diameter hole centred on disc. Cut with a hole saw or coping saw

Cut six holes to suit your cruet set (probably around 62 mm). Space them equally around the ring centred between the inner and outer circles

Glue and cramp the top circles together using PVA woodworking adhesive after fitting the central pillar so that the laminate fits between the discs

92 mm diameter circle to 3 mm depth. You can cut this easily by scribing round the circle and paring away the top laminations of the ply, using a chisel

280 mm diameter circles from 12 mm multiply

90 mm diameter circle from plastic laminate

Four 73mm diameter circles from 12mm multiply. If you use a hole saw to cut out the centres from the upper rings, you can use the waste pieces plus two others. Cut a hole in the top circle to suit your candle. Glue and cramp together

177 mm diameter circle from 6 mm multiply. Cut from the scrap left from the lower ring

6 mm diameter steel balls (you will need roughly 93 to fit round the circle leaving a slight gap)

235 mm diameter circle cut from 6 mm multiply. Cut a 183 mm diameter circle from the centre

235 mm diameter circle from 12 mm multiply

32mm No.8 (4·2 mm) steel countersunk woodscrew

235mm diameter circle from felt. Glue in place with impact adhesive

Cross section of assembly

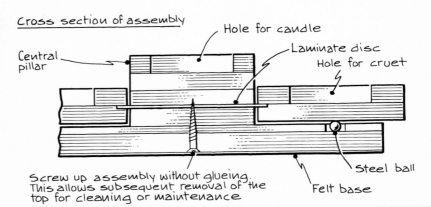

Central pillar

Hole for candle

Laminate disc
Hole for cruet

Steel ball

Felt base

Screw up assembly without glueing. This allows subsequent removal of the top for cleaning or maintenance

Planning a living room

The living room is one of the most overworked areas in the house. But with careful thought and planning you can design a room that is both comfortable and functional, while at the same time attractive and easy to clean

Of all the rooms in a home the living room is the one that most reflects the personalities and interests of its inhabitants. Other rooms have predesignated functions—the bedroom, for instance, is mainly for sleeping and the kitchen is for cooking and often eating. But the living room is the area where any number of family activities take place. No other room requires as much consideration into the individual needs and interests of individual family members in order to create both a purposeful and relaxing environment.

Irrespective of whether you are planning to move to a different house, building a new one, or are simply thinking about making changes in your current home, an honest appraisal of what kinds of things you and your family enjoy doing is the best way to determine what type of living room will suit your family needs.

A good idea in the initial stages of designing a living room is to write out a list of all the activities that your family enjoys. And next to each item note the most comfortable conditions needed for carrying out the particular activity. For example, next to listening to music you will have to consider storage space for records as well as any soundproofing that may be needed to prevent the music from reverberating throughout the house. If you intend to have your TV in the living room then you will have to provide comfortable seating and think about positioning it so that no one will trip over the wiring. (Most TV's are positioned far too low for comfortable viewing, including those attached to the manufacturer's stand. A height of not less than 1200mm from the floor to the base of the set is recommended.)

You will find that a number of the activities such as reading and watching television cannot take place at the same time in the same area. This is where you will begin to notice the limitations that you will have to place on your design. Indeed, many families would be hard put to cope with all the activities that might appear on such a list. At this point you can decide which family activities will be allocated to other rooms in the house. If you find it easy enough to do this, then what you are left with is a room used primarily for entertaining visitors, and the space will go unused a good deal of the time which may not be such a wise idea for a large family.

Once you have determined the type of living room that you want you can

Below: *Sparse furnishings and neutral colours give this spacious living room a really modern look—but definitely not for those with a young family!*

begin to analyse the various components that go into the creation of a well-designed room. But first a word of warning. Many home improvements—such as installing central heating or adding a second bathroom—help to improve the value of your home if you decide to sell it. But as the living room is such a personal design matter, new occupants may wish to totally alter what you have considered to be a home improvement. That major shelving unit you install may be of little interest to a prospective buyer, or your fitted carpets may be removed in favour of laying a tiled or wood panelled floor.

Space

A living room needs to offer freedom of movement. A crowded or cluttered room will detract from the relaxation and comfort that is necessary in family living space. To see best how you will achieve an easy-moving atmosphere make a drawing of your room, preferably on graph paper, where you can mark all the measurements to scale.

Note down the positions of existing doors and windows as well as existing electric points and central heating sources. Many homes often consist of a number of small rooms and with today's demands for more open spaces it may be necessary to remove a dividing wall perhaps to create a living-dining area. With a hallway that leads into the living room, the dividing wall might be removed to give more space.

You may wish to add an additional door that leads to a back garden so that your living room becomes an extension of the garden in the summer. Then, of course, you must think about proper insulation to prevent draughts in the winter. The addition of windows helps to open up a room and adds much needed natural light. If your ceiling is too high and you wish to create a more intimate environment then you may at this early stage make plans for lowering it. If your living room is quite large, then the addition of a stud wall partition or a simple screen or free-standing shelves will break up a long, continuous space.

Certain existing features such as a fireplace or an imposing bay window may be used as the basis for planning the internal layout of your room. Also, make a note of all the characteristics of the room that you dislike—such as poor natural lighting or too boxy a room shape—and begin to consider the ways of correcting bad features. Both good and bad existing features, and what you choose to do with them, will greatly affect the spatial arrangements of your room.

Your main area in the living room will no doubt be for seating, and positioning this so that family traffic does not interfere is your first task when grouping your furnishings.

If your room is used for through traffic, make sure you provide a comfortable walk-way through the room unobstructed by furniture and see that the TV set is not placed behind the traffic flow. Leave enough room—at least 600mm—between various pieces of furniture for ease of movement. Doors should be able to open unobstructed (and this includes the doors and drawers of cabinets as well as doors into the room). Light switches need to be easily accessible to anyone entering the room. If you are planning on a study area in your living room see to it that it is positioned away from main activities—perhaps in an alcove already suggested by the shape of the room—and remember there is no point in having your study area on one side of the room with storage and bookcases on the other.

If you are using your living area combined with a dining area then you must relate the position of your table and chairs to the kitchen in the best way possible for ease of serving.

Heating and lighting

Once you have worked out your furniture groupings on your floor plan, you can determine whether you

Right: *Simple furnishings and plain decor are offset by the unusual hanging light.* **Below:** *Well-placed wall hangings and colourful cushions create an interesting corner seating area*

Elizabeth Whiting

will need extra heating. Or it may be a cost consideration that your furniture arrangements must be situated where they will be in optimum heating conditions. You will want to place furniture away from draughty areas and consider what types of window covering you will need such as heavy drapes, wood shutters or perhaps some form of double-glazing.

With fireplaces you will have to ensure that your seating is not so close to a raging fire that people feel uncomfortable. You may decide that the fireplace causes too great a heat loss when not in use and that you should close off the flue.

Lighting for living rooms needs to be flexible and well-placed and is seldom satisfactorily supplied from a single, central ceiling point. You may need overall illumination for general purposes, and this could be provided by ceiling mounted spots or pendants that are controlled by a dimmer switch to give greater flexibility of mood and atmosphere.

You will need direct light in the areas where people read, write or sew, but take care it does not shine into the room to dazzle other people or create shadows on other areas of the room—even though shadows are a

major way of giving a feeling of depth to a living room.

Decorative schemes

Living rooms being such busy places, decorative schemes are often best kept fairly simple, and this is especially true in a small living room. Bright, contrasting colours and busy patterns run the risk of becoming oppressive and tiresome. Pale, neutral colours often supply the best background for a comfortable environment and will be the least affected by varying degrees of light. Dark colours tend to blur one into the other as light intensity diminishes, but they do contribute towards making a large room look smaller and are less prone to showing signs of wear.

Nowhere is the overall effect of your room more influenced than by its general colour scheme. Once you have decided on it you have a framework in which to select the furnishings.

When choosing colours for your main seating area you may wish them to be similar to your basic scheme—in

Below: *A fireplace, comfortable seating and soft lights are the perfect combination to create a warm and welcoming atmosphere*

Furniture

The various styles of furniture available will either reflect a particular period or the traditional design of a particular country. Some types suggest functionalism, such as the high-tech look, while others—such as a number of modern American designs—suggest casual entertaining. Still others, particularly certain periods of French design, suggest formality.

What you must be concerned with in making your selections is that your furniture is complementary with the architectural layout of your rooms and also compliments any existing pieces of furniture.

You will be selecting items that will be grouped in your living room and that will remain fairly stationary. Other pieces—the occasional chair or the odd table—will be moved around according to the activities going on in the room. With these items you must consider their flexibility. For example, a chair used for studying could also be used for visitors and so should

Left: *Colours, patterns and texture are featured to best advantage in this bright and airy room.* **Below**: *An attractive, streamlined unit neatly houses TV and video equipment*

which case the area will be less of a focal point in the room. By choosing a contrasting colour, and especially if all the seats are of the same colour, the integrity of the grouping will be increased. The use of colour is an important way of isolating areas in your living room or of bringing them together.

Texture adds a different dimension to a living room. It helps to stop schemes from becoming bland and uninteresting and offers the opportunity to create contrasts in a relatively subtle way. Try exposed, coarse, brick against a highly polished wood floor for instance. Smooth surfaces give a cooler and more formal look to a room while deep piles and soft fabrics will add a touch of warmth.

The use of patterns can be one of the cheapest ways of creating the special quality that you want in your room, but too many different patterns used on furniture, curtains and walls will only end up becoming a distraction. The choice of patterns should be one of the last considerations in designing a living room—they should serve more as an enrichment to a room rather than the focus of it. And if you are designing a room with a particular period in mind, your choice of patterns should enhance the effect.

Bill McLaughlin

Above: *Huge floor cushions are not only a good idea for the children, they also make excellent standby seating*

be a design that is complementary to both study area and main seating area. The more uses you can get out of one piece of furniture the better. Tables are very versatile if wisely selected.

You will be interested mainly in supplying comfortable seating in your living room, and here more than anywhere you can easily fall into the trap of succumbing to fashion or a bargain without giving enough consideration to comfort. Low seating with lots of cushions may be tempting in the furniture showroom (especially when you consider that these are also the least expensive), but it may clash with the more traditional pieces that you already have or it may be too large for your room. Wood colours, too, should be chosen to co-ordinate with the overall style of your room and with existing pieces. Generally, the darker colours are more traditional while blonde woods are more modern.

Arranging your seating is crucial to family and guest relaxation. Nothing is more comfortable than people sitting in a row unable to see each other without turning, or people positioned so that they are forced to stare at each other. Having a focal point of interest such as a fireplace eases this tension. Grouping your furniture in a circular fashion or placing pieces at right-

angles to each other contributes to greater relaxation. A sofa that sits more than two will not be good for conversations when three people are sitting in a row. Other seating will be necessary and, after all, the sofa is the best place for stretching out in the living room.

Shelving and storage units should be both pleasing and functional. While units are often situated along a wall, consider whether a free-standing unit will help to break up a large space.

Whether it is a prized collection of antiques or books or an assortment of potted plants or a hi-fi, shelving units provide the space where the family possessions may be put on display. The length and width of your shelves should be designed with the size of the objects you will display in mind, so that things fit securely and easily while still remaining visible.

Items stored in the living room which are regularly used in other parts of the house may be a nuisance if the storage space is best approached through the main seating area. Try to limit your storage items in the living room to what is regularly used there.

A hi-tec standa

Frederick Mancini

This ultra-modern standard lam follows the hi-tec design trend i which industrial materials and tech niques are adapted for home furnishing And yet, it is stylish enough to blend i with more conventional themes.

The materials used make the lam exceptionally easy to build : the basis i a scaffolding system with a ver streamlined finish, held together b Allen screw clamps. You can buy thi in several sizes with a very wide rang

mp

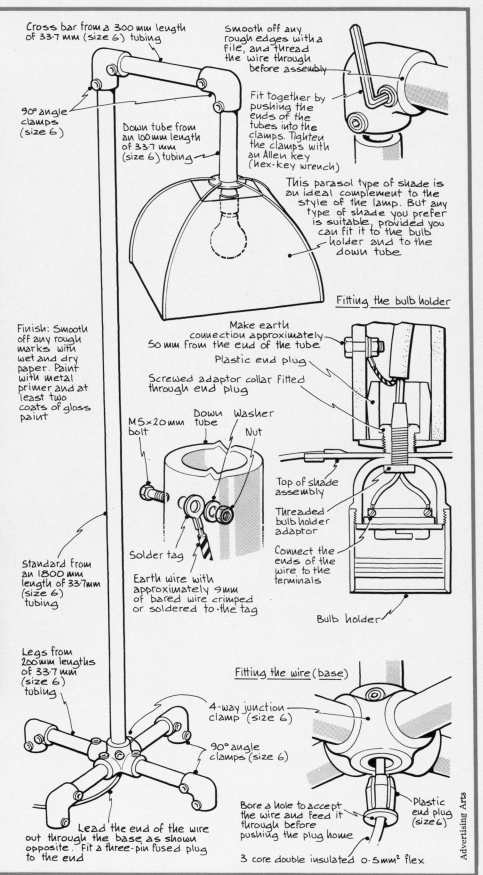

Cross bar from a 300 mm length of 33.7 mm (size 6) tubing

90° angle clamps (size 6)

Down tube from an 100 mm length of 33.7 mm (size 6) tubing

Smooth off any rough edges with a file, and thread the wire through before assembly

Fit together by pushing the ends of the tubes into the clamps. Tighten the clamps with an Allen key (hex-key wrench)

This parasol type of shade is an ideal complement to the style of the lamp. But any type of shade you prefer is suitable, provided you can fit it to the bulb holder and to the down tube

Fitting the bulb holder

Make earth connection approximately 50 mm from the end of the tube

Plastic end plug

Screwed adaptor collar fitted through end plug

M5×20mm bolt

Down tube

Washer

Nut

Top of shade assembly

Threaded bulb holder adaptor

Connect the ends of the wire to the terminals

Solder tag

Earth wire with approximately 9mm of bared wire crimped or soldered to the tag

Bulb holder

Finish: Smooth off any rough marks with wet and dry paper. Paint with metal primer and at least two coats of gloss paint

Standard from an 1800 mm length of 33.7mm (size 6) tubing

Legs from 200 mm lengths of 33.7 mm (size 6) tubing

Fitting the wire (base)

4-way junction clamp (size 6)

90° angle clamps (size 6)

Bore a hole to accept the wire and feed it through before pushing the plug home

Plastic end plug (size 6)

3 core double insulated 0.5mm² flex

Lead the end of the wire out through the base as shown opposite. Fit a three-pin fused plug to the end

of fittings. The drawings on the right show which fittings are needed, and the lengths of tubing used—suppliers will often cut the tubes to length for you. Smooth off rough edges and assemble as shown, threading the wire as you go. You must use a three-core earthed wire, and make an earth connection to the metal.

Finish with gloss paint, then attach a bulb holder and shade via a plastic end plug as shown.

Living room decor

The living room more than any other reflects your family's likes and lifestyle. And because it is where you entertain friends and relations, it is worth giving extra thought to its furnishings and decorations

Because the living room is where most of the family spend their leisure time, the decor here should be comfortable and easy to live with, but should also take into consideration the size and shape of the room itself.

For instance, the high-ceilinged

room shown **left** uses light, natural colours which make the room appear even more spacious. However, the combination of furniture and accessories used helps to maintain a soft and pretty effect. The bay window is left without any form of dressing to let in maximum light and the decorative fireplace forms a prominent feature in the room.

If you want more of a country flavour, pastel shades and a mass of pretty fabrics is an effective answer. The room **above** uses complementary curtains and wallcoverings and, although a variety of different patterned fabrics are included, the colours tone in perfectly.

This style of room gives you an excellent opportunity for using fabrics to co-ordinate accessories too. For example, a motif from the curtain is used to decorate a cushion cover, and fabric from the sofa has been used for a border around the tablecloth and a lining for the magazine bin.

On the other hand, if you prefer the classic style of decoration, the monochrome effect in the room **right** might be more appealing.

The most decorative features—cornice, ceiling rose and window frame—have been picked out in creamy white and the base of the wall seat, which is made from skirting boards, is painted in complementary creamy tones. The lacy curtain provides the perfect window dressing—discreetly shielding off the outside world while still permitting the maximum amount

of light to penetrate into the room.

For a stamp of individuality, why not try your hand at a decorative frieze design **(right)** like the one shown here? The decor and furniture is designed to accentuate the room's dimensions and obvious features. But to add a touch of drama in this otherwise sedately furnished room, an unusual design has been hand-stencilled above and below the picture rail to contrast splendidly with the plain white walls.

If you want a less formal style of room, cane furniture is an excellent choice. it comes in a variety of styles and designs and is reasonably inexpensive to buy. It also has the added advantage of being light and easy to move around and is fairly adaptable to changing colour schemes.

For instance, the combination of seats around the mirror-topped coffee table **below right** provides an attractive setting in a basically neutral room. Touches of colour are brought in quite simply with cushions and wall hangings and the whole effect is perfectly finished off with huge, leafy plants. Again, although the basic colouring is white, the texture of the furniture itself lends a certain warmth and cosiness to the room.

For something very unusual, the room **below** takes the simple uncluttered look to the extreme. But this stark, clinical look can create a calming and restful atmosphere.

Elizabeth Whiting

Leo Ferrante

Martin Palmer

Elizabeth Whiting

A comfy seat cushion

This cushion is simple to make, and will provide you with comfortable seating for very little cost. In its natural state it is soft and floppy, but when you sit in it, it will conform to your shape to give you all-over support.

The filling is expanded polystyrene granules. These are very light, so the finished cushion is easy to move around. They are sold as loose-fill insulation and are also often available from foam suppliers.

All you need to make is a simple cover for the granules. Make this from any close-woven tough fabric, such as a linen union. Choose a colour and pattern to complement your decor. Wash all your fabric before making up to prevent shrinkage later.

The plans show how to make a separate inner liner, so you can remove the outer cover for cleaning. You can save on cost and construction by omitting this liner, but in this case, choose a cover which will not show the dirt.

Make a paper pattern, as shown in the plans, for the five panels which make up the cover. Cut out the pieces and join them as shown, matching the pattern if this is prominent. Next, fit zips to the outer cover.

Stuff the inner liner for fitted cover with the granules and close the final seam. Fit the filled inner liner inside the outer cover and zip closed to complete your cushion.

Materials list

You will need approximately 3.25 metres of 1250mm wide fabric for each cover. You can make the inner liner from a plain close-woven calico. Choose a tough close-woven fabric for the outer cover, suiting the colour and pattern to your decor. You will also need sewing cotton, and, for the removable cover, two 500mm zips. The filling takes about 0.75 cu.m of expanded polystyrene granules, but experiment with this amount until you get a comfortable 'feel'.

Making the reinforcing circles

These fit to top and bottom to cover the joints and reinforce them. Cut out circles 57 mm radius and turn in a 20 mm seam allowance all round. This is easier if you clip the edge as shown. Hem all round. Fit the completed discs in place on the covers and stitch through, 5 mm in from the edge

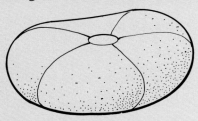

Joining the panels

Lay the panels with their right sides together and seam with a straight stitch, taking in the 20 mm seam allowance. Open out as shown to give the completed seam. Join all panels in the same way and turn out through the zipped opening

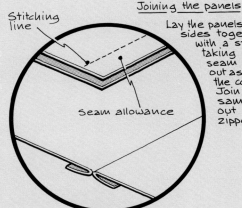

Stitching line

Seam allowance

Reinforcing circle

Fabric panel (5 in all)

Zipped seam

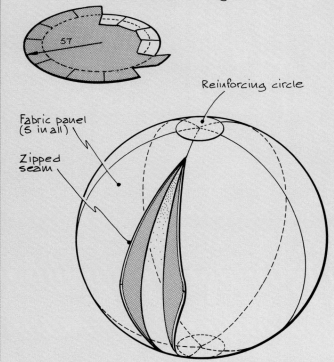

Fitting the zips

Join the two zipped panels first, then add the remaining panels as shown above. Take two panels and turn over the seam allowance. Stitch along to form a hem. Take two 500 mm zips and put their open ends together at the centre line of the panels. Stitch the tape to the edge of the panel through the hem, using a sewing machine with a zipper foot, or by hand. At the closed ends, overstitch the ends of the tape, then join the remaining fabric with a seam in the normal way

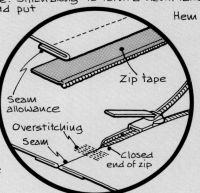

Hem

Zip tape

Seam allowance

Overstitching

Seam

Closed end of zip

This is the layout of the completed outer cover. Make the inner liner in the same way but leave a short section of one seam unstitched. Turn the right way out, and stuff with polystyrene granules until the cushion will adopt a rigid shape and retain it, but without being too full and stiff. About ¼ cubic metre of granules should produce the effect shown below. Slipstitch the seam to close it and fit the inner bag inside the cover. Zip shut, and your cushion is complete. You can later remove the cover for cleaning, simply by undoing the zips and slipping out the liner

Mark out this shape on a large sheet of paper and cut out. Pin to your fabric with dressmakers pins, setting the long dimension (1250 mm) across the width of the cloth. Cut out round the pattern. Make five panels for each bag

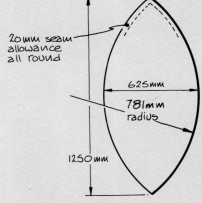

20 mm seam allowance all round

625 mm

781 mm radius

1250 mm

The completed cover is as shown right, forming a complete globe made up five segments reinforced at top and bottom. The outer cover has a zip included in one seam so it can be removed for cleaning. Make an inner liner in exactly the same way but with all the seams completely joined

Cutting out the panels

Better bedrooms

You spend about a third of your life in the bedroom so give it some care when you come to decorating it. Think of practicality, personal style, comfort and visual appeal and remember there are countless approaches

Below: *If it is the dramatic touch you are after, this bedroom with its quite extraordinary stark and streamlined finish, its thorough symmetrical lines and heavy colour scheme, takes drama seriously. In such a scheme furniture should be kept to a minimum*

The bedroom should be a pleasant, restful retreat where you can escape from the hustle and bustle of the outside world. And it is the one room where you can be yourself and express your own personality in the choice of decoration.

A bedroom has far less wear than a living room so the wallpaper, carpets and furniture can be chosen because you like them rather than because they are practical—with a bedroom it does not matter if the wallpaper cannot be wiped clean.

Start by deciding what style of bedroom you want, otherwise you may end up with such a clutter and mixture of styles that the room is anything but restful. Unless you are starting from scratch in a new house, you will probably have to incorporate various items you already possess—like the carpet or some of the furniture—and this may dictate the style.

You may have one area of strong colour that you cannot change, such as the carpet. One way of dealing with this is to blend in the other furnishings with different tones of the same colour —for example if your carpet is deep blue, have the walls a paler blue.

As a rule, try and keep the walls as plain as possible. All-white rooms are always popular, but the bedroom will look cold unless there are some splashes of colour. These can come from curtains, bedspreads, pictures or even make-up bottles and jars on a dressing table. Indian bedspreads add lovely colour to a room and they can also be used as wall hangings, curtains or blinds.

You must also take into account the position of the room in relation to the amount of natural sunlight that will filter through the window.

Rooms with small windows and not very much daylight need warm colours like orange, red and yellow, while rooms which receive plenty of sunlight can take cold colours like blues, greens and greys without making them seem too chilly.

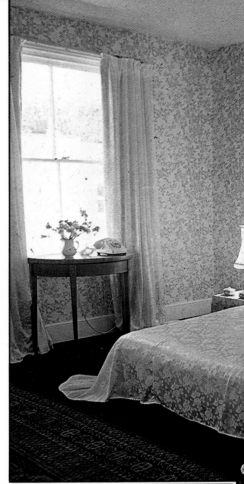

Below: *It is often difficult to know what to do with a young child's bedroom beyond cluttering it with a profusion of homely toys and colours. In this bedroom the monotony of large areas of white wall is broken by a continuous but simple mural while the rest of the area remains functional*

Elizabeth Whiting

chairs and the bed. If possible, have the floor sanded and varnished with one or two pretty patterned rugs by the bed. The very essence of a country-style bedroom is its simplicity—thick carpets and built-in wardrobes would spoil the look.

The glamorous bedroom

If you like the idea of sinking into a deep pile carpet and you want a thoroughly glamorous bedroom, start with as thick a carpet as you can reasonably afford.

A circular, sunken, or raised bed or a water bed lends a real film-star look to a room. The glamorous bedroom look is achieved with soft textures—thick carpet, padded bedhead and lamp shades made in soft materials—rather than bright colours. Cream and white are popular colours for this type of room—both for walls and furniture—colour coming from the carpet, pictures on the walls and plenty of mirrors. Subdued lighting shows these decorative features to their best advantage.

Left: *With the help of a few well-chosen cushions and a long bed canopy hanging elegantly over the bedhead, this bedroom has a smart comfortable style set off by a few accessories only. The two types of carpet also accentuate the bed area*

Bill McLaughlin

The single-colour bedroom

Decorating your bedroom in several shades of one colour can look very effective but you must be sure that you can live with the colour before you change your whole room to this style. Paint the walls and ceiling a paler shade of the main colour and leave the darker tones for the carpet or the bedspread and curtains.

1920s-style room

If you have darker, heavier furniture—walnut or mahogany chests of drawers and wardrobes—you can aim for a 1920s-style room. Cream walls and shades of brown and cream for the rest of the room creates a restful, restrained atmosphere. Bamboo chairs and tables and either wall-lights or tiffany lamps complete the look.

Spare rooms

These are usually the smallest bedrooms so they need to be bright and cheerful and not too fussy. A wide variety of people, all with different tastes, are likely to stay in a spare

Below: *Maximum potential is made of the space in this modern attic bedroom as each item including the bed is placed to achieve its greatest effect. With this kind of space and light, rugs, cushions and plants are the most effective accessories*

Sombre colours like strong greys and browns tend to make a room look cold and business-like instead of warm and inviting. If you must use them, offset their severity with lighter, brighter woodwork or pretty, toning fabrics for bedspreads and curtains.

Bedrooms are usually dominated by feminine taste but this does not mean that they have to be all frills and roses on the walls—there are all sorts of interesting styles to choose from.

Country style

The simple, country-fresh look with white painted walls and bare boards is very popular these days. Flower-patterned wallpaper can also be used for the walls, providing it is the type with tiny sprays of flowers in delicate colours and not full-blown red roses.

Gingham looks pretty in this style of bedroom: matching bedspread, curtains and tablecloth in gingham add a splash of colour to white walls.

Lamps can be old-fashioned brass with a brass base and glass shade. The furniture should be simple and in natural wood—such as stripped pine for chests of drawers, tables,

Elizabeth Whiting

room so it is best to play safe with the decorations. White walls with floral or striped curtains or the single-colour scheme are both sound choices.

Dual-purpose rooms

In most homes space is vitally important—there never seems to be enough. Bedrooms take up a large area and if you use them only for sleeping, that space goes to waste for a large part of the day. If you want a room that is cosy and warm enough to spend time reading, watching television, sewing or studying in, it must be planned with these activities in mind.

A great deal of the floor space will be taken up with the bed. As that may leave very little space for moving around, it is worth considering a bed that can be tipped up and concealed during the day. In an old house with high ceilings, you could have the bed on a platform—leaving space underneath for a desk, dressing table or storage units.

If you want to work in your bedroom, it is important that there is enough storage space to be able to tidy things away—clothes, in particular.

Having a table that folds away or fits into one of the cupboards is a good idea if you want the bedroom to double as a sewing room.

Good light is also important. If you are going to use the room during the day, put your table or desk near the window—set at right-angles to the window rather than facing it.

Planning your room

Before you start changing the whole style of your bedroom, make a scale drawing of the room and put in the furniture—also to scale—where you think you would like it to go.

The position of the bed is important so put this in first. Avoid siting it under the window or in the direct line between door and window or you may well be in a draught.

Now put the rest of the furniture wherever you like then see how it looks on the plan. You can see at a glance if you will have room to sit at the table, or if you will have to move several things before you can get into bed. Remember that low furniture will not seem nearly as crowded as tall furniture.

Work out your ideal lighting too. As well as some form of central light, you need a lamp or bedside light which can be turned off from bed. Dressing tables and work areas need plenty of lighting for use at night.

Elizabeth Whiting

Above: *Having a co-ordinated colour scheme can be extremely attractive in a bedroom. Here the large bedroom has fabrics, carpet, bedspreads, wall paper and even the paintings in a gentle green tone. The overall effect is subtle and pleasing with any hint of monotony dispelled by features such as the bolsters on the carpeted shelf and the symmetrical arrangement*

Left: *Even a quite small room such as this can be easily converted into a functional playroom/bedroom by the economical use of a tier of bunk beds. These are fitted neatly within the accommodating contours of the room and double over as a storage area at the top and bottom leaving the rest of the area free of too much clutter*

Right: *A traditional, rather Victorian looking bedroom can be very appealing if you have the furniture and the ornaments to suit it. The central feature is the brass bed which demands slightly ornate traditional furniture as well as embellished mirrors and pictures with strong frames placed quite high on the walls. To show up these accessories, colours are subdued*

Bill McLaughlin

Bed with the 'four-poster' effect

A four-poster bed adds a touch of elegance to any bedroom, but can be expensive. This 'four poster' uses ordinary curtain rails and brackets to achieve the same effect at a much lower cost.

The curtain rails illustrated are adjustable for both length and height.

To construct this easily-made 'four poster' the first step—before you buy any materials—is to locate the ceiling joists in your bedroom. You can do this either by going up into the attic to look, or by tapping across the ceiling: a hollow sound indicates a gap between the joists.

Where joists are not exactly in the right place for the fixing brackets, you can cut short lengths of nogging—say 75mm × 50mm or 75mm × 38mm—and skew nail them between the joists.

Establish the positions for these noggings by hand drilling through the ceiling from below, then poking a knitting needle through the hole so you can find it easily.

If this is not possible, for example because other people live on the floor above, your only alternative is to move your bed a few cm to one side or the other, if practicable.

Since one curtain rail crosses over another at each corner, the curtains must be cut so that those on the lower rail do not hang below the others. So when cutting out, make the lower curtain (or part curtain) shorter by the diameter of the curtain rod, shortening it from the top.

Elizabeth Whiting

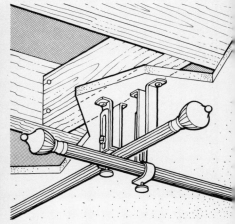

Above: *Noggings—lightweight timber members—cut in between the ceiling joists can be used if the joists themselves are wrongly positioned*

Below: *Where the curtain rails are to be of the 'crossover' type, expandable rail supports are needed*

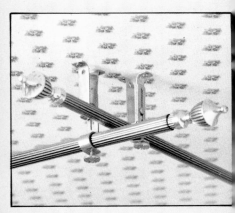

Left: *Bed in an alcove in a similar traditional style—the effect enhanced by two-level lighting*

Tim Street-Porter/EWA

Using the bathroom as living space can help to solve rush-hour problems when everyone is trying to get ready for school and work at the same time. For a family with an open lifestyle, the solution is a combined living room and bathroom, which several members, or even the whole family can use at once.

Designs and styles

The bathroom, perhaps surprisingly, is the best room in the house for letting your fantasies run riot. Even the most avid bather only spends a limited time there, so you are unlikely to find an unusual and imaginative decor too overpowering, as you might in one of the more frequently used rooms.

For the romantic, the possibilities are endless. You might, for example, create an Edwardian boudoir, conjuring up a bygone and more tranquil age with stained glass, wrought iron, hand-painted tiles and pot plants. By contrast, with clever use of modern—and often highly practical—materials, you could create a space age fantasy of the future.

If such ideas are too extravagant for your taste, you can still pamper yourself with up-to-date fabrics, floor coverings, furniture and fitments. This way you can start each day in a relaxed mood in pleasant surroundings.

Walls and floors

Humidity and condensation, while not necessarily problems, must be taken into consideration when planning a bathroom. It is never wise to buy ordinary wallpapers, carpets and other floor coverings without advice on the effects of these factors.

Tiles form an excellent and essential splashback around the bath and basin and can be arranged in more interesting patterns and shapes than the conventional straightforward squares and rectangles. You can of course half-tile or fully tile all the walls, but this will detract from the 'living room' effect. Tiles are available in every imaginable colour, including sophisticated shades such as crimson and cinnamon. They are also available with textured patterns, with individual printed and hand-painted designs, and in sets which form a complete picture mural when positioned on the wall.

Specialist shops which sell only tiles offer the widest choice, but some designs are extremely expensive. Some antique and junk shops sell tiles made during the last century; often very attractive and unusual, these would be ideal for a Victorian-style bathroom. Any tiles that incorporate pictures or patterns help to create the feeling that the room is something more than just a bathroom.

Alternatively, you can choose from an enormous range of vinyl wallpapers, from mock marble to Art Deco. You should be able to find one that suits the style and colour scheme of your bathroom without having to resort to typical and conventional patterns.

Pine panelling and cork tiles (on both

Camera Press

walls and floor) provide a happy combination of the practical and the decorative. The mellow natural colour, plus the sound and heat-insulating properties of the materials make these ideal for a cheerful family room.

Carpet is the most luxurious floor covering and the one most likely to give the true feel of a living room. Buy carpet or carpet tiles which have been specially treated against damp. A silicone spray can be used with ordinary carpet to prevent rotting, but this does not provide total protection.

A delightful casual look can be achieved with stripped or varnished floorboards and two or three rugs. Do make sure, however, that there is no possibility of splinters and that the rugs have a slip-proof backing.

Bathroom fitments

Baths, basins and bidets are now available in all colours and in an enormous range of shapes and sizes. Choosing an unconventional colour or a pretty pattern helps to get away from the utilitarian image of the bathroom and gives you the opportunity to mix and match colours in the decor.

A cheaper, but still interesting, treatment is to renovate an old bath. Remove any side panelling and paint the outside and the feet of the bath in your own choice of colours and patterns. In other words, make a feature of it.

You will require two or more basins for a family-style bathroom. Set these at different levels for adults and children. Flexible pipes will enable you to alter the heights as the children grow. Alternatively, fit the basins at the same height and provide adjustable steps for the younger members of the family.

In a free and easy household, a double

Left: *Setting the bath on a raised platform is perfect in a spacious room. Terracotta tiles provide a decorative finish for floor, dais and window sills*

Right: *Brown floor covering contrasts beautifully with white paintwork and soft pastel wallpaper to create a warm and friendly atmosphere in the bathroom*

Below: *A simply constructed vanity unit provides decorative bathroom storage as well as handy towel rails*

Liz Farrow/Jessica Strang

Syndication International

Above: *A stripped pine chest provides a decorative and practical addition to this bathroom. Leaded lights and a view of roses add a country flavour*

Above: *A variation on the four poster theme—this unusual bath surround uses tinted glass panels in a decoratively carved framework with brass supports*

bath can also speed up the morning rush. But luxury, rather than speed, is your criterion, you might consider a sunken bath or one with an unconventional shape —round or shell-shaped for instance. Remember though that these can be very expensive and that you must check yourself that they comply with local drainage regulations—there is nothing to prevent suppliers selling costly bathroom fitments with outlet or flushing arrangements which cannot be fitted legally.

There are two approaches to the layout of bathroom fixtures and fitments. For privacy keep the bath, basin and so on in one part of the room, perhaps concealed by a screen or a low wall. Use the rest of the room as a living area, furnished with chairs, a dressing table and whatever else you want. More extrovert people can make the bath the focal point of the room. Instead of fitting it against a wall, for instance, have it jutting out into the room, or even positioned in the centre.

Furniture
The addition of furniture not normally seen in bathrooms helps to create the

right mood. Once again, the keynote is to combine the practical and the decorative. Items such as tables, chairs, a dressing table, a screen and a free-standing cupboard can all be incorporated to create the right effect.

Bamboo and cane furniture will not be affected by the humid atmosphere and is easy to keep clean and dust-free. The kind of melamine-faced furniture designed for bedrooms is also an excellent choice. Wood is attractive, but avoid veneers which can easily be damaged. Upholstered chairs or sofas would certainly add a touch of luxury, but should be positioned away from the bath area and protected with an anti-damp spray. Brightly coloured deck chairs and other garden furniture would be ideal and make an unusual and extremely eye-catching display.

It is worth looking for furniture in junk shops and at auctions. Pieces which

might be unsuitable for the rest of the house may be just right for this sort of bathroom. You could be lucky enough to find such appropriate items as an old-fashioned wash-stand or else a carved wooden clothes horse which would make an interesting towel rail.

Lighting and heating
Abandon all ideas of a central, globe light and fluorescent tubes which are inevitably associated with bathrooms as bathrooms, rather than as living areas. Subtle, recessed lighting or several wall-hung lamps which throw a soft glow over the room are much more suitable. There is a wide choice of styles, from plain, circular lamps for a modern decor, to opalescent, shell-shaped shades for a more romantic effect. Ceiling spotlights and downlights are also a good feature, because they can be used for practical illumination and also dramatic highlights. But

Michael Nicholson/EWA

Right: *Plain and simple, yet highly practical. The corner bath and storage chests make good use of limited space in a neat and comfortable bathroom*

hanging one with a large ornate wooden frame or perhaps buy a cheval glass. An entire wall of mirror glass would complement a modern look and be especially useful in a small bathroom.

A selection of pretty china and glass pots and bottles can be used to store toiletries and to add charm to the decor. Do not simply line them up on a shelf or conceal them in a cupboard, but scatter them about the room.

Pot plants add tremendously to the mood. Hang them on trellis on the wall or stand them in attractive cachepots and planters around the room. Most house plants will thrive in a humid atmosphere and, if the room is warm and light, you can grow some really exotic flowering specimens.

Hang inexpensive pictures and posters on the walls. Protect them with frames and perspex, otherwise they will wrinkle and stain. Old-fashioned 'pub' mirrors and glass pictures are ideal and many modern reproductions are available fairly cheaply.

Look around your living room to see what makes it cosy and welcoming. Then try transferring the same ideas to your bathroom. Whether you choose to include vases of flowers, a decanter and glasses, a collection of Toby jugs or an 'executive' toy, give your creative flair full rein and design an unexpected haven of comfort.

remember that, for safety, there must not be direct access to the light switch inside the bathroom.

Heating presents similar safety problems. Electric wall heaters with a pull-cord are completely safe, but rather out of keeping with the desired effect. For a truly relaxed and cosy look nothing compares with an open coal fire or a closed wood or coal burning stove, but this is not always a practical choice. Lamps which also provide heat, specially designed for bathrooms and kitchens, are another possibility. An unobtrusive radiator is undoubtedly the easiest solution even if it does not have the visual impact of the other alternatives.

Accessories

Clever use of accessories will make all the difference. Mirrors are really important, but do not confine your choice to plain ones screwed directly on to the wall. Try

Bill McLaughlin

Pine bathroom accessories

This practical and attractive set of bathroom accessories is cheap and easy to make from standard softwood boards. You can design your bathroom around the complete set, made as one project. Or—much more fun—treat each item as a quick, one-day project in its own right

A good set of accessories can make a big difference to the comfort and decorative 'feel' of your bathroom. Our featured set is made of pine for a solid and durable finish which will tone with many different decorative schemes. Each item is perfectly co-ordinated with all the others, so you can either make the complete set or mix and match to suit your needs.

As well as the fittings shown here, the set includes a combined seat and linen box, a towel rail, a mirror frame and a toilet roll holder—all detailed in a later chapter. The wall cabinet and linen box are quite complicated, but the smaller fittings are simple to make and use a minimum of materials. They are also based on a modular system, with many interchangeable parts.

The working drawings overleaf give full details for the fittings shown. The three shelf fittings on page 53 are all built in exactly the same way, using glued and screwed butt joints and standard 100mm × 19mm softwood boards. Cut the boards to the length required and profile the edges as shown. The two smaller fittings have holes cut in the shelves to accommodate a mug, toothbrushes and a soap dish. When you have cut all the parts, drill the backboards and screw them together using a waterproof adhesive such as urea formaldehyde and brass screws to avoid problems with rust. Finish with at least two coats of lacquer, including the back of the backboards, then screw to the wall using mirror or coverhead screws.

The cabinet is a more complicated construction, using housing joints, bridle joints and rebates. Cut all the parts to size as shown. You can make them all, except the backboard and the door panels, from 150mm × 19mm softwood cut or planed down to size. If you prefer, buy the nearest stock size above, and plane down.

Assemble the frame in the order shown and fit the backboard. Make up the doors, checking their size exactly against the frame. Sand all the timber, and, as above, lacquer thoroughly. Hang the doors, fit knobs and catches, then screw to the wall.

Left: *The golden tones of natural pine will blend with almost any colour scheme. All the fittings are made on a modular system to look well, however many or few you use*

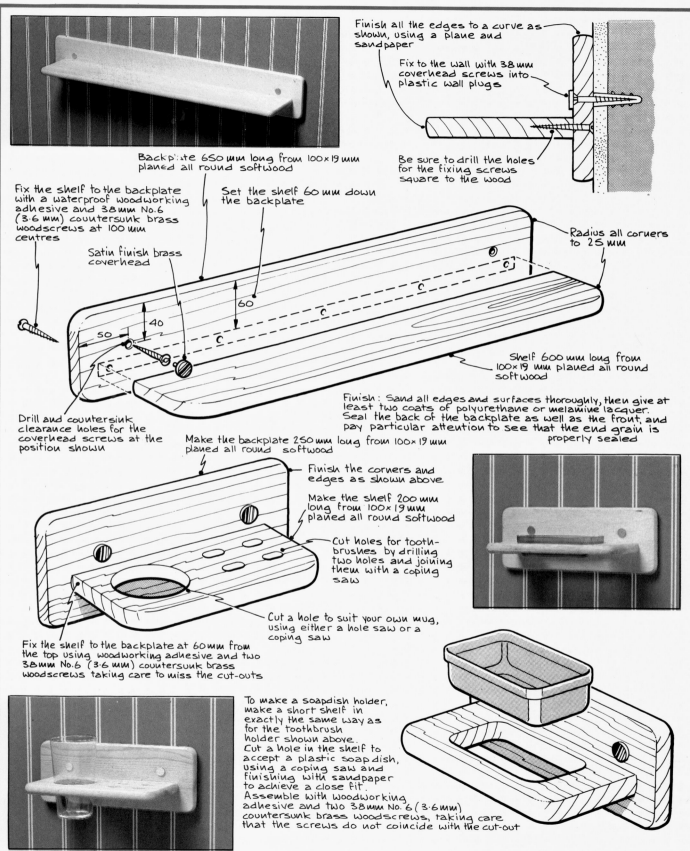

Finish all the edges to a curve as shown, using a plane and sandpaper

Fix to the wall with 38mm coverhead screws into plastic wall plugs

Be sure to drill the holes for the fixing screws square to the wood

Backplate 650 mm long from 100 × 19 mm planed all round softwood

Fix the shelf to the backplate with a waterproof woodworking adhesive and 38mm No.6 (3.6 mm) countersunk brass woodscrews at 100 mm centres

Set the shelf 60 mm down the backplate

Satin finish brass coverhead

Radius all corners to 25 mm

60

40

50

Drill and countersink clearance holes for the coverhead screws at the position shown

Shelf 600 mm long from 100 × 19 mm planed all round softwood

Finish: Sand all edges and surfaces thoroughly, then give at least two coats of polyurethane or melamine lacquer. Seal the back of the backplate as well as the front, and pay particular attention to see that the end grain is properly sealed

Make the backplate 250 mm long from 100 × 19 mm planed all round softwood

Finish the corners and edges as shown above.

Make the shelf 200 mm long from 100 × 19 mm planed all round softwood

Cut holes for toothbrushes by drilling two holes and joining them with a coping saw

Cut a hole to suit your own mug, using either a hole saw or a coping saw

Fix the shelf to the backplate at 60mm from the top using woodworking adhesive and two 38mm No.6 (3.6 mm) countersunk brass woodscrews taking care to miss the cut-outs

To make a soapdish holder, make a short shelf in exactly the same way as for the toothbrush holder shown above. Cut a hole in the shelf to accept a plastic soap dish, using a coping saw and finishing with sandpaper to achieve a close fit. Assemble with woodworking adhesive and two 38mm No. 6 (3.6 mm) countersunk brass woodscrews, taking care that the screws do not coincide with the cut-out

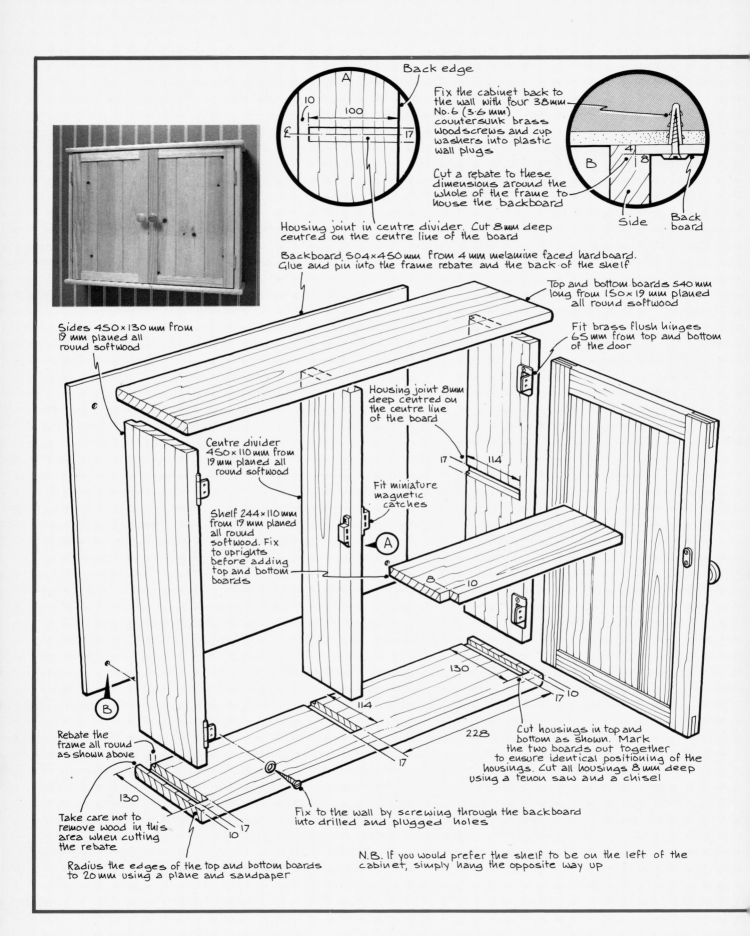

Back edge

A

10

100

17

Fix the cabinet back to the wall with four 38mm No.6 (3·6mm) countersunk brass woodscrews and cup washers into plastic wall plugs

Cut a rebate to these dimensions around the whole of the frame to house the backboard

2

4

B

18

Side

Back board

Housing joint in centre divider. Cut 8mm deep centred on the centre line of the board

Backboard 504×450mm from 4mm melamine faced hardboard. Glue and pin into the frame rebate and the back of the shelf

Top and bottom boards 540mm long from 150×19 planed all round softwood

Sides 450×130mm from 19mm planed all round softwood

Fit brass flush hinges 65mm from top and bottom of the door

Centre divider 450×110mm from 19mm planed all round softwood

Housing joint 8mm deep centred on the centre line of the board

17   114

Fit miniature magnetic catches

Shelf 244×110mm from 19mm planed all round softwood. Fix to uprights before adding top and bottom boards

A

8   10

130

17   10

114

228

17

Rebate the frame all round as shown above

B

130

10   17

Cut housings in top and bottom as shown. Mark the two boards out together to ensure identical positioning of the housings. Cut all housings 8mm deep using a tenon saw and a chisel

Take care not to remove wood in this area when cutting the rebate

Fix to the wall by screwing through the backboard into drilled and plugged holes

Radius the edges of the top and bottom boards to 20mm using a plane and sandpaper

N.B. If you would prefer the shelf to be on the left of the cabinet, simply hang the opposite way up

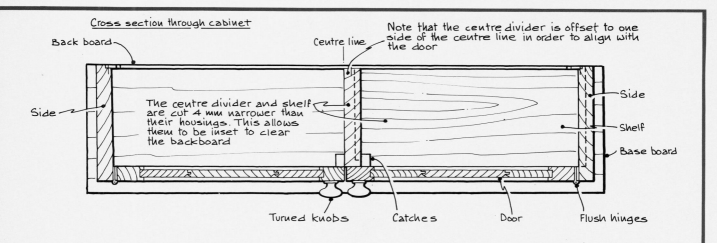

Cross section through cabinet

Back board

Note that the centre divider is offset to one side of the centre line in order to align with the door

Centre line

Side

The centre divider and shelf are cut 4 mm narrower than their housings. This allows them to be inset to clear the backboard

Side

Shelf

Base board

Turned knobs   Catches   Door   Flush hinges

Finish: Sand all surfaces and edges thoroughly. Finish all timber with polyurethane or melamine lacquer, paying particular attention to see that end grain is properly sealed.   Mask the back board or finish before fitting in place

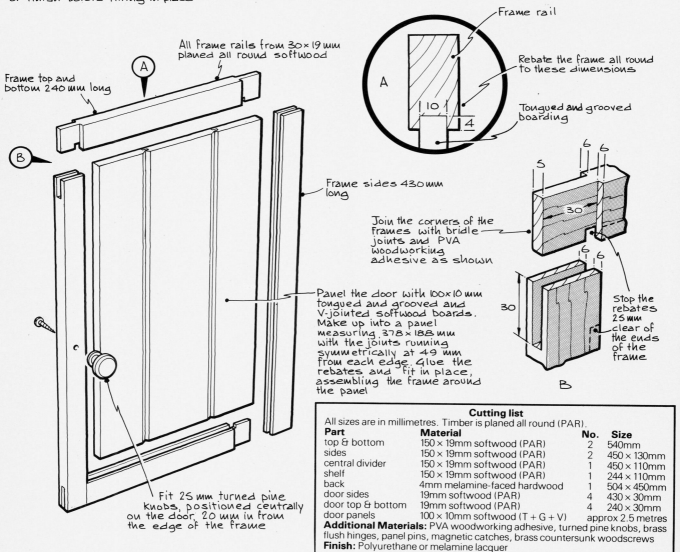

All frame rails from 30 × 19 mm planed all round softwood

A

Frame top and bottom 240 mm long

B

Frame sides 430 mm long

Frame rail

Rebate the frame all round to these dimensions

A   10   4

Tongued and grooved boarding

Join the corners of the frames with bridle joints and PVA woodworking adhesive as shown

Panel the door with 100×10 mm tongued and grooved and V-jointed softwood boards. Make up into a panel measuring 378×188 mm with the joints running symmetrically at 49 mm from each edge. Glue the rebates and fit in place, assembling the frame around the panel

Stop the rebates 25 mm clear of the ends of the frame

5   6 6

30

30   6 6

B

Fit 25 mm turned pine knobs, positioned centrally on the door, 20 mm in from the edge of the frame

Cutting list

All sizes are in millimetres. Timber is planed all round (PAR).

Part	Material	No.	Size
top & bottom	150 × 19mm softwood (PAR)	2	540mm
sides	150 × 19mm softwood (PAR)	2	450 × 130mm
central divider	150 × 19mm softwood (PAR)	1	450 × 110mm
shelf	150 × 19mm softwood (PAR)	1	244 × 110mm
back	4mm melamine-faced hardwood	1	504 × 450mm
door sides	19mm softwood (PAR)	4	430 × 30mm
door top & bottom	19mm softwood (PAR)	4	240 × 30mm
door panels	100 × 10mm softwood (T + G + V)		approx 2.5 metres

Additional Materials: PVA woodworking adhesive, turned pine knobs, brass flush hinges, panel pins, magnetic catches, brass countersunk woodscrews.
Finish: Polyurethane or melamine lacquer

More bathroom accessories

Completing the set of co-ordinating pine bathroom accessories featured on pages 52-55, this chapter gives construction details for a towel rail, toilet roll holder, mirror and a linen box

Below: All the accessories are designed to co-ordinate, so you can fit out your bathroom completely or choose your favourite items
Below left: The mirror, towel rail and toilet roll holder which complete the set are featured in the following pages

Malcolm Robertson

As with the other fittings, all the items featured here can be made from standard softwood boards. The linen box is a panelled frame construction and is quite complicated to build, but the three wall-mounted accessories are simplicity itself.

The towel rail and toilet roll holder are constructionally identical—the only difference is in length. Both have back plates identical to those used for the shelves. Use screws and glue to butt joint the two end boards, drilled to take a dowel rod. The end knobs are a push fit, and can be removed to change the roll.

The mirror frame is a simple rebated section with mitred corners. Fit the mirror in place and screw through the frame into the wall.

Make up the frame for the linen box, panelling with tongued-and-grooved boards. Cover a piece of plywood with foam and vinyl, then frame to form the lid. Hinge it in place.

Finish all the fittings with lacquer, making sure that they are thoroughly sealed all round.

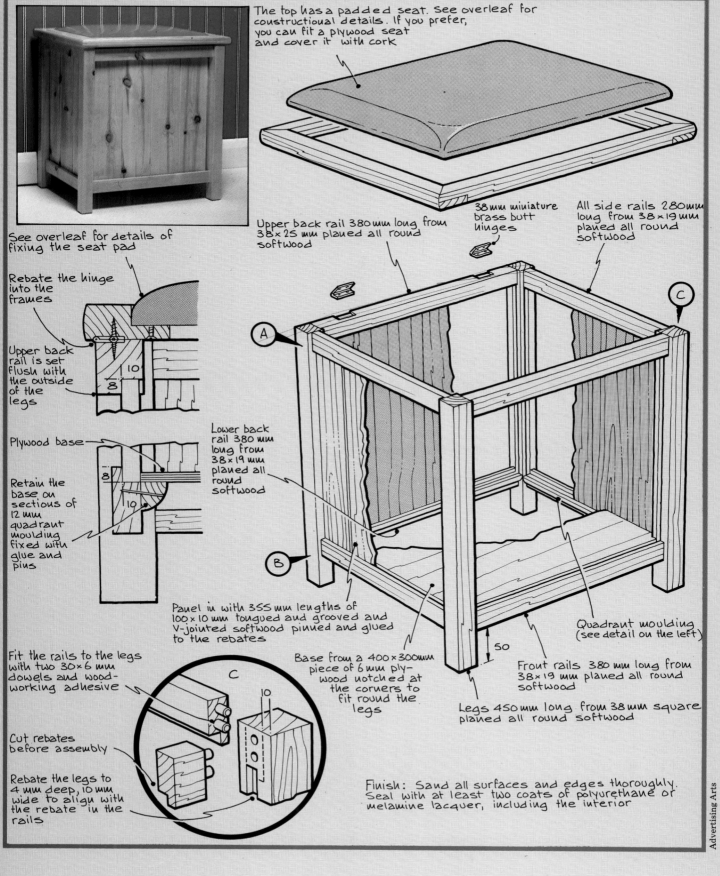

The top has a padded seat. See overleaf for constructional details. If you prefer, you can fit a plywood seat and cover it with cork

Upper back rail 380 mm long from 38 × 25 mm planed all round softwood

38 mm miniature brass butt hinges

All side rails 280 mm long from 38 × 19 mm planed all round softwood

See overleaf for details of fixing the seat pad

Rebate the hinge into the frames

Upper back rail is set flush with the outside of the legs

10

8

Plywood base

Retain the base on sections of 12 mm quadrant moulding fixed with glue and pins

8

10

Lower back rail 380 mm long from 38 × 19 mm planed all round softwood

A

C

B

Panel in with 355 mm lengths of 100 × 10 mm tongued and grooved and V-jointed softwood pinned and glued to the rebates

Fit the rails to the legs with two 30 × 6 mm dowels and woodworking adhesive

Cut rebates before assembly

Rebate the legs to 4 mm deep, 10 mm wide to align with the rebate in the rails

C

10

Base from a 400 × 300 mm piece of 6 mm plywood notched at the corners to fit round the legs

50

Quadrant moulding (see detail on the left)

Front rails 380 mm long from 38 × 19 mm planed all round softwood

Legs 450 mm long from 38 mm square planed all round softwood

Finish: Sand all surfaces and edges thoroughly. Seal with at least two coats of polyurethane or melamine lacquer, including the interior

Cover the seat with a piece of vinyl fabric measuring 515 × 415 mm

Make the seat pad from a piece of 25 mm foam measuring 415 × 315 mm

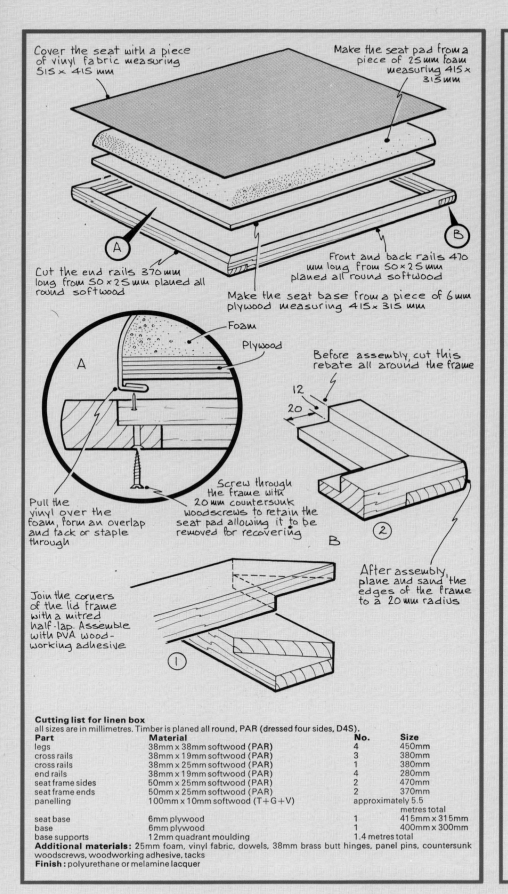

Cut the end rails 370 mm long from 50 × 25 mm planed all round softwood

Front and back rails 470 mm long from 50 × 25 mm planed all round softwood

Make the seat base from a piece of 6 mm plywood measuring 415 × 315 mm

Foam

Plywood

A

Before assembly, cut this rebate all around the frame

12
20

Pull the vinyl over the foam, form an overlap and tack or staple through

Screw through the frame with 20 mm countersunk woodscrews to retain the seat pad allowing it to be removed for recovering

B

2

After assembly, plane and sand the edges of the frame to a 20 mm radius

Join the corners of the lid frame with a mitred half-lap. Assemble with PVA woodworking adhesive

1

Make sure that the support bracket aligns with the lower edge of the profile of the backplate

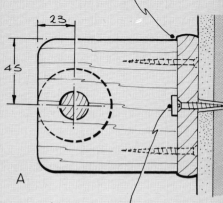

23
45

A

Screw through the backplate into drilled and plugged holes in the wall. On cavity walls use cavity fixings

Join the corners of the mirror frame with a mitred half-lap. Glue together with PVA woodworking adhesive and pin from behind

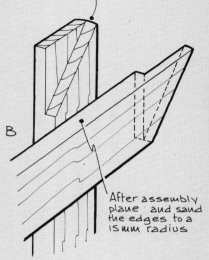

B

After assembly plane and sand the edges to a 15 mm radius

Cutting list for linen box
all sizes are in millimetres. Timber is planed all round, PAR (dressed four sides, D4S).

Part	Material	No.	Size
legs	38mm x 38mm softwood (PAR)	4	450mm
cross rails	38mm x 19mm softwood (PAR)	3	380mm
cross rails	38mm x 25mm softwood (PAR)	1	380mm
end rails	38mm x 19mm softwood (PAR)	4	280mm
seat frame sides	50mm x 25mm softwood (PAR)	2	470mm
seat frame ends	50mm x 25mm softwood (PAR)	2	370mm
panelling	100mm x 10mm softwood (T+G+V)	approximately 5.5 metres total	
seat base	6mm plywood	1	415mm x 315mm
base	6mm plywood	1	400mm x 300mm
base supports	12mm quadrant moulding	1.4 metres total	

Additional materials: 25mm foam, vinyl fabric, dowels, 38mm brass butt hinges, panel pins, countersunk woodscrews, woodworking adhesive, tacks
Finish: polyurethane or melamine lacquer

210 mm length of 18 mm dowel

Back plate 250mm long from 100 × 19mm planed all round softwood. Finish the corners and edges as shown on page 28

General constructional details are identical to the towel rail shown below

Chamfer the end of the dowel slightly

Curtain rod end knob. Glue to one end of the dowel, push fit the other end

Support bracket 100 × 90 mm from 100×19 mm planed all round softwood with profiled corners and edges

Assemble the parts by gluing and screwing from behind with 38 mm brass countersunk woodscrews

Back plate 650 mm long from 100 × 19 mm planed all round softwood with profiled corners and edges

Drill a 19 mm hole for the rod

150

A

40

610 mm length of 18 mm dowel

Fix back to the wall with coverhead screws and satin finish brass coverheads

Curtain rod end knob. Glue to end of the dowel, push fit the other end

B

Fix to the wall with coverhead screws and satin finished brass coverheads fitted through the frame

Frame top and bottom from 50×19 mm planed all round softwood, 520 mm long

Make the backing board from a piece of 4mm hardboard measuring 450×300 mm

Plain mirror cut to 450 × 300 mm

Glazing sprigs

Hardboard backing

Mirror

Retain the mirror and backing with glazing sprigs

15

8

Cut out this rebate before assembly

Frame sides from 50×19 mm planed all round softwood 370 mm long

C

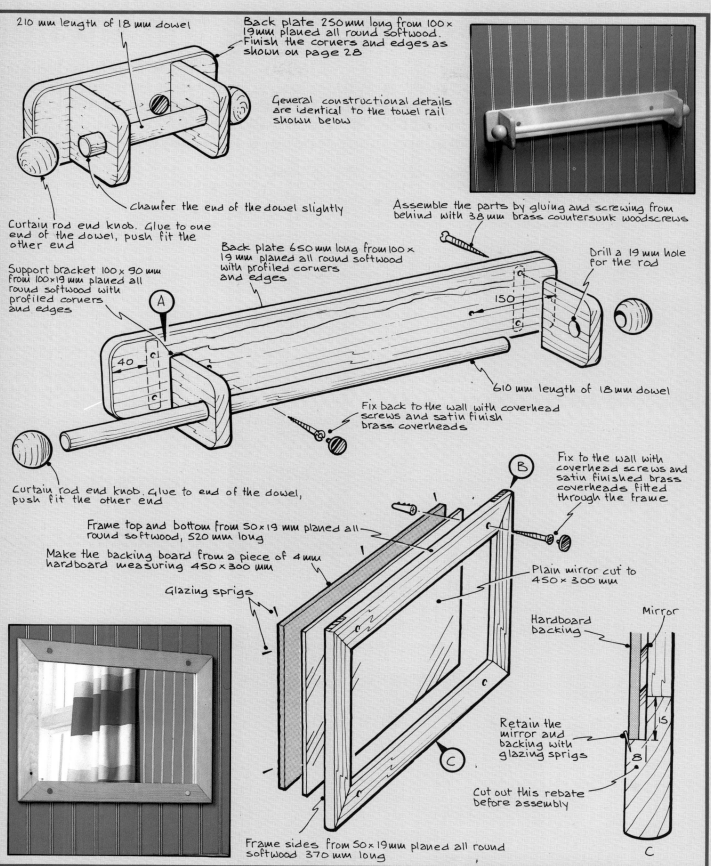

Redesigning the kitchen

● **Deciding on kitchen activities** ● **Kitchen design theory** ● **What can go and what can stay in the kitchen** ● **How to make the best use of the space available** ● **Deciding on the scope of your improvement scheme** ● **Basic layouts**

A Left and below: *This small galley kitchen contains only the barest essentials and has several problem fixtures, yet careful planning and tasteful decorations make the most of the room. With the main appliances on one wall, much needed worktop space is provided on the opposite wall and this doubles as a breakfast bar. Seating takes the form of stools (the bar is worktop height) which can be stowed under the worktop when access to the back door is needed. The ugly boiler and flue have been well disguised by a worktop and cupboards and the existing old gas cooker blended in nicely by combining it with traditional-style units in natural wood. The glass panelled back door and casement above provide plenty of natural light*

Elizabeth Whiting

This is the first part of a major Home improvements course series on how to refurbish, modernize or restructure your kitchen—generally the most heavily used room in the house, and often the one most in need of improvement. Although it is designed to help anyone improve their kitchen—whether through drastic structural modifications or just simply by revamping old units—the emphasis of the series is away from the now 'traditional' fitted kitchen, so often the ideal of designers only. Instead it lays stress on designing and building a kitchen yourself, with just you and your family in mind. This should give you a room which meets your needs almost exactly but does not cost the earth—something designers and mass producers cannot do.

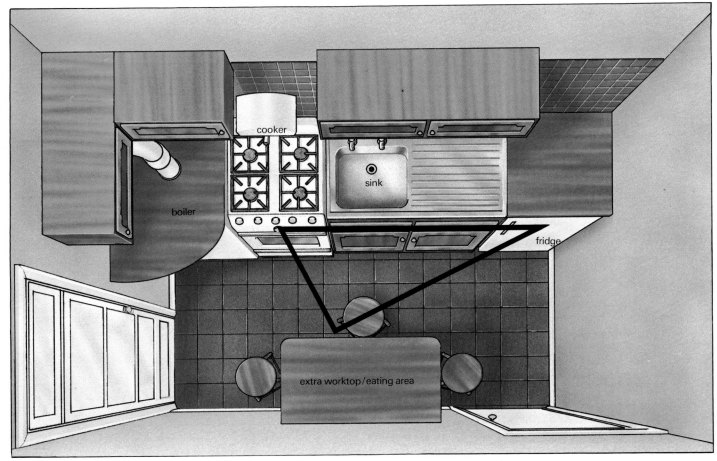

cooker

sink

boiler

fridge

extra worktop/eating area

Steve Cross

B. Right and below: *A classic U shaped kitchen for the convenience cook. All the appliances are grouped neatly around a semi-circle with plenty of worktop and drainer space between them, despite the room's small size. Furthermore, the core triangle is well out of the access way to the back door. The space taken up by the appliances makes floor to ceiling storage essential—here, neat off-the-shelf units finished in hardwood*

The first part of the series deals with designing your kitchen around your family and the space at your disposal, inside the existing room and elsewhere in the home. The next part covers appliances, fittings, services and decoration. The final part gives a 'plan of action' and profiles successful modifications to two problem kitchens, showing how the theory can be put into practice.

Kitchen activities

Start your planning by thinking about what you do – or will want to do – in the kitchen. The panel on page 65 lists the usual activities, so study it and relate it to the needs of your family. Some of those mentioned are essentials, and one way or another you must accommodate them. But others are strictly optional: you may not have had the space or the inclination to practise them under the present set-up, but this does not necessarily exclude them from the new design. At this stage it suffices to say that you should decide what you want, then see if you can design a kitchen to fit those requirements.

Cooking is a quite obvious kitchen activity, but different cooks have different needs and this in turn must influence your design. 'Convenience' cooks need the kind of space in which to instal the gadgetry that makes cooking easy—a modern oven and hob, a food processer, a freezer, perhaps even a microwave. They also need cupboard space for bulk food storage and for packing things out of the way.

More traditional cooks tend to need more work surfaces and plenty of shelves so that fresh foods and kitchen utensils are close to hand.

Laundry and washing facilities should be looked at carefully. In Canada, these are traditionally carried out in a basement, freeing the kitchen for its primary use as somewhere to prepare food. In the UK, the kitchen is generally used as a laundry as well—but in small kitchens, it is well worth thinking about moving the washing facilities elsewhere; perhaps to a bathroom or a small spare room which offer the same services.

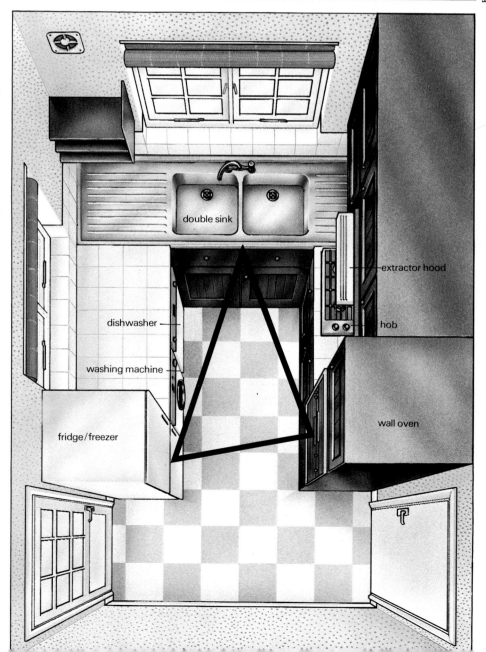

double sink

dishwasher

washing machine

fridge/freezer

extractor hood

hob

wall oven

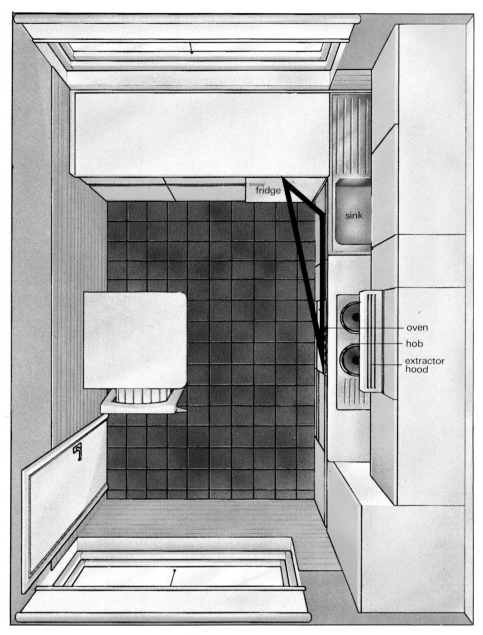

fridge

sink

oven
hob
extractor
hood

Camera Press

If your kitchen is large enough, eating and entertaining are very important activities because people always gravitate to where there is food and warmth. A lot depends on what goes on in the rest of the house. For example, in a house with no dining room the kitchen makes a natural substitute; and where dining is not a problem, the kitchen could make an ideal second living room.

The kind of space and facilities needed for the activities above can often be adapted—or made adaptable—to fit in with leisure requirements or the needs of a young family. Some hobbies are just too messy for anywhere else in the house yet they often end up there just because the kitchen facilities cannot cope. The same applies to young children. The kitchen is the ideal place for them to play while being kept an eye on, yet if the environment is harsh the space will be wasted.

There are of course many other considerations of this sort to be taken into account at this stage. The end result is bound to be a compromise, but you can make sure that this is in your favour.

Design theory

Kitchen design theory is just that—theory. Only you can interpret and modify the various rules and guidelines to arrive at your own ideal.

The basis is the *core or work triangle* —an imaginary area encompassing sink, cooker (range) and fridge around which the main kitchen activities are centred. The units can be arranged in a U shape, at right-angles or in line, but they must have work surfaces between them (how much depends mainly on how the cooking is done), and the total distance around the work triangle should not exceed 7m.

The idea behind the core triangle is that it places everything within easy reach and saves you having to move about more than you have to. Having work surfaces between units enables you to prepare then cook, unpack then store, or stack then wash, without too much confusion. It applies to large and small kitchens alike because you only do so much at one time in one place: once the limit is reached, further work surfaces and units often become superfluous.

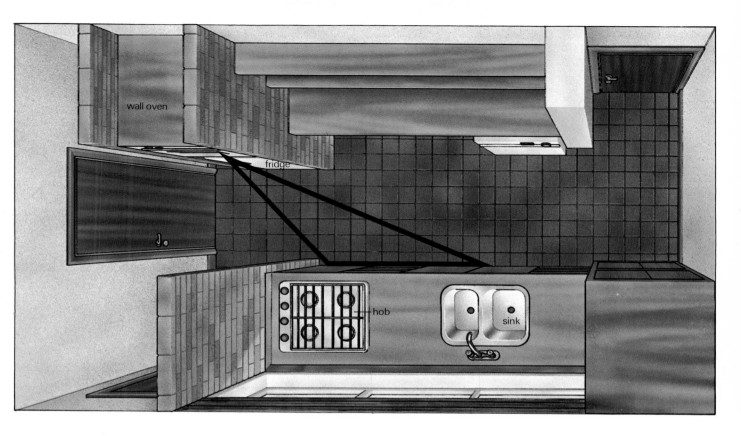

wall oven

fridge

hob

sink

If you are tempted by the thought of streamlined, fitted units on all four walls, think again. Ask yourself if the space they would take up might be put to better use as, say, a dining area. This would still leave you with the core triangle, which could be as streamlined as you like.

What goes, what stays

Before you go any further towards positioning the core triangle, adding other appliances and storage, or allocating space for activities, consider what you might be able to move out of the kitchen. The question is all-important in small kitchens where space is tight, but even in larger rooms it might actually be more convenient to place certain items or appliances elsewhere.

Freezer: If you have (or plan to get) a freezer for economical bulk buying rather than day to day use, it may be able to go in the garage or an outhouse, in the hall, or down in a basement.

Crockery and utensils: Items of this sort which are used only occasionally make ideal candidates for banishment to a sideboard or dresser in a living room or to a cupboard in the hall. But those in everyday use must remain close to the core triangle.

Washing machine: As mentioned above, this may be more convenient in another room. In the UK, the bathroom is an obvious choice, but if this is not

large enough, some other nook or cranny currently going to waste may do just as well. Your main consideration will be drainage arrangements.

Preserves and bulk foods: Like the freezer, there is no point in having these crammed into the kitchen unless you need to get to them frequently. A shallow cupboard under the stairs or in the hall would be ideal; so might shelving in a garage or outhouse.

Problem kitchens

Problem kitchens and kitchen problems are two different things. Whereas the second can be eliminated by skilful and thoughtful redesigning, the first exist because the usual rules do not apply.

The almost universal complaint is that the kitchen is too small, but this can be compounded by its having far too many doors opening into it, by the fact that it has to act as a thoroughfare to the back door, or even by the need to house many large appliances – some of which you may have mistakenly installed yourself.

The obvious solution in nearly all cases is drastic structural modification – knocking through, extension, removal or repositioning of doors – so that the design ideals can be accommodated. But this is not something to rush into, and it can often be avoided if you are prepared to compromise or relocate things elsewhere.

If you take a look at your existing

D. Above and below: *Although the layout of this pretty little galley kitchen might at first seem strange, it has been designed with extra appliances in mind. The dishwasher on the inside wall is plumbed into an internal waste pipe to be joined later by a washing machine and dryer. The wall oven and fridge can safely obstruct the back door because they will not all be in use simultaneously*

Elizabeth Whiting

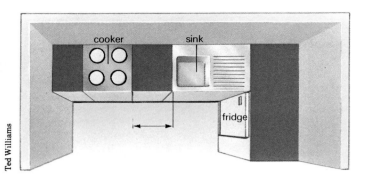

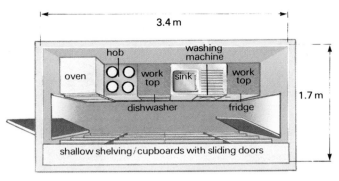

cooker sink fridge

3.4 m

oven hob washing machine work top sink work top dishwasher fridge 1.7 m

shallow shelving / cupboards with sliding doors

Ted Williams

Elizabeth Whiting

E. Above: *A small L shaped arrangement incorporating the basic core triangle and (right) a narrow galley designed to hold a full complement of appliances*

F. Right and far right: *A larger kitchen along traditional country farmhouse lines—the obligatory kitchen table is joined by a smaller one to cater for a wide range of activities. The core triangle centres cooking in one corner of the room with good worktop space and plenty of open shelves for storage. The large fridge/freezer is within the core but is easy to reach from elsewhere*

kitchen, it is likely to fall into one of four types: L shaped with appliances and fitments on adjacent walls; U shaped with three walls in use; galley shaped with opposite walls only housing all fittings and equipment; or I shaped in which the room is exceptionally narrow and only one wall can be used.

Bearing in mind the idea of the core triangle, consider if the existing layout eases the problem or makes it worse. For instance, if your existing galley shaped kitchen is more than 2.4m wide and is not a through traffic zone, a U shaped layout would make better use of the space.

A tiny room is no cause for despair. If your cooking consists of preparing instant meals using convenience foods you may not need more than a minimal work surface between sink and stove. This style of cooking works perfectly well in a room where the walls are so close together that there can only be work surfaces down one side. Fig. E shows a neat arrangement for essentials with the fridge flanking the main spread.

For more ambitious cooks, a perfectly satisfactory kitchen for preparing quite large and elaborate meals can be created in a room as small as 3.4m × 1.7m. The tight galley arrangement shown in fig. E includes floor to ceiling shallow storage covering one wall while the opposite wall houses many labour saving appliances— sink, dishwasher, washing machine— and still gives generous, well distributed work surfaces.

Making a decision

Armed with the information about core triangles and layouts in relation to room shape, and with some idea of what activities the new kitchen is going to have to cater for, you are almost ready to make a survey of the existing room and decide roughly on the design.

The one thing you have yet to decide is the scope of your project—whether you want to make major structural alterations, just to gut the existing room and start again from scratch, or simply to refurbish and modify what is already there. Because all three overlap to some extent, and to avoid repetition, the survey guide below starts with the simplest.

Refurbishment: Start by considering the kitchen sink and its relation to the cooker and fridge. You do not want to have to move it if at all possible and it may be that the other two units already form a core triangle in a layout that suits the room shape. If they do not, you will have to move them and plan for new work surfaces in between.

At the same time consider doors and windows. Try if you can to keep the core away from any thoroughfare—such as the back door—and leave it well lit by natural daylight. While you are working, your

shadow should not fall over your work and you should not obstruct entrances.

Do not necessarily be restricted by the walls: the shape of your kitchen might allow part of the triangle to be formed by an island unit—with perhaps the fridge on one side and room for some kind of breakfast bar on the other. Its final form is not important at this stage—just its function and the space it takes up.

With the core triangle established, turn your attention to other appliances. The most inflexible of these are washing machines and dishwashers because they both need drainage facilities (water supplies are much easier to arrange). If you are concerned only with refurbishment, it is generally safer to plan for them near the sink and thus near an existing drainage point. Bear in mind that the easiest places to plumb in the drainage outlets of these appliances is at a gully or at the existing sink outlet.

Next comes storage around the core triangle. Here you will need space for everyday foods, much of the crockery and kitchen utensils, and also cleaning materials. Some of it can probably go under the sink, and more under the work surfaces, but beware of having to stoop or bend too much. Wall storage is generally

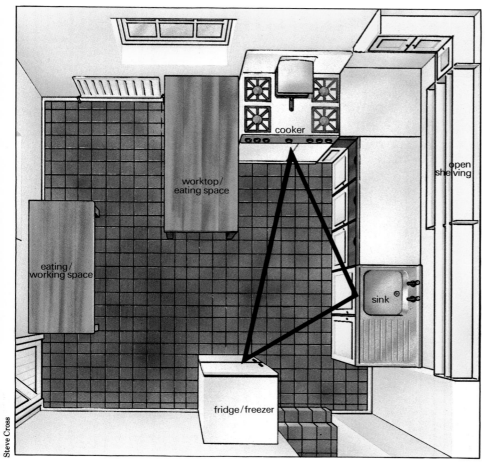

Steve Cross

Labels on image: cooker, worktop/eating space, open shelving, eating/working space, sink, fridge/freezer

more practical and helps to keep the area compact, though you may want to leave space to fit a drainer above the sink and an extractor over the cooker.

Once the main work area is complete you can 'spread out' to embrace the other kitchen activities being planned for, which should by now be very much easier. Narrow and long rectangular rooms lend themselves naturally to some form of bar—along or across the room—for eating and leisure. In square rooms there is often a better case for a traditional kitchen table—once out of fashion, but still unrivalled for versatility and flexibility.

Any door to the exterior can now be given some thought. Unless there is a porch or lobby, some kind of storage and hanging space would be useful here.

Finally come the fixtures and fittings tailored very specifically to your own requirements. These offer plenty of flexibility anyway, but if you have got the 'basics' right they should fit in easily.

Gutting: In this case all the above considerations apply, but you will have more freedom as to where to site the core triangle. Again start with the sink. The traditional place for this has always been on an outside wall near a window, mainly because it gives a pleasant view while

working but also because drainage arrangements are generally very much simpler in this position.

However, modern work patterns call for less and less time to be spent at the sink and if you have a window with a good view it might be better employed as the centrepiece of, say, a dining area. Drainage is always a difficulty but you can get a better idea of where your options lie by making a sketch of the drainage system as it might affect the kitchen. Sketch in the parts you cannot see if necessary, bearing in mind that drains always follow simple, straight routes and that there will be inspection covers at any junctions.

The actual technicalities of reconnecting the sink are in the next section of the series, but at this stage it is helpful to know that you need a gully, waste water pipe or combined waste/soil stack (in newer homes). Of these, the gully is the easiest to connect to, followed by PVC stacks. Cast-iron stacks are difficult to break into, but are often worth replacing in their entirety. Underground pipework presents the greatest problem, though if the pipes run through the kitchen it is usually possible to instal a short sub-stack at some point on the run.

While you are thinking about drainage, consider possible locations for a washing machine or dishwasher on the fringes of the core triangle.

You should now have some idea of where the core triangle is to go. Before you make a final decision, reconsider the key questions:

● Does the arrangement and the layout that will develop from it make best use of the room's shape?
● Does the core interfere with access or through traffic (and can this be avoided)?
● Does it leave you enough room to cater for the activities you want?

Structural alteration: If you are planning to revamp your kitchen on this scale, the important thing is to make sure that the alterations serve some useful purpose. The main considerations should always be to increase the amount of usable space and to improve access—but both depend on what you want the kitchen for.

If knocking through features in your plans, make sure that the new room will work for you along the lines described above. Extending a long narrow room might do no good at all; nor might adding a small lobby to a large square room.

The same applies to extensions: if you think purely in terms of adding extra space and overlook how that space is going to be used, you could come unstuck.

Structural alteration does of course give you the most freedom, and once you have decided what you need, you can start drawing up your own personal plans. There is no reason why you should not aim for the ideal of separate work, eating and access areas. But always remember that it is what you want that counts: the theory is there only to help you achieve it.

KITCHEN ACTIVITIES

Primary
Food preparation and cooking
Serving meals
Washing dishes and pots
Storing food—perishables and bulk
Storing cooking and eating utensils
Housing kitchen appliances

Secondary
Laundry:
housing washing machine and drier,
facilities for hand laundry

Optional Extras
Dining area
Place for children's play
Entertaining friends
Hobbies/workshop

Planning the kitchen

● **The importance of planning** ● **Laying out the central appliances** ● **Access to fringe appliances** ● **Fitting a twin-tub sink** ● **Installing the services** ● **Data panels for materials and equipment** ● **Cross-referenced index to skills courses**

Redesigning your kitchen involves a network of decisions about appliances, fittings, services and decorations. This second section of redesigning the kitchen explains the choices you need to make before settling on your new layout. Bear in mind both what you already have, what you can afford to instal now and also what you may want to include if your family or finances increase.

As explained in the first section, the most functional kitchens group the essential appliances – sink, cooker and fridge – close together with well-lit, generous work surfaces all around. But kitchens come in as many shapes and sizes as people and each family makes different demands on the room – especially in housing additional equipment. Because of this it is only possible to give guidelines for your improvement scheme, not a formula for the perfect layout. But even so it is worth looking at two successful designs (figs A and B) to see how appliances dictate the space arrangement and what can be achieved with careful planning.

Although the next section explains how to draw up a plan of action for your improvements scheme, it is useful to keep in mind when considering planning possibilities that 600mm × 600mm is the conventional measurement for depth and width of appliances and furnishings, surfaces and units. Note how this works in the various examples which, probably like your own room, are not exact multiples of this measurement. Work surfaces cover extra space which can then be used for racks for vegetables, tea towels, or trays. If space is very limited and you are buying new appliances and units, you can find them only 500mm wide or even 500mm deep also, so you can proportionately scale down your kitchen altogether.

Central appliances

However large the range of appliances you intend to include in your kitchen, the priority should be to put sink, cooker and fridge in the most convenient places for each other. Take a fresh look at your existing layout to see which, if any, you need to or are able to move.

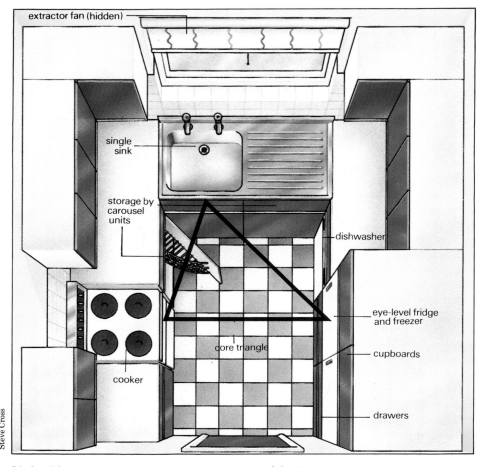

extractor fan (hidden)

single sink

storage by carousel units

dishwasher

cooker

core triangle

eye-level fridge and freezer

cupboards

drawers

Steve Cross

Sinks: If you intend to replace a worn-out sink, think about repositioning it at the same time. Many places other than the conventional outside wall location are feasible by extending the drainage. Radical changes can be made if you can use the 'clearing eye' system, as explained below. However, this will not be necessary if the modification to drainage is minimal. For instance you may be able to move the sink unit much closer to work surfaces, while still retaining a view outside and good lighting, by putting the sink at right angles to its present window wall location. A short move sideways is sometimes necessary to replace a single sink with double bowls. A double sink – even if one is only half-size – is especially

useful if you are installing a waste disposal unit. Always remember that a space for a wall-mounted drainer above the draining board is a great advantage.

Figs 1 to 9 show how to set two bowls into a worktop – including cutting and tiling the worktop, connecting two wastes into a single drain and fitting a mixer tap. Fitting separate bowls or a drainer into a worktop is not only more stylish and adaptable but also considerably cheaper than buying a complete sink unit.

Cooker and fridge: It is simpler to move the cooker (range) than the sink, either by repositioning the electric outlet or by having the gas outlet extended by means of a flexible tube running behind floor cupboards. The same applies to gas and electric fridges.

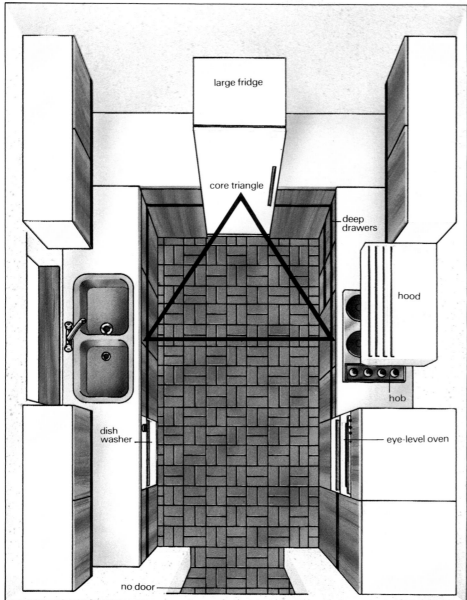

large fridge

core triangle

deep drawers

hood

hob

eye-level oven

dish washer

no door

1 When replacing a single sink with a twin-tub unit start by laying the new worktop in place and checking that it is properly levelled

2 Lay the two tubs and the mixer tap you are using in their respective positions and check that the tap reaches both tubs comfortably

3 Now mark the positions of the tubs on the worktop by drawing a pencil line around the inside of the units as they lie upside down on the surface

Sometimes you can achieve the best kitchen layout only by placing the fridge and cooker side by side. In this case allow in plans for a 50mm thick board of fire retardant expanded polystyrene to be wedged firmly between the two – but not fixed, as it should be removable for cleaning. The same principle applies to the space-saving arrangement of a bank of built-in appliances with a wall oven above a small fridge. If separate hob and oven are adjacent, there should be a minimum of 300mm setting down space between them. Wall ovens are an especially good choice for anyone who cannot squat easily or if you want to make the kitchen safer for your children. They also allow you more freedom when choosing storage and cooking facilities.

Fringe appliances

Certain other appliances need to be close to the core of the kitchen without interfering with the central work area. These may be items you do not yet have but if you are changing the electrics and furniture in the room, this is the best time to prepare the way for them so you do not have to rip out your current improvements in the near future.

Dishwasher: A dishwasher should be where you can load it while standing at the sink, as dirty crockery may need a preliminary rinse. Also, of course, it has to be plumbed into water supplies and drains. If you have a choice of either side of the sink, choose the side where unloading clean dishes to storage is a simple movement.

4 *To cut the apertures, drill a series of 10mm holes inside the pencil line and join them all up using a padsaw. Do not cut outside the circle*

5 *Now lay the tubs in position and check that they fit properly. If their holes are too small enlarge them slightly with a half-round file*

6 *If you are fitting a waste disposal unit do it now. Secure the upper part of it to the sink before fitting the rest*

7 *Now connect the hot and cold water supplies to the mixer tap, and the plastic overflow pipes to the overflow outlets at the backs of the tubs*

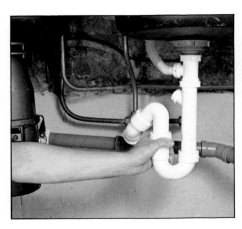

8 *When the waste disposal unit is finally fitted you can connect the waste pipes and traps. Connect both wastes together for convenience*

9 *When all the water supplies and wastes have been connected seal the tubs, the tap unit and the worktop itself with a suitable mastic sealant*

Freezer: If you decide to keep your freezer in the kitchen, do not be bound by the convention of placing it next to the fridge. If you already have a tall fridge and freezer and can only put them side by side, keep the fridge nearest the central core area. The most remote corner of the kitchen is perfectly suitable for a freezer, particularly the top-loading locker type which cannot be used as a worktop.

Washing machine and dryer: These have to be close to each other but as far from the food area as possible. The problem usually lies in drainage, which means any machine not plumbed in to its own separate water supply and waste has to stand next to the sink unless it can be completely disconnected and wheeled away on castors for storage.

A top-loading machine is only suitable for very spacious kitchens though a hinged worktop can be fitted over it. Any machine which discharges its waste via a pipe looped into the sink is unhygienic because germs can come into contact with food so you should try to avoid this.

The most space-saving and hygienic arrangement is a front loading machine plumbed permanently into a fixed waste pipe with a dryer mounted directly over it. But whatever the arrangement of your appliances, if you have to do laundry in the kitchen try to ensure that one worktop area can be reserved exclusively for the clean and dirty washing.

Work surfaces

Give priority to work surfaces over storage – cupboards and shelves can be slotted in to any unused spaces later. Make sure, too, that they are close to the centre of work activities and key appliances. There should be adequate space for food preparation – such as vegetables – near the sink, a place for mixing food, and also a serving area to set down dishes and plates close to the cooker so these do not have to be carried. These can all be combined, as in the town kitchen (fig. A).

However, resist the temptation to have more work surfaces than you really need. The kitchen in fig. B has as much as most families will ever need at one time; vast areas created by ranges of floor cupboards just get filled up with items which could better be stored out of sight. The space is better used by installing wall to floor storage, leaving space for a generous kitchen table.

The ideal worktop height depends on the height of the person using it and what they are accustomed to. The average recommended is 900mm and, if in doubt, try this out and vary it between 850mm and 1000mm.

The sink top is best at a slightly higher

Simon Butcher

George Wright

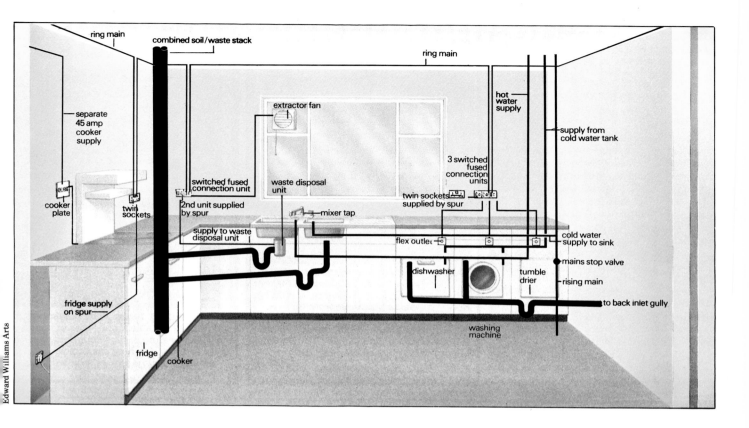

level—900mm to 1050mm—as arms go over the edge and into the sink. Ideally the bottom of the sink should be comfortably at fingertip level of whoever uses it – but of course, in most families this is impossible.

Solid units are best equipped with simple timber plinths to provide toe space. Plinths are also useful for 'averaging out' units of different heights or for raising 900mm units to a level which suits you better.

Not all kitchen jobs are best done at the standard levels. Standing jobs requiring a down-from-above direction – such as cake or breadmaking – are easiest at a kitchen table or surface of similar height (around 635mm). This can also be a good level for setting a hob into a worktop, as it is easier for stirring, frying or looking into pans. Try to leave knee space under any low work surface as this can be as useful as a table for sitting down food preparation jobs.

Flap down worktops are space-savers in very small kitchens for extra laying out or eating space. But in large kitchens they tend to be left down and accumulate unnecessary objects, so they should be reserved for occasional tasks like ironing. This is also a risk with slide-out cutting boards, and the alternative – often cheaper – is to store these in vertical racks.

One effective way of making the most

of a heavily used worktop is to put in a narrow shelf about 250mm above the surface. This is kept free for ingredients and utensils in use during food preparation so these do not clutter up the larger work surface but are spread out ready for use. The shelf should be high enough to clear any mixers or similar equipment used on the work surface but well below wall units which usually start at 1350mm above the ground.

The normal overall depth of most appliances – cookers, fridges and dishwashers is 600mm, and where these form a line with floor units, you need a worktop up to 700mm deep to achieve a smooth run. So decide first on the layout of appliances before buying or making the work surface. Where appliances do not dictate depth and space is limited, a worktop depth of as little as 400mm can be very useful. Remember though that this means storage both above and below has to be much shallower than the conventional units.

Storage

Slot storage into, around, below and above the 'core area' of work surfaces and appliances. Choose either open shelves, cupboards, drawers or hanging racks – or preferably a mixture of all – according to space available and the items to be stored. Your choice should suit the type of cooking you usually do.

C. A typical layout of the services in an L-shaped kitchen showing how the requirements of cooking, washing up and laundry can be accommodated with a neat and orderly arrangement of plumbing and drainage pipes, and electric cables. Note that the plumbing and electricity arrangement shown applies solely to the systems in use in the UK and not those in other countries.

Wall and floor cupboards already in your kitchen can all be repositioned according to your new layout if you need them. Remember that a work surface does not have to have anything under it and most people find it less strenuous to reach things above 900mm than to bend down. Floor cupboards are most useful for storing large, deep objects which will not fit into a 300mm deep wall cupboard or for anything not frequently used. If you want to use this level for food storage, the only really convenient arrangement is a two storey carousel which makes use of an otherwise difficult corner.

Another sensible use for under worktop space is for deep easy-sliding drawers for storing large but light objects like saucepans and flour sieves. These can be useful either near the sink or the stove. The conventional stack of shallow drawers should be avoided, especially in a small room: only one drawer – for cutlery

Final kitchen design

The decision-making process ● Tackling the jobs in the correct order ● Two conversions of a galley kitchen ● Working out the core area of the kitchen ● Alternatives for a larger kitchen ● Drawing up working plans properly

Armed with all the information supplied in the previous two sections, you should now be ready to plan and start work on your own kitchen. The order of deciding on the design is quite different from the order of work (see the panels below). You will also be ready to start drawing up your own scale plans; special advice on what to consider and where to start when doing kitchen plans is given below.

However, as you may now be feeling confused by the options open and where to begin, this last detailed section begins by

A. Below: *The kitchen that was the base for conversions A and B. Very little thought had gone into its layout and basic considerations such as worktop height and the core triangle seem never to have crossed the planner's mind*

following through how two kitchens were remodelled, giving alternative plans for two very different households in each case. Although you can never find the perfect solution to your own kitchen by copying another, analysing the design and renovation processes can be both instructive and inspiring.

The small kitchen

First consider a kitchen as inconvenient and antiquated as anyone is likely to have to tackle. It measures only 3m × 1.85m and has a single frosted window overlooking the neighbour's wall. Two doors at either end open inwards, one directly on to steps down to the garden and the other into a hallway with a small larder. It is typical of kitchens in semi-detached two storey houses built in the UK in the 1920's, though it has plenty in

common with—and many of the same problems as—small kitchens throughout the world (fig. A).

For all its limitations even this kitchen can be modified to serve either a young couple on a very tight budget or a large family with many bulky appliances to accommodate and the money to make necessary changes.

Conversion A

Fig A shows the kitchen the young couple took over. An array of antiquated fitments were lined up against the window wall: a miniature dresser and old stove at one end, a scratched enamel sink and drainer served by an erratic gas water heater at the other. A fridge had taken up the gap, plugged by a long flex into a single socket high up by the internal door. The opposite wall had a high shelf and radiant electric fire fixed to it; against it was a table used for eating despite the doors. The garden door had wet rot and the window wall streamed with condensation during cooking because it was brick faced with thick plaster and shiny paint. The floor was surfaced with cold tiles in bad condition.

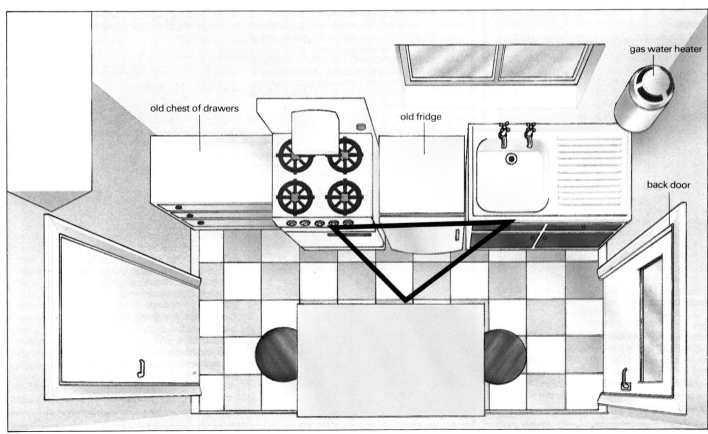

old chest of drawers
old fridge
gas water heater
back door
Steve Cross

Considerations: The couple had to use the larder for household storage so all food, crockery and utensils had to be found places in the new kitchen. This was not a major problem as they shopped regularly and kept few bulk items. However, they had to house their giant washing machine in the kitchen and also wanted to eat breakfast there.

As their finances were limited, they could not spare cash for insulation or ventilation at this stage. Their carpentry skills were also limited so any alterations had to be simple. Consequently their design had to incorporate off-the-shelf kitchen fitments and secondhand appliances wherever possible. Unfortunately the only item they could retain was the radiant fire as everything else was either too worn, or wasted valuable space.

The couple's solution: Nevertheless, by careful planning they were able to make a neat bank of fitments along the window wall forming the core area of the kitchen (fig. B). This was the only place for a smooth, long run of work surfaces. As it was exactly 3000mm and their self-assembly tops and units came in

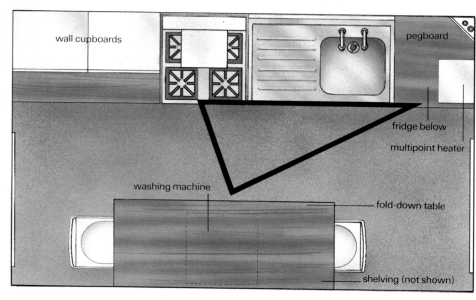

B. Above: *A plan view of conversion A as carried out by a young couple on a limited budget. With a little thought they have created a core area along one side with more setting-down space*

C. Below: *Conversion A carried out on a galley kitchen by a young couple with a limited budget. This view shows the core area with all the major appliances ranged along the outside wall*

Ray Duns

D. Above: *Looking in the opposite direction you can see the multipoint gas heater and the glass-paned outside door*

E. Below: *This view shows the folding breakfast table/worktop, with the washing machine removed for clarity*

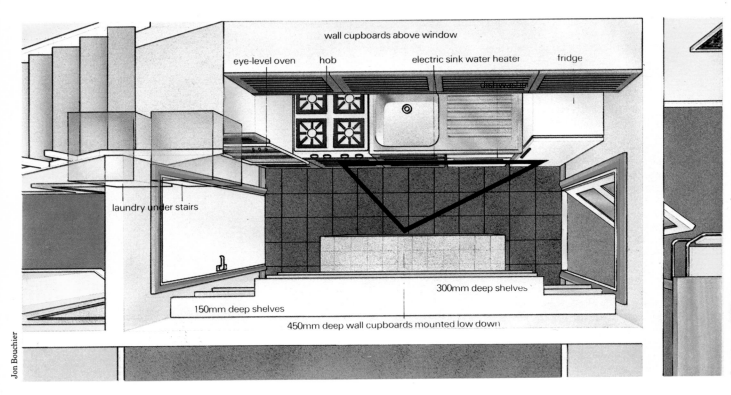

wall cupboards above window

eye-level oven   hob   electric sink water heater   fridge

laundry under stairs

300mm deep shelves

150mm deep shelves

450mm deep wall cupboards mounted low down

Jon Bouchier

F. *Conversion B: a plan for the same galley kitchen but now with a dining room added on at the back. The laundry is now under the stairs leaving more room for food preparation, storage, and an automatic dishwasher*

multiples of 500mm, they decided to buy a cooker and fridge less than 500mm wide to give maximum worktop space. Even so, to allow for clearance space on both sides of the stove and fridge, they had to remove the skirting boards (baseboards) either side of the run of units.

The run in conversion A is formed by two 1000mm knock-down base units with space between for the cooker and a gap by the garden door for the fridge. One unit is topped by a stainless steel sink and drainer, the other has a wall cupboard over it and gives a spacious surface con-

veniently near to the cooker. Another 500mm of work surface is created by fixing a worktop with battens screwed to the garden wall and sink unit over the fridge. Above it a pegboard with hooks gives vertical storage for frequently used pots, pans and utensils.

More work surfaces are provided on the other wall by fixing a standard 1500mm × 600mm worktop on folding brackets. This also serves as a breakfast bar and storage area for the washing machine. When the latter is wheeled to the sink for use, the worktop is folded down to allow access to the fridge and garden.

Rehanging the inner door gives more space for eating—chairs are pushed under the worktop at other times. The swing of the outer door can not be changed because of the steps, but the door itself is replaced by an off-the-shelf glass

panelled door, double glazed for warmth and fitted with a roller blind. The wall above the breakfast bar is covered with adjustable shelves to house the crockery. The radiant heater is mounted on brackets to clear the shelves beneath.

It can be seen that this arrangement required minimal alteration to services. The waste for the new sink was easily connected to the yard gulley as only the position of the drainer was changed. A new gas multipoint water heater with balanced flue replaced the old heater and this also serves the bathroom upstairs. Connections were taken from the cooker's gas pipe and mains water to the sink, brought up in the corner of the worktop and boxed in discreetly.

More electric power points were installed—a double one above the longer worktop for small appliances and another by the garden door for the fridge and washing machine. The single socket by the internal door was replaced by a double one to serve the radiant fire and other appliances.

Note that decoration in the conversion is kept simple and natural—the colour dictated by the new vinyl flooring. The base units are left white and 'wood effect' laminate is chosen for all work surfaces. The walls are painted with white 'anti-condensation' paint and this makes the room bright enough to be lit adequately by two pendent lights taken from the central ceiling rose. Bright colour is restricted to lampshades, stools covers and plants on the window.

The works
1. Order new appliances, fitments or taps; delay further work until arrival
2. Strip out old plumbing (gas, hot and cold water); waste pipes; electric wiring; loose plaster; obsolete fitments and appliances
3. Instal new electrics—socket outlets; other power outlets; lighting outlets and switches (but not light fittings)
4. Renew or repair surfaces to ceiling, walls or floors but do not paint yet
5. Fit all new appliances
6. Fix all new fitments, including worktops over appliances
7. Decorate ceiling and walls—paint, tiles, paper
8. Decorate old and new fitments
9. Lay new floor covering
10. Fit new light fittings
11. Put in loose equipment and furniture

Conversion B

Costs and structural alterations do not always have to be kept to an absolute minimum as they were in conversion A. With wider scope, and by making full use of the available wall space, the same small kitchen can be converted to serve a family of five (Fig. F).

Limitations: In this case the kitchen improvements were part of extensive alterations to the house. A dining room extension was built outside the garden door so that this could be rehung to swing outwards. The family planned to eat in the living room next to the kitchen, so a hatch was knocked between the two. Central heating was installed, with the gas-fired boiler being positioned in the living room fireplace.

The kitchen had to accommodate an electric wall oven, gas hob, dish washer and a large fridge—plus generous storage for bulk provisions and lots of crockery and utensils. The larder was not available as it had to be converted into a laundry room to take a washing machine and dryer (achieved by putting a vent in the external wall).

The solution: A close look at the conversion shows all the appliances ranged along the window wall: the tall fridge by the garden door with a mechanical air extractor above it, the wall oven built-in with cupboards above and below at the opposite end. Between the two is an 1800mm space to take the gas hob and a stainless steel sink. Beneath are the dishwasher and a small electric

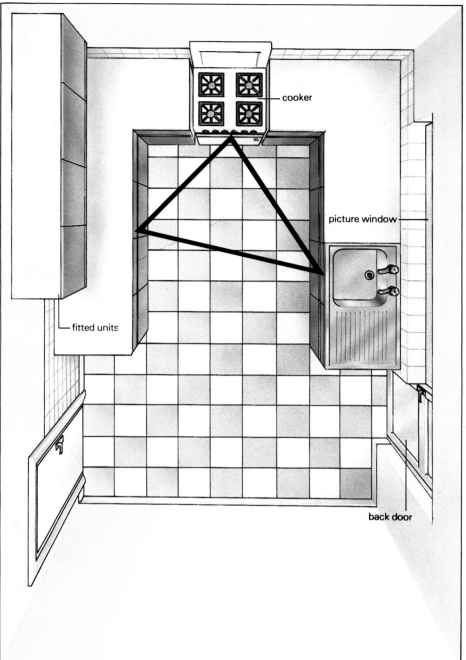

cooker

picture window

fitted units

back door

Steve Cross

G. This fitted kitchen in a new house under-utilizes the space available, and is inflexible in its layout. In many households a complete redesign of the kitchen area would be necessary in order to make it conform with the requirements of the average family

hot water heater—installed for economy as the boiler and main hot water tank are positioned so far away from the kitchen sink.

Purpose-built melamine faced shelving between the dishwasher and under-oven cupboards stores bulky items in everyday use. Things which are needed less frequently can be stored at high level on the 600mm wide length of melamine faced blockboard spanning the entire wall above window level. All the shelves and cupboards on this wall are fronted with louvred doors to streamline the rather complex arrangement. A 100mm removable plinth is fitted in front of everything except the fridge, and both the fridge and dishwasher are on castors for easy cleaning. Even the centre wall spaces are utilized: a cooker hood over the hob; a pegboard between oven and window for utensils; and glass shelves across the window for plants.

The opposite wall—except the spaces for the hatch and central heating radiator—is also put to good use, but only for storage and work surfaces. The main work surface—fixed to the wall by brackets—is cut from a standard 2000mm × 450mm worktop; this allows for the maximum possible length between the radiator and a flap-down table by the garden door. Adjustable shelving covers the top half of the wall in various depths, and three cupboards are fixed directly to the wall below the worktop.

Drainage in this conversion had to be changed considerably. The dishwasher waste was plumbed into the sink waste at the top and both were then connected to the existing gulley. The washing machine waste could not easily run along the external wall to the gulley because of a soil vent pipe. So it was taken in 38mm plastic pipe low along the inside wall before discharging into the gulley. Cold water taken off the mains supply to the sink supplies both machines. Water for the small electric heater below the sink was also taken off the mains supply—a special dual-flow sink mixer tap allows for this arrangement.

Many extra socket outlets were needed. The 30 amp outlet for the wall oven and cooker hood switch were put on the side of the oven housing. A double socket outlet for the water heater and dish washer was installed under the sink, with another pair for the fridge and mechanical air extractor by the garden door. Two pairs of socket outlets for small appliances were put over the long worktop, beside the serving hatch. Lighting was restricted to overhead pendent lights.

Again, decor is simple but cheerful; the ceilings and walls (including the pegboard wall covering) are painted white and all joinery, including the plinth and skirting board, is dark green. The work surfaces, window reveal and splashback are all tiled in a green and white pattern to match and the floor is cork tiles over tongued-and-grooved chipboard. Brightly coloured lampshades provide contrast.

Conversion B is very compact, yet it is not oppressive because of the plentiful natural light from the window—and also because the now-glazed garden door and the hatch give a feeling of space extending beyond the kitchen. The excellent ventilation makes the room comfortable and the open-plan storage aids accessibility. The work surface area is large enough for meals and despite the tight galley shape it is safe for the cook to have helpers because sink and hob are close at hand.

Larger kitchens

Some kitchens do not have such a tight restriction on space but nevertheless need remodelling to make them more workable. This can even be true of a brand new room like the U shaped fitted kitchen shown in fig G which is very wasteful of the available space.

H. *Conversion C as carried out by a family who wanted to eat in their kitchen and had to keep several appliances to hand as well. Theirs is now a traditional UK-type layout*

Conversion C

Fig H shows the way a family who wanted to eat in the kitchen—and house a large fridge, a dishwasher, and a washing machine and dryer—made the room suit their needs. The sink and cooker locations remain unchanged but half the U is removed. One 500mm wall cupboard is left between window and cooker but all other units have been banished to elsewhere in the house; new storage space can also be created by installing narrow shelving on adjustable brackets above the dining area.

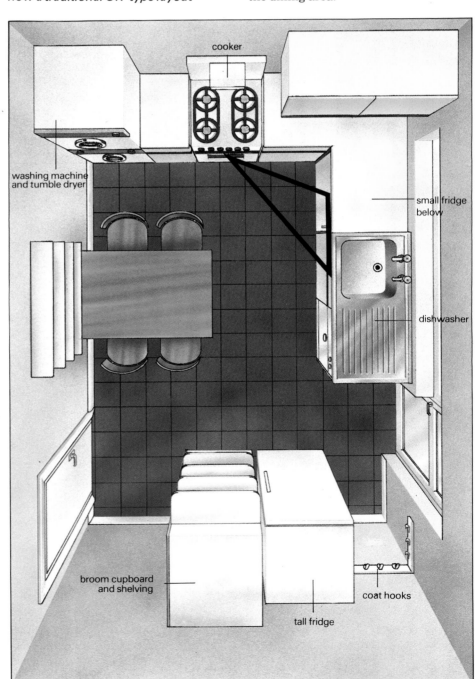

cooker

washing machine and tumble dryer

small fridge below

dishwasher

broom cupboard and shelving

tall fridge

coat hooks

Steve Cross

78

As the table is large – 1200 × 800mm – and a maximum of 800mm from the perimeter worktops, it also serves as a sit-down work surface and laying out space. The empty space next to the cooker is filled by an off-the-shelf floor cupboard and by the washing machine with the dryer mounted above. As this is an external wall, the dryer vent can be let into it and the washing machine waste plumbed via a 'clearing eye' to the gulley serving the kitchen sink.

Some of the base units on the sink wall have been removed to house the dish-washer – plumbed into the sink waste – and a very small fridge. This was bought because the old, giant fridge had to be on the far side of the room and so used more as a larder. Shelving bolted to the adjacent broom closet takes food en route to the fridge. The area by the back door is reserved for coats and dirty shoes.

I. *Conversion D: a more functional layout with food preparation and laundry areas carefully separated. This is a less homely kitchen designed purely for speed and efficiency in every task*

Conversion D

The same basic kitchen can also be very successfully modified so that laundry and food areas are kept completely separate and quite different appliances included in the layout (fig. I).

In this case the washing machine with dryer above is located by the garden door with a worktop for sorting clothes beside them. The same leg of the U is demolished as in conversion C, but some worktops are re-used to form a peninsula dividing the kitchen zones with a fridge freezer at the end. This gives a neat 'core' triangle between the hob and the double sink which replaces the original sink and drainer. The dishwasher is fitted under the peninsula worktop and the wall oven is installed in the far corner, separated from the hob by 300mm of setting down space with storage below.

Drawing up plans

You might already have acquired some basic knowledge previously on how to draw up scale plans for room alterations but for a complex room like the kitchen it is worth drawing a 1:20 plan using the 1:20 section of a metric scale. Also it is better to use tracing paper so that you can make a separate plan later for the room's permanent fixtures and use moveable cut-outs for trying other fitments and appliances in various locations.

If you use tracing paper you will have to make your own grid. Mark it off at 300mm intervals from the 1:20 metric scale. Begin your drawing in the corner of the kitchen and start measuring where the lines of the grid meet. As the floor and elevation plans will be complicated, it may be easier to make freehand sketches first and put measurements on to these.

Be prepared to measure at several levels to include wall fixtures and power supplies – both for the floor plan and elevations. Fitments obscuring corners should be shown in section on elevation plans. Include information about drainage outside too as this is important when considering changing the positions of 'wet' appliances.

When you have settled on your new layout and checked that you can buy any new fitments and appliances in the sizes you want, draw up a final set of plans – floor and elevations – and consult the two 'action' panels for an exact timetable.

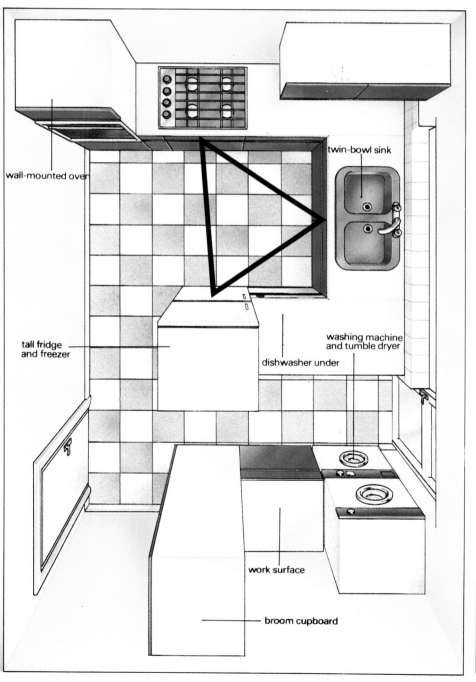

wall-mounted oven

twin-bowl sink

tall fridge and freezer

washing machine and tumble dryer

dishwasher under

work surface

broom cupboard

Warning
Before starting any work, check that your plans will conform to relevant regulations for plumbing, drainage, electricity and building work.

Lighting for kitchens and bathrooms

Zefa

Light fittings are decorations on their own. There are a great many ways of lighting your kitchen and bathroom to make them efficient, as well as stimulating to live in

The ideal kitchen and bathroom should combine efficiency with personality, atmosphere and visual appeal. And with a little careful planning this can be achieved simply by clever lighting. There are many possibilities in both rooms: floodlighing, spotlighting, concealed and strip lighting all prove their use in different areas.

Natural and artificial light
The kitchen might be the nearest room to a workshop in the home but it is just as much a living area and the correct lighting is essential.

Good general light without glare is needed here, with direct light for specific working areas. The right combination should light the room efficiently while at the same time allowing you to feel comfortable and at ease.

Although a great deal of work in the kitchen is carried out during daylight hours some additional artificial lighting is often needed. Your first

consideration should therefore be how to combine the two as efficiently as possible without creating problems.

Artificial light which is too brilliant or warm will look entirely out of place during the day. But some forms of electric lighting offer particularly good simulation of natural light—at least in terms of its tone and colour. These tend also to diffuse light more evenly than daylight so that shadow contrasts are less clear cut and vibrant than normal.

A dimmer switch will enable you to reduce the daylight glare of annoyingly bright artificial light and can be gradually adjusted to match approaching nightfall.

Similarly, the use of low wattage spotlighting and concealed lighting can give you the necessary clarity in certain areas without irritation.

You can help to establish your lighting requirements quite simply by simulating the varying strengths of natural daylight. On a clear day with

Above: *Spotlights in this kitchen are well placed to illuminate the sink, the cooker and the built-in breakfast bar. These silver-bowled spotlights dramatically highlight the subdued colour scheme*

plenty of sunlight, hold a net curtain or a fine gauze over the window. You will find that more light is thrown on some areas than others, giving you a good idea which parts of the kitchen are going to need particular highlighting.

Oddly enough, some kitchens in direct sunlight still require artificial daytime lighting to make up for the brilliant rays of light that fall in sharp contrasting shadows on certain areas of the room.

Overall light
Good general light, usually from a central overhead fitting, should provide an even distribution which illuminates most of the kitchen reasonably well for most purposes.

The two most common types of general lighting are the fluorescent tube, which is anything from 200mm to 2.4m in length, and the tungsten lamp.

Fluorescent tubes provide up to

three times as much light as tungsten bulbs and, as they last an average of 5000 hours, are the most economical form of overall lighting. There is a wide selection of fluorescent tubes available, either straight or circular and in a variety of colours.

The best choice for the kitchen is a colour 27 de luxe warmwhite tube, especially when diffused through a perspex baffle of similar shade. Tubes designed to simulate natural daylight are ideal where artificial light is necessary at all times, though they can flatten the contours of the room.

However, certain types of fluorescent light does tend to distort colour and can have an adverse effect on the look of both food and your complexion. You need to offset this by carefully planning and choosing your direct lighting (see below).

General light bulbs with tungsten filaments range from 15 to 200 watts and have an average life of 1000 hours. These come as clear, pearl frosted and silica-coated. For a fitting with an efficient reflector the clear bulb is usually best. The silica-coated bulb can provide a nicely diffusing light through a translucent opal or easy-clean fabric shade.

Direct lighting
Direct lighting for specific areas is best provided by spot lights, which may be mounted on special 'tracks'. Special light fittings can be clipped at various positions along the track and angled at the oven, table, ironing board or any work surface needing efficient light without glare.

Spotlight fixtures come in various styles and house several different types of bulb. One of the most common types is the internally silvered lamp with a built-in reflector. This gives a controlled beam for flood lighting effects and has an average life of 800 hours.

For spotlighting areas where food is likely to be prepared, choose the type with a pressed armoured glass reflector. This helps to reduce the heat given out in the beam and avoids 'cooking' salad vegetables during preparation. The heat is conducted to the holder so it requires a special fitting for absolute safety.

Worktop lighting
Apart from the standard, semi-concealed fluorescent tube above the sink area, there are numerous ways of lighting work areas.

Before making any final decisions about your lighting, you might find it useful to draw a plan of your kitchen

and then—bearing in mind the various jobs you will be carrying out there—pick out the worktop areas that will require specific light.

Most refrigerators and ovens have their own internal lighting but you could also think about similar light fitments for other storage cupboards and deep alcove shelving areas.

Probably the most efficient method of lighting worktops is with small fluorescent tubes linked together and concealed underneath wall-mounted cupboard units. Some manufacturers leave a lip at the front of their units designed for this purpose. Otherwise, a batten to hold the tubes can be fixed underneath along the underside of the cupboard quite easily.

One or more wall-mounted spotlights set on a track or fixed separately can do the same job and, depending on the style of the kitchen, look more attractive. However, they usually have to be set further away from the surface they are illuminating and some people find them a little too powerful for comfort.

A spotlight set at an angle at the side of the worktop might be better, though working in its beam can cause awkward shadows.

Suiting your style
The style, shape and decor of your kitchen are important points to consider before making a final decision on your lighting system. For example, colours and textures can be enhanced with a 'wash' of light directed on to the wall or ceiling.

You can add to the appeal of a

Above: *An adjustable overhead light in the centre of the room helpfully supplements daylight in the kitchen*

modern, streamlined kitchen by lighting all areas individually. The separate effects are then combined and softened by bathing the whole kitchen in a spread of gentle, overall light from a central source.

Take care not to throw out the balance in a particularly colourful kitchen by using too many high-lighting effects. You can ruin the successful combination of several matching or contrasting colours that complement each other if you highlight only one.

In a rustic-styled, wood-panelled kitchen, on the other hand, no end of visual appeal can be introduced by highlighting features. And a selection of upward-pointing spotlights can be used to flood walls, ceiling and corners. Again, these effects can be brought into unity when supplemented by one overall light.

As with colour, light may be used to visually alter the appearance of a room. In an ill-proportioned kitchen for instance, lamps or spotlights mounted on walls or corner tables with wide, diverging baffles pointing towards the ceiling will make the room appear higher.

A lampshade on an overhead light, set low so that no light shines through above it, will seem to 'lower' the ceiling for a more cosy effect. And for a feeling of width, a wall-washing light can be mounted so that it illuminates a large area of one wall.

Light for eating

Whatever the mood of your kitchen by day—clinical, functional, cluttered, adventurous—you can create something entirely different at night with simple lighting effects.

The rise-and-fall type of lamp is an excellent choice in a kitchen dining area. And the addition of a dimmer switch enables you to create a softer atmosphere for a dinner party. Without a dimmer, choose bulbs between 60 and 100 watts combined with a shade which will give an even spread of light.

Side-angle spotlights are another good idea for the dining area but take care when positioning them: some seating positions at the table might become 'victimized' while others remain too shadowy.

An excellent way of creating a bit of atmosphere while adding a touch of colour at the same time is to use a coloured light-filter on the face of a spot lamp. This can be especially effective when the dining table itself is bathed in candlelight.

And with a number of spotlights fitted to the same ceiling rose, either attached to a central vertical rod or on a ceiling track, you can change the atmosphere of the room simply by setting the main beams of light at different levels and areas. Again, a dimmer switch makes the change of mood doubly effective.

Perhaps the most subtly attractive atmosphere effect is caused by reflected light: whole areas can be illuminated just by the light bounced off walls, ceilings and corners.

Even the most simple fitting—the single bulb—can be used to cast symmetrical or assymetrical shadows on the ceiling with the aid of a lampshade.

Bathroom lighting

Like the kitchen, a bathroom needs good overall light combined with some localized, direct light for working by —in this case around the mirror for make-up application and safe shaving. But more often than not space is at a premium in the bathroom, and this may restrict your choice. But whatever you choose, be extra-careful about safety— water and electricity are a lethal combination. In the UK, for example, switches should be of the pull-cord type.

A central ceiling light usually provides the main light source and for safety reasons, this should be of the enclosed type. Inset lamps in frosted or opal glass shades are a good choice and are easy to keep clean. They

B. Baert

Above: *The reflective mosaic surface in this bathroom makes the most of minimal lighting over the mirror*
Right: *Spotlights positioned over the mirror and on the ceiling are powerful features here and provide a good deal of localized light*

Elizabeth Whiting

provide a bright overall light without any glare and fitted with a 60 watt bulb, should be perfectly adequate for a small bathroom.

In a larger room you can afford to be a little more ambitious with your lighting effects. Rather than one central fitting for the main light source you could have two or perhaps more and even consider wall fittings.

Mirror lighting

In the bathroom, lighting for shaving and making-up by is inevitably concerned with mirrors. A wall-mounted bathroom cabinet with built-in illuminated facing mirror is a good investment for the small bathroom, as it provides both direct light and storage without taking up valuable space.

If you have a mirror already, enclosed tungsten or fluorescent strip lights positioned on each side will give the most efficient illumination. And

Elizabeth Whiting

recessing the mirror and lights into a panel on the wall makes the whole arrangement more attractive.

Where you have no choice but to position a single strip light above the mirror, make sure that it is long enough to throw light on both sides of the face. Many of the larger bathroom strip lights available include a shaver point for added convenience.

If there is no room at all for strip

Above: *In a kitchen with streamlined modern fittings, the semi-concealed lighting under the shelves and the units is an eye-catching light source*

lighting around the mirror or bathroom cabinet, you may be able to fit spots on the ceiling which are angled to shine on either side of the face—but check this point first with your local authority.

Automatic cupboard lights

Ray Duns

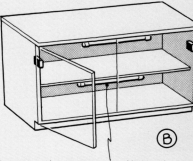

Each pair of lights is operated by the switch on that side

N.B. For these designs see the wiring diagrams opposite

Ⓐ

Central lights are switched on when either door is opened

Ⓑ

Where shelf is not full depth of cupboard, striplights can be fitted as shown

Ⓑ

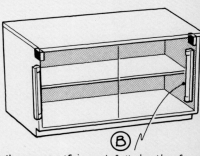

Sliding doors operate integral switches in lamp holders

Ⓒ

If you have a dark cupboard which is hard to see into, fitting interior striplights with door-operated switches is the ideal solution.

The cupboard shown is typical of many kitchen units and has a single, deep, central shelf. Two striplights have been used here—concealed behind false valances to protect them and act as light baffles. The diagrams opposite show how to arrange this and give the circuit diagram for the connections.

The other diagrams show arrangements for different cupboards, including those in bathrooms, where you must use a pull-cord switch. Also shown are lamp-holders with integral door-operated switches which can be fitted instead of striplights.

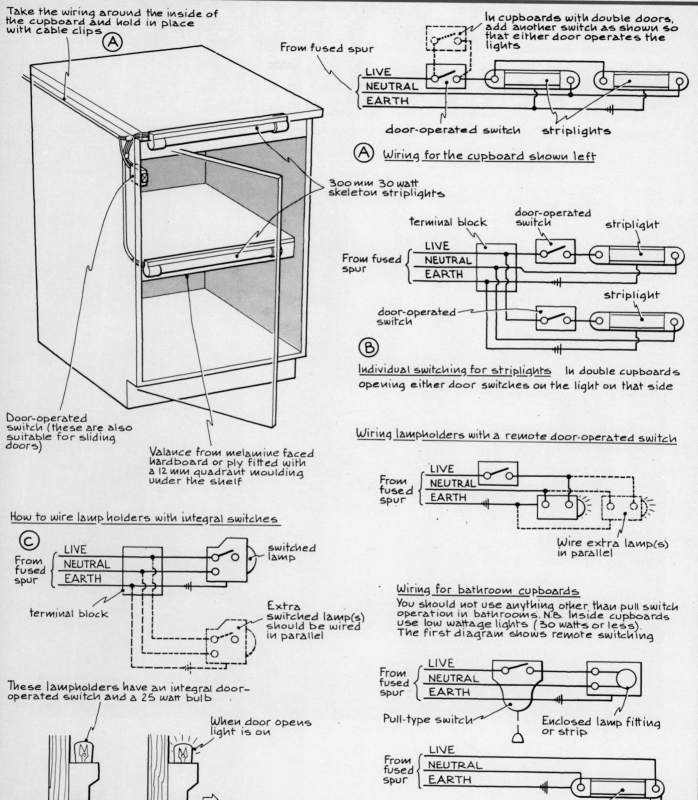

Take the wiring around the inside of the cupboard and hold in place with cable clips

(A)

From fused spur

In cupboards with double doors, add another switch as shown so that either door operates the lights

LIVE
NEUTRAL
EARTH

door-operated switch   striplights

(A) Wiring for the cupboard shown left

300 mm 30 watt skeleton striplights

terminal block   door-operated switch   striplight

LIVE
NEUTRAL
EARTH

From fused spur

door-operated switch

striplight

(B)

Individual switching for striplights   In double cupboards opening either door switches on the light on that side

Door-operated switch (these are also suitable for sliding doors)

Valance from melamine faced hardboard or ply fitted with a 12 mm quadrant moulding under the shelf

Wiring lampholders with a remote door-operated switch

LIVE
NEUTRAL
EARTH

From fused spur

Wire extra lamp(s) in parallel

How to wire lamp holders with integral switches

(C)

LIVE
NEUTRAL
EARTH

From fused spur

switched lamp

terminal block

Extra switched lamp(s) should be wired in parallel

Wiring for bathroom cupboards
You should not use anything other than pull switch operation in bathrooms. N.B. Inside cupboards use low wattage lights (30 watts or less). The first diagram shows remote switching

These lampholders have an integral door-operated switch and a 25 watt bulb

When door opens light is on

LIVE
NEUTRAL
EARTH

From fused spur

Pull-type switch

Enclosed lamp fitting or strip

LIVE
NEUTRAL
EARTH

From fused spur

All the door-operated switches shown will work with sliding doors

Alternatively you can fit an enclosed striplight with integral pull switch as shown

CHILDREN'S ROOMS AND PLAY AREAS

Planning a child's bedroom

Susan Griggs

Children's and teenagers' rooms need to be multi-purpose and flexible. Careful planning is necessary to pack in all the beds, desks and cupboards they need

Two things make designing children's bedrooms different from designing other rooms in the house. The first is that while children come in all shapes and sizes, they never stay the same for long. The second is that children do all kinds of things in their bedrooms—the least problematic of which is sleeping.

Children's bedrooms need to be infinitely-adaptable, multi-function living spaces. And no room can ever satisfy these requirements unless a great deal of imagination goes into its design. This means planning with foresight, as well as carefully selecting the furniture, fittings, fabrics and materials for the room.

Which room?

If you are fortunate enough to be starting from scratch, either with a new-born baby, or a new house, think carefully before choosing the room. Make sure it is big enough for the child: a small bedroom may be suitable for a baby, but beyond the age of two, children need space to play. As they grow older they need space to entertain friends and ultimately somewhere to indulge their interests and do their homework.

Few of us have enough overall space to provide separate rooms for such activities, we must make the most of the bedroom itself. The larger it is, the more versatile you can make

it. And the more that children can be encouraged to do in their rooms, the less the rest of the house will be cluttered up with their toys, their friends and their noise.

Safety is an important consideration. For example, a bedroom with low window sills may be potentially hazardous for small children. And since toddlers barely able to walk are notoriously able when it comes to climbing, you should think about installing some means of preventing the child from climbing out. Vertical wooden bars are a good idea and are easy to make up.

Window latches should always be checked for security, and electric and

Above: *This neat solution to the problems of a very small bedroom still provides plenty of privacy and desk space for each child. A completely symmetrical arrangement divides the bedroom fairly*

heating appliances for safety. Free standing heaters and any electric, gas or paraffin heater which has an exposed element, even if it is barred, can be highly dangerous and should be replaced. For absolute safety use fully enclosed radiators or perhaps a convector heater.

Wall and floor coverings

Children of all ages need hardwearing floor and wall coverings. Mud, water-colours, pencil drawings, glue, even food, may all find their way on to the walls and floor of the bedroom, so washable products are a must. It is usually a good idea to decide on the type of coverings you want well before you consider the actual decoration.

Buying a carpet in a roll is not necessarily the best choice. Carpet tiles are easier to lay and can be replaced if one or two get completely ruined or particularly worn. Bear in mind though that after a year or two of constant use, the carpet overall may have lost some of its original colour and texture, and that replacement tiles may be a poor match.

Other good alternatives for a tough, clean floor covering are cork tiles or one of the many varieties of vinyl floorings. Entirely washable and largely stain resistant, they are attractive and hardwearing although perhaps a little uncomfortable for bare feet on a cold morning.

The variety of patterns available in vinyl floorings is enormous and you can add a few soft rugs to give comfort to bare feet.

Wall coverings, too, require careful consideration since both wallpaper and emulsion paints have their good and bad points. A busy wallpaper, for example, may conceal some of the graffiti which a child might inflict on the walls but could work out expensive. Emulsion paints are much cheaper and if you buy a vinyl matt, silk or satin finish, you can be sure it is washable and will paint over any offending marks which may appear.

Whatever paint you use, make sure it is not toxic especially if the room is for a small child. Teething toddlers have been known to chew lead painted window ledges with unhappy results.

Lighting

If the child's bedroom is to be a real living space, the lighting in it needs to be given as much thought as any of the other fittings. For small children, remember that free standing bedside lamps with trailing wires can be hazardous. It is better to install a wall or ceiling fitting with a ceiling-

Above: *Not only does this classic space saving idea provide a comfortable bed space, it creates a cosy work and storage area under the bed*

mounted pull switch for safety.

For young children who will only sleep with night lights there are numerous low-light lamps available set in fairy-tale pottery cottages or owls. But you might consider the alternative of using a dimmer switch on the main light.

An older child's bedroom, which is designed for specific uses, perhaps for reading or homework, would certainly benefit from the clever use of spotlights. These are available in all kinds of combinations, from singles to clusters, as wall or ceiling fittings, table lights and on ceiling tracks. Spotlights give you the great advantage of being able to direct the light as you wish, picking out particular

areas or even, in a teenager's bedroom, creating two distinct spaces—one for sleeping, one for living.

Furniture and fittings

Before turning to the decorative styles and colours in the bedroom, give some thought to the fittings and fixtures. This is where the greatest difference between children's rooms in the house becomes apparent.

Although small children do not need tall wardrobes or big beds, beware of buying or building furniture which will have only limited use. Think ahead to the child's likely needs in the future. If your children are teenagers, consider other uses for the bedroom, and the furniture you will need when they eventually leave to set up their own homes.

With space at such a premium in most family houses, whatever your children's ages you should consider the value of space-saving beds and

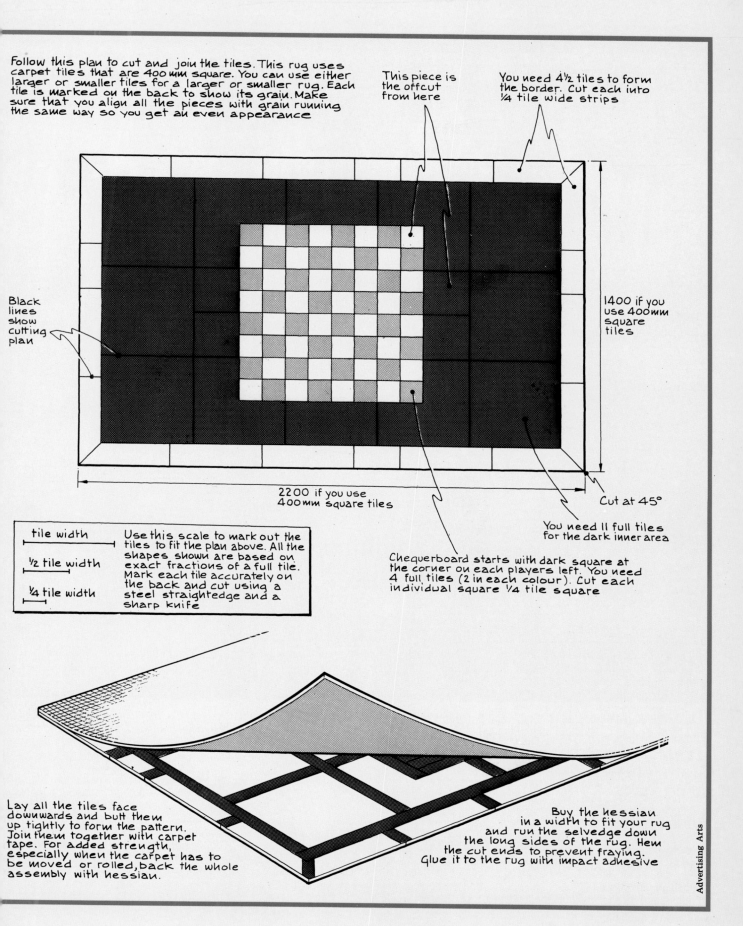

Follow this plan to cut and join the tiles. This rug uses carpet tiles that are 400mm square. You can use either larger or smaller tiles for a larger or smaller rug. Each tile is marked on the back to show its grain. Make sure that you align all the pieces with grain running the same way so you get an even appearance

This piece is the offcut from here

You need 4½ tiles to form the border. Cut each into ¼ tile wide strips

Black lines show cutting plan

1400 if you use 400mm square tiles

2200 if you use 400mm square tiles

Cut at 45°

You need 11 full tiles for the dark inner area

Chequerboard starts with dark square at the corner on each players left. You need 4 full tiles (2 in each colour). Cut each individual square ¼ tile square

tile width

½ tile width

¼ tile width

Use this scale to mark out the tiles to fit the plan above. All the shapes shown are based on exact fractions of a full tile. Mark each tile accurately on the back and cut using a steel straightedge and a sharp knife

Lay all the tiles face downwards and butt them up tightly to form the pattern. Join them together with carpet tape. For added strength, especially when the carpet has to be moved or rolled, back the whole assembly with hessian.

Buy the hessian in a width to fit your rug and run the selvedge down the long sides of the rug. Hem the cut ends to prevent fraying. Glue it to the rug with impact adhesive

Advertising Arts

Nursery furniture

Jon Stewart

Just the thing for a doll's tea party, this bright toy table and chair set can be used for all sorts of games—or even for a real meal. Largely made from plywood, it is inexpensive and very simple to construct with only basic tools

Young children will love to sit down to a meal at their very own table—whether it is a real tea or just pretend. This set is sturdy enough to take years of punishment, and it can be used for drawing or board games as well.

You can make up to four chairs—they will pack snugly away as the triangular seats are designed to fit into the spaces between the table legs. For even neater packing, just unscrew the table top and slot the legs apart to allow it to stack flat. Each chair also has a handy toy box concealed under its lift-off lid.

Most of the parts are cut from 12mm plywood—the table is just three pieces. The seats are slightly more complicated to make, using softwood supports as well as plywood. Many of the parts are small enough to make from offcuts, and you can economize on materials by cutting them out together—for example, putting four of the seat triangles together to form a square.

Assemble according to the working drawings. As with all children's projects, take great care to remove all sharp edges or roughness—even inside the seat. Finish in your chosen colour scheme.

Workplan

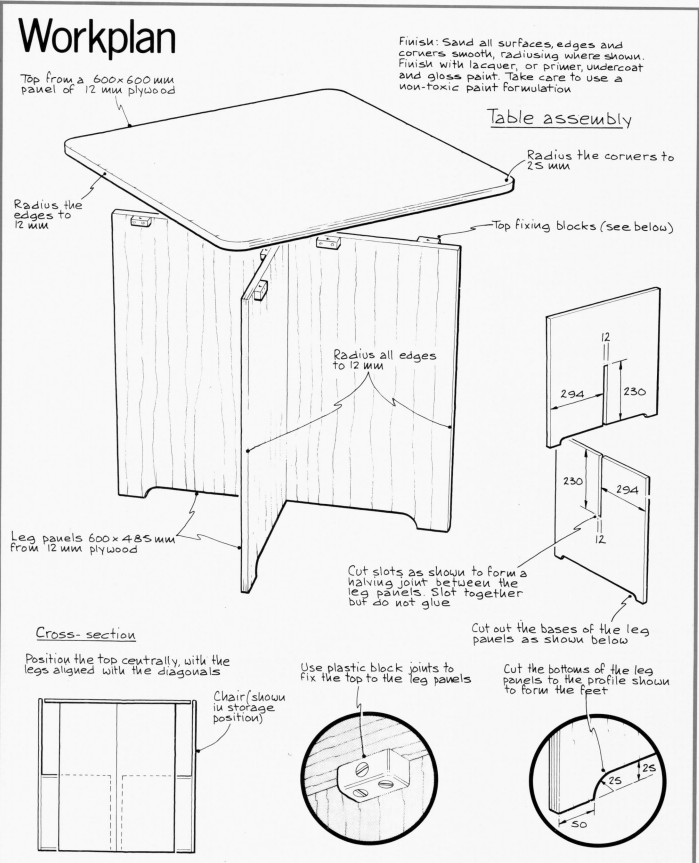

Top from a 600×600 mm panel of 12 mm plywood

Finish: Sand all surfaces, edges and corners smooth, radiusing where shown. Finish with lacquer, or primer, undercoat and gloss paint. Take care to use a non-toxic paint formulation

Table assembly

Radius the corners to 25 mm

Radius the edges to 12 mm

Top fixing blocks (see below)

Radius all edges to 12 mm

12

294   230

230   294

12

Leg panels 600×485 mm from 12 mm plywood

Cut slots as shown to form a halving joint between the leg panels. Slot together but do not glue

Cut out the bases of the leg panels as shown below

Cross-section

Position the top centrally, with the legs aligned with the diagonals

Chair (shown in storage position)

Use plastic block joints to fix the top to the leg panels

Cut the bottoms of the leg panels to the profile shown to form the feet

25

25

50

Advertising Arts

Cross-section of chair

Numbered parts indicate the panels shown in the diagrams below

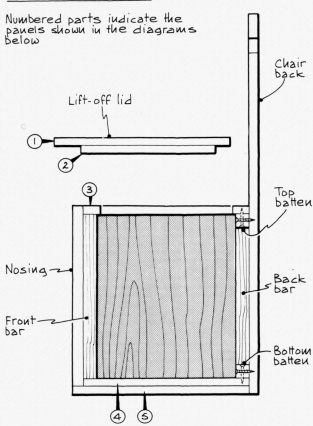

Lift-off lid

Chair back

Top batten

Nosing

Front bar

Back bar

Bottom batten

Cutting list

All sizes are in millimetres. Timber is planed all round, PAR (dressed four sides, D4S). Chair parts are for one chair only. Note that if the triangular panels are cut out together, less material will be used.

Part	Material	No.	Size
table top	12mm plywood	1	600 × 600mm
leg panels	12mm plywood	2	600 × 485mm
chair back	12mm plywood	1	500 × 500mm
chair base	12mm plywood	1	500 × 250mm
bottom panel	12mm plywood	1	488 × 231mm
seat base	12mm plywood	1	438 × 231mm
lid	12mm plywood	1	500 × 250mm
side panels	4mm plywood	2	329 × 276mm
nosing	38 × 13mm ½-round moulding	1	276mm
front bar	75 × 25mm softwood (PAR)	1	252mm
back bars	25mm triangular moulding	2	264mm
battens	25 × 25 softwood (PAR)	2	438mm

Additional materials: PVA woodworking adhesive, panel pins, countersunk woodscrews, plastic block-joints
Finish: Primer, undercoat and gloss paint

Chair panel details

Cut all the panels shown from 12mm plywood and fit to the chair in the order indicated above by the numbered code

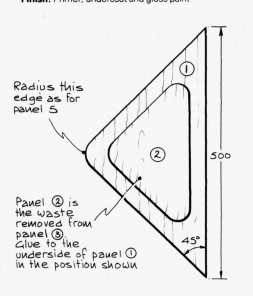

Radius this edge as for panel 5

Panel ② is the waste removed from panel ③. Glue to the underside of panel ① in the position shown

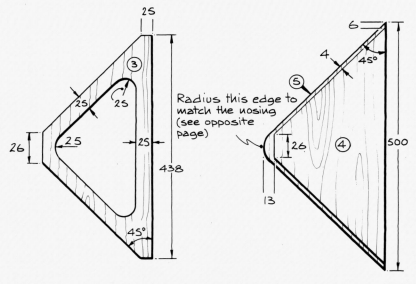

Radius this edge to match the nosing (see opposite page)

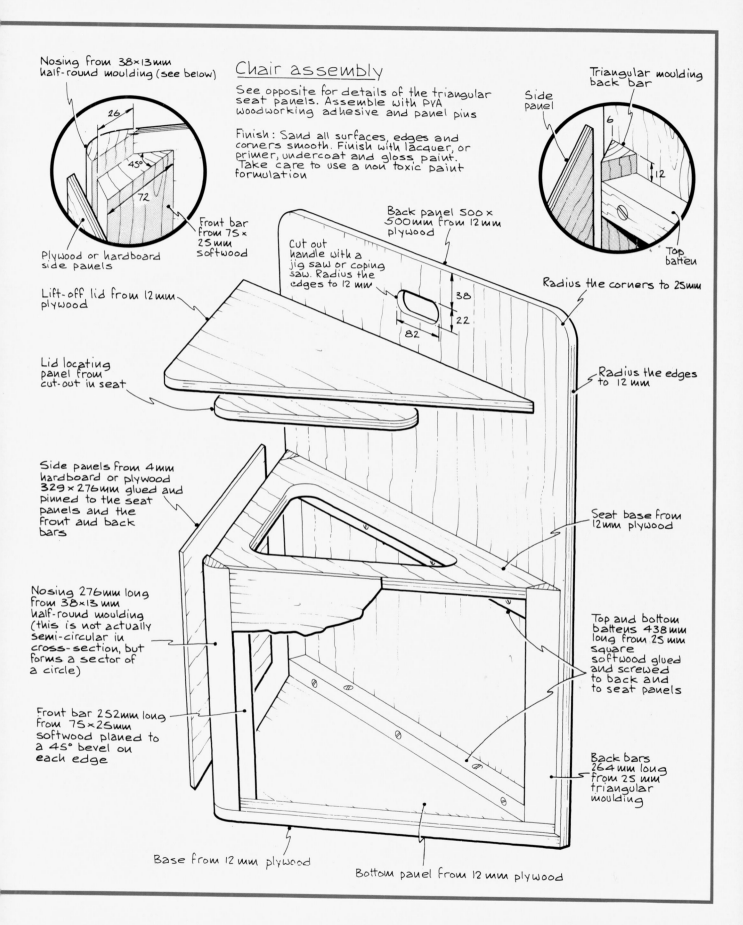

Nosing from 38×13mm half-round moulding (see below)

26

45°

72

Plywood or hardboard side panels

Front bar from 75 × 25 mm softwood

Chair assembly

See opposite for details of the triangular seat panels. Assemble with PVA woodworking adhesive and panel pins

Finish: Sand all surfaces, edges and corners smooth. Finish with lacquer, or primer, undercoat and gloss paint. Take care to use a non toxic paint formulation

Side panel

Triangular moulding back bar

6

12

Top batten

Radius the corners to 25mm

Lift-off lid from 12mm plywood

Back panel 500 × 500mm from 12mm plywood

Cut out handle with a jig saw or coping saw. Radius the edges to 12 mm

38

22

82

Radius the edges to 12 mm

Lid locating panel from cut-out in seat

Side panels from 4mm hardboard or plywood 329 × 276mm glued and pinned to the seat panels and the front and back bars

Seat base from 12mm plywood

Nosing 276mm long from 38×13 mm half-round moulding (this is not actually semi-circular in cross-section, but forms a sector of a circle)

Top and bottom battens 438mm long from 25 mm square softwood glued and screwed to back and to seat panels

Front bar 252mm long from 75×25mm softwood planed to a 45° bevel on each edge

Back bars 264mm long from 25 mm triangular moulding

Base from 12 mm plywood

Bottom panel from 12 mm plywood

A child's rocking chair/table

Nelson Hargreaves

This attractive dual purpose toy will give endless fun to growing children. You can easily build it in a weekend from a single sheet of 12mm plywood and decorate it with your own colourful and eye-catching designs.

Young children really love toys which give them a chance to use their imagination—and there is plenty of scope with this attractive project. One way up it forms a double rocking seat, the other way a really practical table or desk unit.

98

It is extremely simple to make, and requires the minimum of materials. All you need is a single standard (2440mm × 1220mm) sheet of 12mm plywood, adhesive and a few panel pins (common brads). Mark out your sheet following the plans overleaf and cut out all the pieces. A power jig saw will make really light work of this, but it is simple to use hand tools. Take care to mark out and cut the slots and tongues accurately, as this will make secure joints.

Assemble all the parts as shown, using panel pins and PVA woodworking adhesive. You can hold the parts temporarily with sash cramps (bar clamps) which you can hire or by binding strong cord around them.

When you have completed the assembly, sand off all the corners to make sure that there are no sharp projections or splinters on which a child could injure itself. Finish the surface by painting it with primer and undercoat, being sure to use a lead-free composition. You can then use simple, bright colours or paint designs like those shown, using gloss paint.

A further use for the rocker is in the garden, where it would form the basis of an attractive swing. Here, however, you must fit the additional boards shown to prevent a child's legs slipping off the base board.

Kuo Kang Chen

Cutting list

Make all the panels from a single standard (2440mm × 1220mm) sheet of external grade (water and boil-proof) 12mm plywood. Use the plan on the left to mark out the sheet for minimum wastage.

Part	No.	Size
Sides	2	1000mm × 500mm
Back rests	2	670mm × 370mm
Seats	2	670mm × 250mm
Table/footrest	1	670mm × 400mm

Additional materials: PVA woodworking adhesive, 25mm panel pins (common brads)

Finish: Primer, undercoat and gloss paint. Use lead-free paints

<u>Marking out the plywood</u>

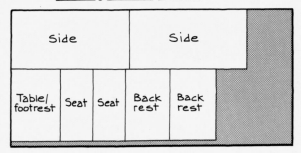

The shaded area represents one full sheet of plywood (2440 mm × 1220 mm) Fit the panels in as shown for the minimum wastage of wood. The offcut which is left over is large enough to use for other projects

Assembly

When you have cut out the seven plywood panels fit them together as shown. Try a dry assembly first to make sure that everything fits properly, easing the joints if necessary. When all is well, dismantle and reassemble with PVA woodworking adhesive in the joints. Pin through as shown between the tongues, punching the heads below the surface. You can hold the assembly together temporarily with sash cramps, or by binding with strong cord

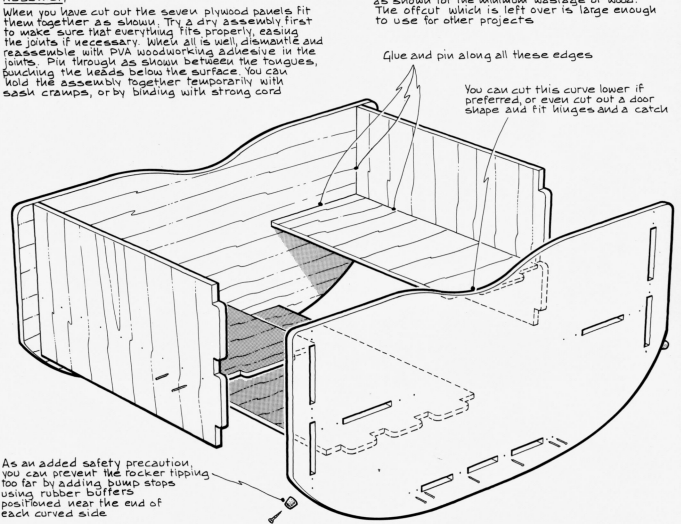

Glue and pin along all these edges

You can cut this curve lower if preferred, or even cut out a door shape and fit hinges and a catch

As an added safety precaution, you can prevent the rocker tipping too far by adding bump stops using rubber buffers positioned near the end of each curved side

Finish

After the glue has dried, sand off all the exposed edges of plywood, including the projecting tongues. Sand the entire surface lightly, and paint with primer. Follow this with undercoat, then finish with gloss paint. You can use simple bright colours, or paint on complete designs, like the car and the boat shown in the photographs. Sketch the designs on the undercoat using a soft pencil, and fill in using gloss paint. Allow each colour to dry before adding details on top

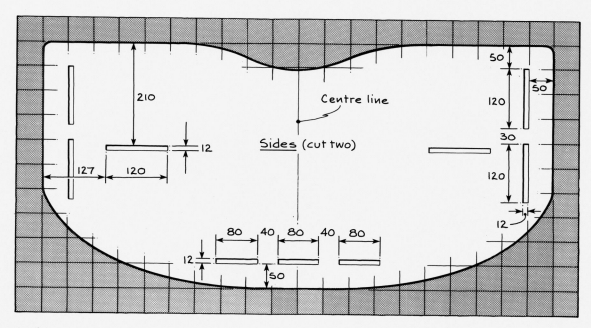

210

Centre line

Sides (cut two)

50

50

120

30

120

12

127   120

12

12

80 40 80 40 80

12

50

Cutting out the plywood

Make all parts from 12mm external grade (water and boil-proof) multiply. Mark out all the pieces together on the sheet. The plan opposite shows how to fit them in. Use the grid above to mark out the curved shape for the sides. Each square on the plan represents 50 mm on the finished side. Mark out the plywood with 50 mm squares and copy the curve. Measure out and mark all the slots. Cut around all the outlines with a power jigsaw or panel saw and coping saw. Cut the slots with a jigsaw or by using a chisel

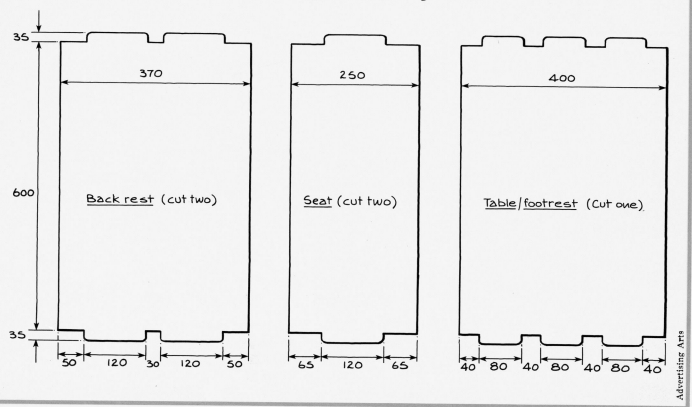

35

370   250   400

600

Back rest (cut two)   Seat (cut two)   Table/footrest (Cut one)

35

50 120 30 120 50   65 120 65   40 80 40 80 40 80 40

Advertising Arts

Above: *A sandpit simply constructed from timber will keep a child happily entertained for hours. And you do not need vast areas of space—this one fits very nicely in a small patio area*

Outdoor play areas

Nothing gives greater pleasure than to see a group of children playing boisterously in the garden. But a play area needs to be planned with care if it is to provide safety and security without restricting the child's freedom

Children need somewhere to play out of doors, so that they can 'let off steam' without causing damage to furniture and furnishings. But even in the garden tiny feet can inflict staggering damage on a prize lawn and quickly destroy months of work spent raising flowers and plants.

At the same time a low hanging branch or a thorny rose twig can inflict nasty injuries on children deeply immersed in a game. Fishponds, paved areas and stone steps are all potential hazards.

Territory for toddlers

Children up to the age of about seven or eight need the greatest supervision. And tempting though it may be to banish all their paraphernalia and noise to the far end of the garden, it is far wiser to select a site which is clearly visible from the house – preferably an area with an uninterrupted sightline from a frequently used room, such as the kitchen.

A physical barrier of some sort will prevent children from wandering off into the main part of the garden and will also conceal the play area from the lawn or patio. From the point of view of appearance, a fairly low hedge is best and also enables you to see into the play area from other parts of the garden.

Evergreen hedges blend in well with most styles of garden and are fairly easy to maintain. Alternatively, a flowering hedge, such as lavender, is both pretty and practical. Avoid using prickly plants like holly which can easily scratch children and, of course, stay right away from any poisonous plants. Yew is particularly dangerous and even the common privet has poisonous berries.

Fences are less suitable barriers because of the danger of splinters. They are also less durable, especially if a child climbs on them or throws a ball against them. If you require a more solid barrier than a hedge, a brick wall is a better choice. A solid wall can often look obtrusive, so think about pierced screen walling or grow climbing plants on the garden side. Again, make sure that the plants are not poisonous.

If there are stone or concrete steps between the play area and the rest of the garden, then a gate is essential. More often than not, a child will unwittingly choose the most dangerous place to take a tumble. If the garden is level, then a gate is not a necessary safety factor, but would be useful to keep the children's games confined to the area intended for them.

Above: *A tree house is great fun for children of all ages – but be sure the platform is firmly supported and the 'house' is surrounded by a sturdy fence*

Below: *Portable paddling pools come in a variety of sizes and are ideal on the garden lawn for tiny tots to splash about in on hot summer days*

A busy mother cannot spend her day watching the children and the garden to make sure that neither of them get unduly damaged. Equally, it is unreasonable to expect children to stay indoors when the sun is shining. The simple answer is to create a play area, designed to keep the children safe while at the same time allowing them the maximum freedom of movement.

Although this is most practical in a large garden where a play area does not seriously diminish the space for cultivation or sunbathing, it is usually possible in most gardens to set aside a small area where the children can play safely. Even so, really active ball games, like cricket and football, might best be practised in the local park.

Roger Perry/MC Library

Spectrum

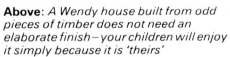

Above: *A Wendy house built from odd pieces of timber does not need an elaborate finish – your children will enjoy it simply because it is 'theirs'*

If the play area is sited on a solid surface then it is probably best to have it grassed over in case of accidents. Choose a variety of grass that is tough and resilient and which does not grow luxuriously long.

Make sure that there are no open drains in the area. Children are bound to satisfy their curiosity with an unhygienic investigation, and there is always the possibility that they could be badly scalded. If it is not possible to site the play area away from drains – outside a kitchen, for instance – then make sure the drains are securely covered and that small fingers cannot become trapped.

Organized activities

There are a number of toys and activities you can provide within the play area, depending on the number and ages of the children and, of course, the amount of available space.

A climbing frame will keep young children happily occupied for hours. You can buy ready-made metal or wooden frames or erect one yourself using your own design. Be sure the base is securely bolted down and set in concrete so that it cannot tip over, and seal or paint the frame because it will have to withstand all kinds of weather. A number of mats such as those used by gymnasts can provide further protection for budding amateur athletes and can be easily stored away during wet weather.

A swing is a firm favourite with children of all ages. Again, the frame

Above: *A collection of colourful cardboard tubes screwed together with nuts and bolts creates a novel arrangement for a child's play area*

Jessica Strang

Michael Boys/Susan Griggs

Below: *A child's vivid imagination can turn a simple wooden structure like this into anything from a castle to a sea-going battleship*

Camera Press

Camera Press

should be securely bolted down and set in concrete. Site it so that there is adequate clearance both behind and in front of the swing, bearing in mind the positions of doors, gates, walls and windows. Check suspension ropes or chains from time to time, and especially after bad weather. Removable ropes or rods which hook into chains are best as these can easily be detached from the main frame and stored away for the winter.

A sandpit brings the seaside to a child's own garden, especially if it is combined with a paddling pool. These can be any size and shape, with a minimum of about 900mm diameter. A depth of 300mm for the pool and 150mm for the pit is quite sufficient. Site the pool in full sunlight, not too far from a tap and drain for easy filling and emptying.

Ready-made pools are suitable only for ornament and cannot stand up to hard wear. Both paddling pools and sandpits are best made of concrete and lined with non-slip tiles to provide a smooth and easily cleaned surface. A concrete or paved area around the pit and paddling pool will be easier to keep clean than a grass verge. Choose a non-clinging, fine sand for the sandpit and use detachable covers to keep the sand and water clean.

Above: *Solid logs form a very definite barrier around this play pit to create a well-secluded hideaway which any young child would love*

Creating for juniors

In many ways, play areas for older children are much easier to plan, although they usually require rather more space. In fact, older children are generally happier in an area which has not had too much planning. They can safely be banished to the end of the garden – and if this is something of an overgrown wilderness, they will like it even better.

Make sure that the area is safe, however, and check long grass for any old and rusty tools that may still be concealed there. Check, too, that any overhanging branches of trees are solid and that fallen trunks will not roll over when climbed upon. If they are secure, leave the branches and trunks in place to provide part of an adventure playground.

Although older children will have outgrown the babyhood tendency to put colourful berries and leaves in their mouths, it is still best to remove and destroy any poisonous plants and weeds in the area, especially if it has been

105

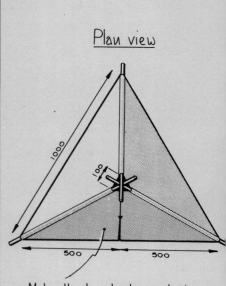

Spectrum

neglected for any length of time. Obviously, the play area should be separated from bonfire sites, rubbish tips and compost heaps.

Grass is nicer underfoot, but the safety factor which precluded concrete or paving for young children no longer applies. Perhaps a combination is best for junior play areas, providing both soft and hard surfaces to cope with any activity.

Again, a physical demarcation of the area is advisable to at least try and deter children from straying over the rest of the garden. Walls, fences and hedges are all suitable here.

One of the things that children seem to like best is a mini version of an army-style assault course. This need not be elaborate and could include such things as a couple of old car tyres hung on a rope from a tree, a low, wooden ramp, a length of plastic 'tunnel' and an overhead rope suspended from posts or trees.

Another great favourite is a tree house, which you can create quite simply using a secure platform, a rain-proof roof and sufficiently high 'walls' to prevent

Above: *A traditional climbing frame is great fun for children of any age, but add a slide to the construction and it becomes doubly exciting*

anybody falling out. Most children will value such a simple structure as a palace, although, of course, more complex designs are possible.

The house should be built on one of the lower branches and the ladder leading up to it must be firmly fixed. Be sure too that the house itself is securely fastened to the tree and check ties at regular intervals, especially after the winter.

If a tree house is too ambitious or if there are no trees in your garden, then a play house on the ground can also be great fun. Build it in a similar way to an ordinary garden shed and paint the outside in bright colours, perhaps including the child's name on the front door. A couple of old chairs, a rug and a pair of bright curtains will furnish the interior. But make sure that the children cannot lock themselves or each other inside the house.

Plan view

Make the two back panels in one piece. Cut the front in two parts and seam down the centre as far as the opening of the flaps. If the fabric you are using has a reversible pattern, the two parts can be made from the offcuts of the back panels.

Corner detail

Make the pole tubes from a 100mm wide strip of fabric, folded double and stitched into the seam.

Stitch the long edges together, catching the edges of the pole tubes in the seam.

Make the poles from garden bamboo canes, about 2 metres in length.

Hem the edges of the fabric to 20mm.

You can make the wigwam from almost any fabric 1 metre or more wide. For economy, use old curtains or sheeting. You can dye a plain fabric, or decorate with fabric paints.

Overstitch the top of the opening to strengthen the seam

A

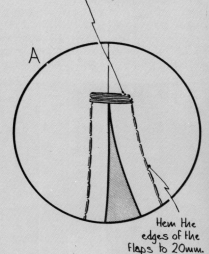

Hem the edges of the flaps to 20mm.

Bamboo cane poles

Tie around the canes at the point where they cross.

Ray Duns

Front view

650

A

Door flaps

Stitch 300mm lengths of tape to the edge of the flap and the pole.

700

Push the ends of the canes into the ground.

Make a wigwam

This traditional Indian wigwam design for younger children will give them hours of fun and enjoyment during the summer months. Because it takes up little room it is ideal for smaller gardens, and it can be folded up neatly.

The framework consists of three bamboo poles. Get them from a garden centre, and choose sturdy examples. Any fabric can be used for the covering, as long as it is a metre wide—you can even consider using old curtains or sheets. For a waterproof wigwam, use canvas and spray the finished article with tent waterproofer.

If you are using a plain fabric, you can decorate it with traditional Indian motifs using fabric paint and cardboard stencils—zig-zag edging around the base looks most effective and other patterns can be found in books and comics.

Make up the covering as shown on the workplan, using a single piece of fabric for the sides and another—seamed down the middle as far as the opening—for the front. Add strips of tape to form ties to close the flaps. If you prefer, you can use a zip fastener stitched to the flaps on each side.

Insert the poles and drive their feet into the ground, making sure that the sides are taut. Tie off the poles where they cross at the top of the wigwam. It is a good idea to bind the ends to avoid the risk of splinters.

A sledge and a cart

This traditional sleigh or sledge with bentwood runners is just the thing for a white Christmas. For warmer months, the plans include a design for a cart with real steering

The sledge is sturdily made from hardwood with mortise and tenon joints and steel bracing. Take care to mark the angles accurately with a bevel gauge.

Make the curved runners by laminating thin strips around a former. Add metal strips and the deck then finish carefully.

Most of the cart is constructed from 12mm plywood. The base is a sandwich construction to contain the steering gear. Assemble this completely on the lower base plate as shown. Many different patterns of wheels are suitable, and you should adapt the axles to suit those you are using. Make up the bonnet complete with steering gear and fix to the top base plate. Fix to the lower assembly, engaging the arm with the track rods.

Make sure you remove all rough edges before applying the finish. As with all children's toys this should be lead-free.

Simon Butcher

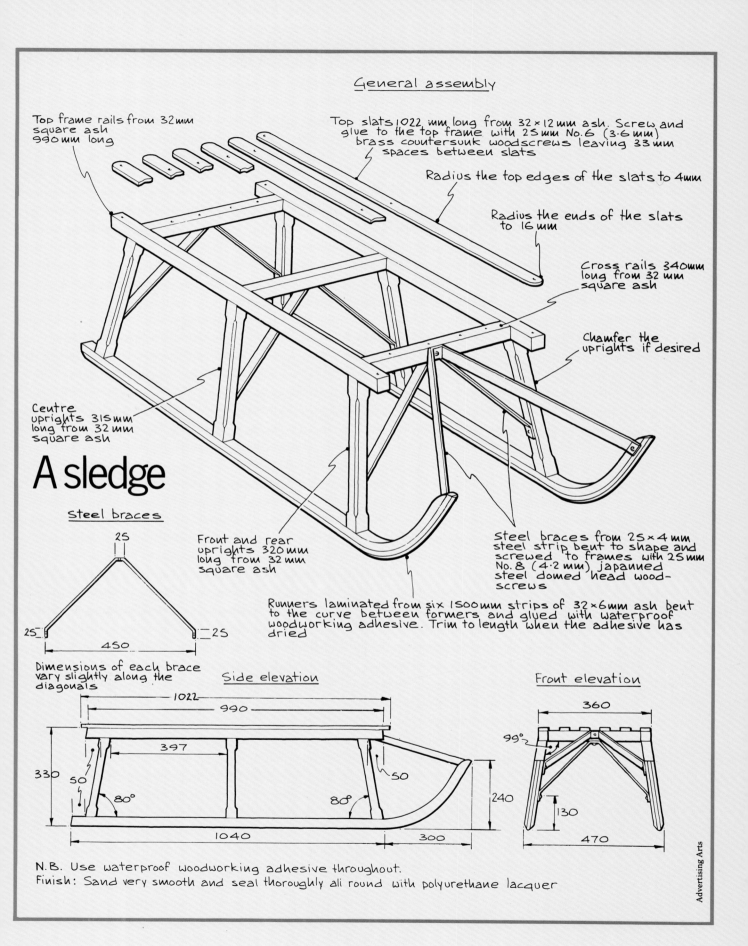

General assembly

Top frame rails from 32mm square ash 990mm long

Top slats 1022 mm long from 32×12 mm ash. Screw and glue to the top frame with 25 mm No.6 (3.6 mm) brass countersunk woodscrews leaving 33 mm spaces between slats

Radius the top edges of the slats to 4mm

Radius the ends of the slats to 16 mm

Cross rails 340mm long from 32 mm square ash

Chamfer the uprights if desired

Centre uprights 315mm long from 32 mm square ash

A sledge

Steel braces

25

25 — — 25

450

Dimensions of each brace vary slightly along the diagonals

Front and rear uprights 320mm long from 32 mm square ash

Steel braces from 25×4 mm steel strip bent to shape and screwed to frames with 25 mm No.8 (4·2 mm) japanned steel domed head wood-screws

Runners laminated from six 1500mm strips of 32×6mm ash bent to the curve between formers and glued with waterproof woodworking adhesive. Trim to length when the adhesive has dried

Side elevation

1022
990
397
330
50
50
80°
80°
1040
300

Front elevation

360
99°
240
130
470

N.B. Use waterproof woodworking adhesive throughout.
Finish: Sand very smooth and seal thoroughly all round with polyurethane lacquer

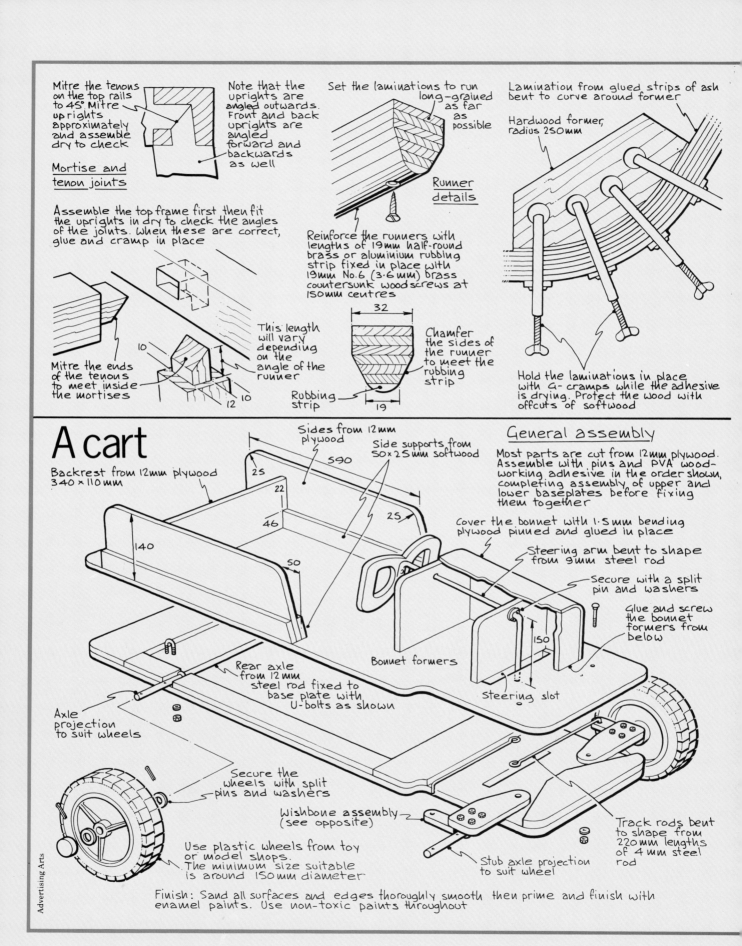

Mitre the tenons on the top rails to 45°. Mitre uprights approximately and assemble dry to check

Note that the uprights are angled outwards. Front and back uprights are angled forward and backwards as well

Mortise and tenon joints

Assemble the top frame first then fit the uprights in dry to check the angles of the joints. When these are correct, glue and cramp in place

Mitre the ends of the tenons to meet inside the mortises

10
10
12

This length will vary depending on the angle of the runner

32

Rubbing strip

19

Chamfer the sides of the runner to meet the rubbing strip

Set the laminations to run long-grained as far as possible

Runner details

Reinforce the runners with lengths of 19mm half-round brass or aluminium rubbing strip fixed in place with 19mm No.6 (3·6mm) brass countersunk woodscrews at 150mm centres

Lamination from glued strips of ash bent to curve around former

Hardwood former, radius 250mm

Hold the laminations in place with G-cramps while the adhesive is drying. Protect the wood with offcuts of softwood

A cart

Backrest from 12mm plywood 340 × 110mm

Sides from 12mm plywood

590

25

22

46

50

140

25

Side supports from 50 × 25mm softwood

25

General assembly

Most parts are cut from 12mm plywood. Assemble with pins and PVA wood-working adhesive in the order shown, completing assembly of upper and lower baseplates before fixing them together

Cover the bonnet with 1·5mm bending plywood pinned and glued in place

Steering arm bent to shape from 9mm steel rod

Secure with a split pin and washers

Glue and screw the bonnet formers from below

Bonnet formers

150

Steering slot

Rear axle from 12mm steel rod fixed to base plate with U-bolts as shown

Axle projection to suit wheels

Secure the wheels with split pins and washers

Wishbone assembly (see opposite)

Stub axle projection to suit wheel

Track rods bent to shape from 220mm lengths of 4mm steel rod

Use plastic wheels from toy or model shops. The minimum size suitable is around 150mm diameter

Finish: Sand all surfaces and edges thoroughly smooth then prime and finish with enamel paints. Use non-toxic paints throughout

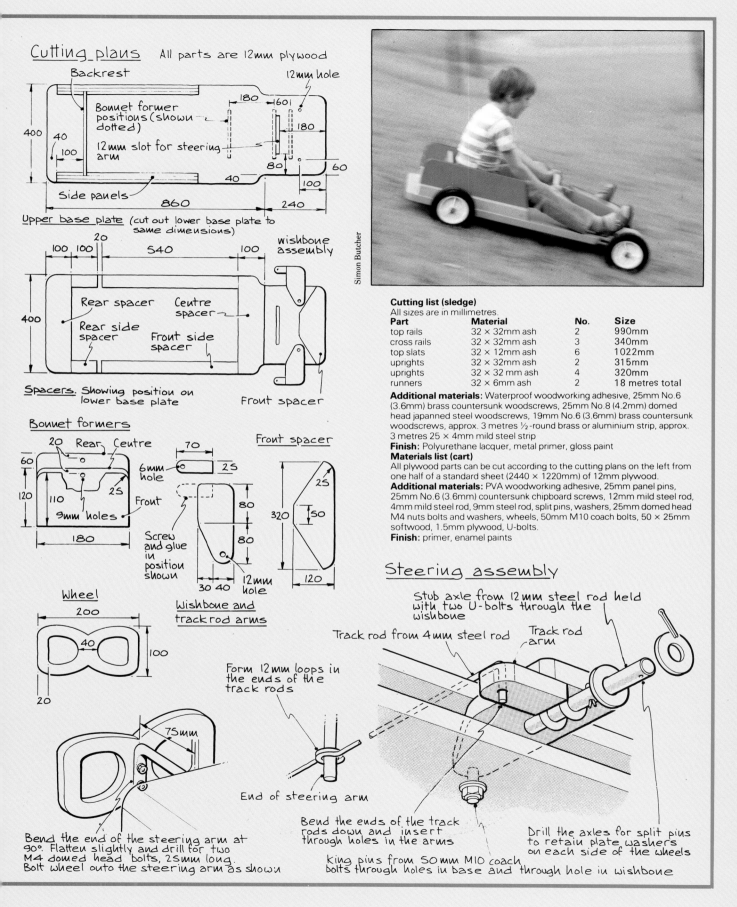

Cutting plans
All parts are 12mm plywood

Backrest
Bonnet former positions (shown dotted)
12mm slot for steering arm
12mm hole
400
40
100
180
601
180
80
60
40
100
Side panels
860
240

Upper base plate (cut out lower base plate to same dimensions)

20
100 100
540
100
wishbone assembly
400
Rear spacer
Centre spacer
Rear side spacer
Front side spacer

Spacers. Showing position on lower base plate

Front spacer

Bonnet formers
20 Rear Centre
60
120
110
25
9mm holes
Front
180
6mm hole
70
25
Screw and glue in position shown
30 40
12mm hole
80
80

Front spacer
320
25
50
120

Wheel
200
40
100
20

Wishbone and track rod arms

75mm

Bend the end of the steering arm at 90°. Flatten slightly and drill for two M4 domed head bolts, 25mm long. Bolt wheel onto the steering arm as shown

Form 12mm loops in the ends of the track rods

End of steering arm

Bend the ends of the track rods down and insert through holes in the arms

King pins from 50 mm M10 coach bolts through holes in base and through hole in wishbone

Simon Butcher

Cutting list (sledge)
All sizes are in millimetres.

Part	Material	No.	Size
top rails	32 × 32mm ash	2	990mm
cross rails	32 × 32mm ash	3	340mm
top slats	32 × 12mm ash	6	1022mm
uprights	32 × 32mm ash	2	315mm
uprights	32 × 32 mm ash	4	320mm
runners	32 × 6mm ash	2	18 metres total

Additional materials: Waterproof woodworking adhesive, 25mm No.6 (3.6mm) brass countersunk woodscrews, 25mm No.8 (4.2mm) domed head japanned steel woodscrews, 19mm No.6 (3.6mm) brass countersunk woodscrews, approx. 3 metres ½-round brass or aluminium strip, approx. 3 metres 25 × 4mm mild steel strip
Finish: Polyurethane lacquer, metal primer, gloss paint
Materials list (cart)
All plywood parts can be cut according to the cutting plans on the left from one half of a standard sheet (2440 × 1220mm) of 12mm plywood.
Additional materials: PVA woodworking adhesive, 25mm panel pins, 25mm No.6 (3.6mm) countersunk chipboard screws, 12mm mild steel rod, 4mm mild steel rod, 9mm steel rod, split pins, washers, 25mm domed head M4 nuts bolts and washers, wheels, 50mm M10 coach bolts, 50 × 25mm softwood, 1.5mm plywood, U-bolts.
Finish: primer, enamel paints

Steering assembly

Stub axle from 12mm steel rod held with two U-bolts through the wishbone

Track rod from 4mm steel rod
Track rod arm

Drill the axles for split pins to retain plate washers on each side of the wheels

111

A sandpit in the garden

This easy-to-build garden project combines a shady picnic spot with a child's sandpit. It is made of low cost timber, and the boarded decking has removable lids which cover the pit at one end and a small storage area at the other

Building this boarded platform is extremely simple, yet the finished result is attractive and practical. Built around a tree, it provides a shady sheltered spot for outdoor meals or just for sitting and reading a book, magazine or newspaper.

Begin by choosing a firm, level, well-drained site. If you have no tree which is suitable to build around, any other spot which meets these requirements will do. Next, you will need to carefully plan and set out the eight stakes which support all the structure. Note that the stakes around the pit are longer to allow for the excavation. You should make the excavation at the same time as sinking the stakes which surround it.

If you are concreting the pit and lining with boards, do so at this stage. It is possible to use an unlined pit, but the sand will tend to become contaminated with soil. The alternative is to line it with a plastics sheet, which will be effective for some time but will eventually deteriorate.

Cover the frame with 150mm × 25mm boards nailed in place. Use galvanized nails to resist rust. You can use either new timber, or, as a cheaper but effective substitute, buy old floorboards from a demolition site. Whichever you choose, treat the timber thoroughly with a wood preservative. If the timber is very rough, it is advisable to give it a thorough sanding to remove most of the roughness and splinters. This is particularly important in the pit area where children will be playing.

Make the two lids to fit on each side of the fixed decking using more boards braced with battens. The lids will keep the worst of the weather from the pit and storage area, but it is as well to use a polythene sheet too.

If you are lining the pit with plastics, fit it as shown, using a batten to secure the top edge. Allow for drainage to prevent the sand from becoming soaked. Fill the pit with sugar sand, obtainable from builder's merchants. Check the walls of the sand pit particularly carefully for splinters and sand down any rough areas.

Alternative ideas

You can build these two attractive tree seats using the same method as for the sandpit.

The picture on the left shows a bench seat and backrest built up against the trunk. Make this on a framework of stakes. However make sure that you do not attach the backrest to the growing trunk or you may damage the bark.

Build the picnic table and benches shown on the right in the same way, but using longer stakes to support the table top. Set the top at about 750mm high, and the bench at around 500mm.

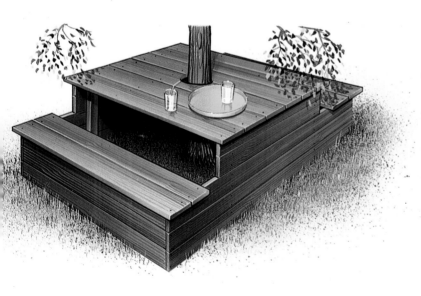

Workplan

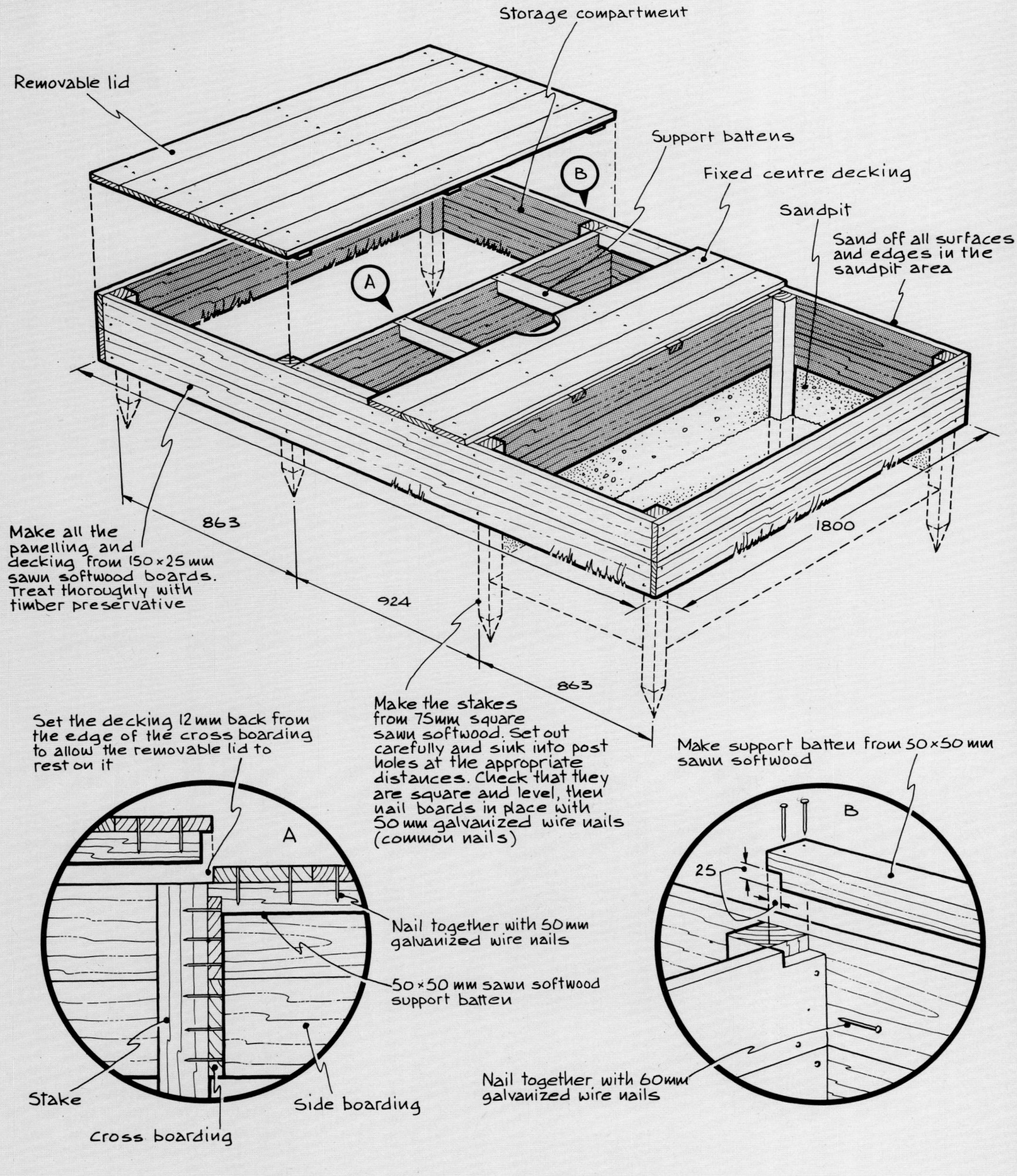

Removable lid

Storage compartment

Support battens

Fixed centre decking

Sandpit

Sand off all surfaces and edges in the sandpit area

Make all the panelling and decking from 150 × 25 mm sawn softwood boards. Treat thoroughly with timber preservative

863

924

863

1800

Make the stakes from 75 mm square sawn softwood. Set out carefully and sink into post holes at the appropriate distances. Check that they are square and level, then nail boards in place with 50 mm galvanized wire nails (common nails)

Set the decking 12 mm back from the edge of the cross boarding to allow the removable lid to rest on it

A

Nail together with 50 mm galvanized wire nails

50 × 50 mm sawn softwood support batten

Stake

Cross boarding

Side boarding

Make support batten from 50 × 50 mm sawn softwood

B

25

Nail together with 60 mm galvanized wire nails

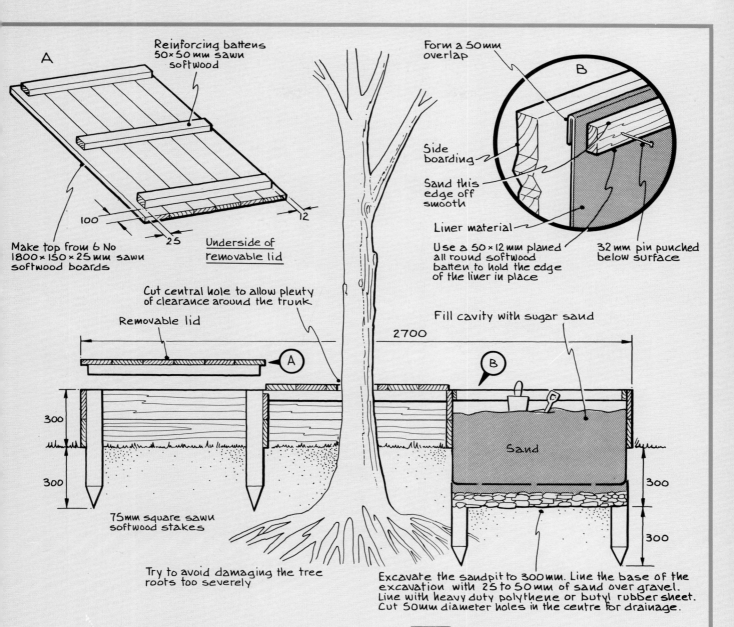

A

Reinforcing battens
50×50 mm sawn
softwood

Make top from 6 No
1800 × 150 × 25 mm sawn
softwood boards

100   25   12

Underside of
removable lid

Cut central hole to allow plenty
of clearance around the trunk

Removable lid

A

300

300

75mm square sawn
softwood stakes

Try to avoid damaging the tree
roots too severely

Form a 50mm
overlap

B

Side
boarding

Sand this
edge off
smooth

Liner material

Use a 50 × 12mm planed
all round softwood
batten to hold the edge
of the liner in place

32 mm pin punched
below surface

Fill cavity with sugar sand

2700

B

Sand

300

300

Excavate the sandpit to 300mm. Line the base of the
excavation with 25 to 50mm of sand over gravel.
Line with heavy duty polythene or butyl rubber sheet.
Cut 50mm diameter holes in the centre for drainage.

Alternatively, you can line the excavation as
shown. Continue the boarding down the stakes
(either nail through from the inside, or dig a
larger excavation, nail then fill up to the
boards. Line the base with concrete over
hardcore for drainage.

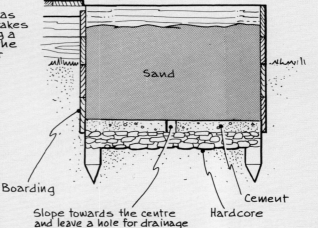

Sand

Boarding

Cement

Hardcore

Slope towards the centre
and leave a hole for drainage

Cutting list

All sizes are in millimetres. Timber is either planed all round, PAR
(dressed four sides, D4S) or sawn.

Part	Material	No.	Size
Stakes (short)	75mm × 75mm sawn softwood	4	600mm
Stakes (long)	75mm × 75mm sawn softwood	4	900mm
Side boarding	150mm × 25mm sawn softwood	4	2650mm
End boarding	150mm × 25mm sawn softwood	4	1800mm
Cross boarding	150mm × 25mm sawn softwood	4	1750mm
Support battens	50mm × 50mm sawn softwood	4	925mm
Reinforcing battens	50mm × 50mm sawn softwood	6	863mm

Additional materials: Pit lining (timber or plastic), cement, hardcore,
sugar sand, 50mm galvanized wire nails, timber preservative, 50mm × 12mm
batten

A childrens' climbing frame

This sturdy and attractive climbing frame should provide years of pleasure and exercise for growing children. It is simple to put together but if space is limited, you can just as easily pack it away for storage

Children love to climb, and can get useful exercise from their games. This traditionally constructed climbing frame provides an environment where they can play safely and under the watchful eyes of their parents. It will fit comfortably into a small garden, and can be dismantled in an hour or so to make four panels which can be easily and compactly be packed away during the winter months.

The frame is sturdily constructed in timber and is based around the four collapsible panels. These are rigidly held together when the climbing frame is assembled by fitting bolted-on cross-beams. All the joints are either screwed and glued or bolted, so construction is very simple. Only basic woodworking tools are needed, but the dowel rods which form the climbing rails are run through holes in the uprights, so you will need a large (32mm) drill. You can use a brace and bit to bore the holes, but a powerful electric drill, preferably with a drill stand, makes the work much easier.

Following the plans, cut all the timber to length then mark each piece with a letter or a number so you can identify its position. Construct the four fixed panels first. These are shown shaded on the plans. Drill all the uprights with the holes for the

dowel rails running across the panel. Note that the holes on the outer uprights are stopped at 30mm depth, so fit a depth guide to the drill.

Now fit the cross dowels. These should be hardwood for maximum strength, but well selected Parana pine can be used instead. Glue the dowels in position with urea formaldehyde adhesive, which is suitable for exterior use. Fit the top and bottom rails of 75mm×25mm softwood, and glue and screw them to the uprights.

When all four panels are complete, mark them out and drill the holes for the dowels, noting which are stopped and which are through. Also, drill the holes for the bolts which hold the top and bottom rails in position.

To assemble the frame, thread the dowels through the panels. Fit the top and bottom rails in position, and secure with coach (carriage) bolts. To prevent the dowels from turning, lock them by inserting a thin cross dowel into a hole drilled through one of the uprights and into the rail.

The main assembly is now complete. You can dismantle it by unbolting the cross rails and removing these and the dowels. The panels will then pack flat for storage.

Before use you should sand all the surfaces smooth, paying particular attention to the edges—you can round these off with a plane. Treat all the timber with a timber preservative, using a non-toxic formulation; you can use paint or lacquer but if this wears off, the timber underneath will be unprotected. If you use timber preservative, retreat every two years.

Add a rope ladder and a swing made from an old tyre, using strong rope, and making sure that the knots are secure. You can also fit a movable platform made from lengths of batten as shown. This will fit between any adjacent pair of dowels and is quite secure once dropped into place.

The frame should be stable when free-standing, but on an uneven surface, you can secure it further by lashing it to stakes set into the ground.

Alternative idea

You can easily make a useful addition to your climbing frame by adding a slide. Make it from 12mm plywood, lined with plastic laminate or highly polished. Fit hooks at the top to hold it to the frame.

Cutting list

All sizes in millimetres. Timber is planed all round, PAR (dressed four sides, D4s)

Part	Material	No.	Size
outer uprights	50mm × 50mm softwood (PAR)	12	1800mm
centre uprights	50mm × 50mm softwood (PAR)	4	2250mm
fixed cross dowels	32mm diameter hardwood dowel	11	1768mm
fixed cross dowels	32mm diameter hardwood dowel	3	1170mm
through dowels	32mm diameter hardwood dowel	12	1170mm
fixed cross rails	75mm × 25mm softwood (PAR)	4	1800mm
fixed cross rails	75mm × 25mm softwood (PAR)	2	631mm
cross rails	75mm × 25mm softwood (PAR)	8	1995mm
cross rails	75mm × 25mm softwood (PAR)	2	677mm
ladder rungs	50mm × 25mm softwood (PAR)	5	400mm
platform sides (optional)	75mm × 25mm softwood (PAR)	2	710mm
platform deck (optional)	50mm × 25mm softwood (PAR)	10	580mm

Additional materials: Rope, old tyre, 72 No. 75mm × 10mm coach (carriage) bolts with nuts and washers, 72 No. 50mm No. 10 (4.9mm) countersunk wood-screws, urea formaldehyde adhesive, 25mm × 6mm dowels.

Finish: Timber preservative.

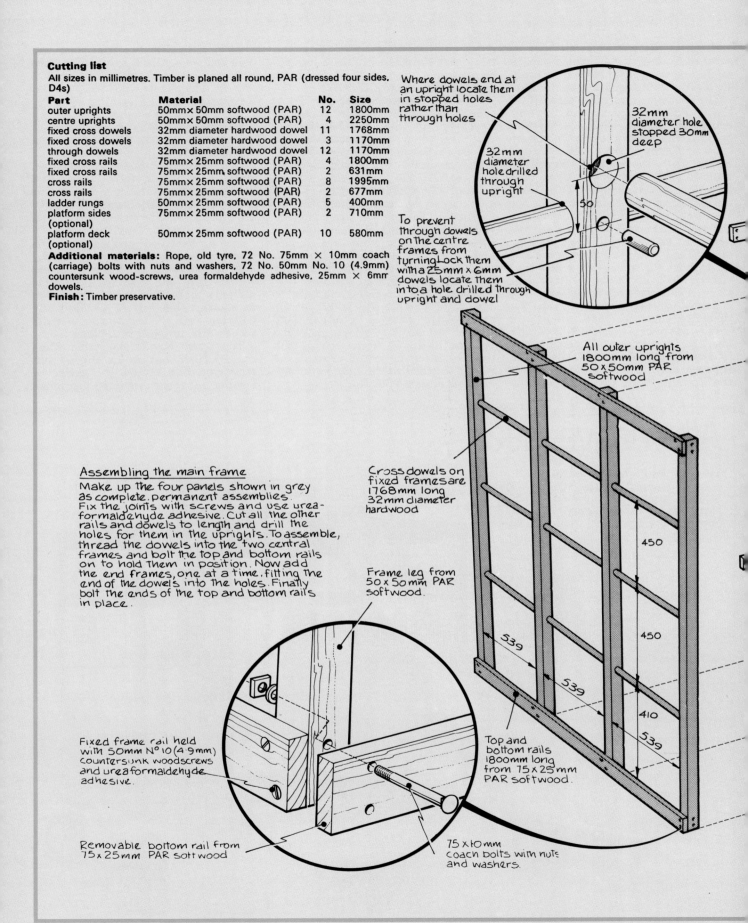

Where dowels end at an upright locate them in stopped holes rather than through holes

32mm diameter hole stopped 30mm deep

32mm diameter hole drilled through upright

50

To prevent through dowels on the centre frames from turning lock them with a 25mm × 6mm dowels locate them into a hole drilled through upright and dowel

Assembling the main frame

Make up the four panels shown in grey as complete, permanent assemblies. Fix the joints with screws and use urea-formaldehyde adhesive. Cut all the other rails and dowels to length and drill the holes for them in the uprights. To assemble, thread the dowels into the two central frames and bolt the top and bottom rails on to hold them in position. Now add the end frames, one at a time, fitting the end of the dowels into the holes. Finally bolt the ends of the top and bottom rails in place.

All outer uprights 1800mm long from 50 x 50mm PAR softwood

Cross dowels on fixed frames are 1768mm long 32mm diameter hardwood

Frame leg from 50 x 50mm PAR softwood.

450

450

539

539

410

539

Top and bottom rails 1800mm long from 75 x 25mm PAR softwood.

Fixed frame rail held with 50mm N°10 (4.9mm) countersunk woodscrews and urea formaldehyde adhesive.

Removable bottom rail from 75 x 25mm PAR softwood

75 x 10mm coach bolts with nuts and washers.

118

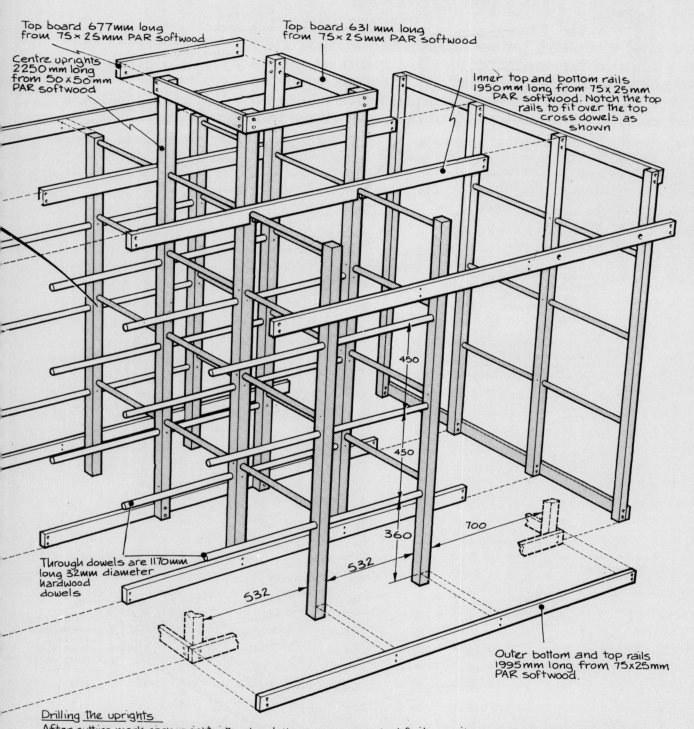

Top board 677mm long from 75 × 25mm PAR softwood

Top board 631 mm long from 75 × 25mm PAR softwood

Centre uprights 2250 mm long from 50 × 50mm PAR softwood

Inner top and bottom rails 1950 mm long from 75 × 25mm PAR softwood. Notch the top rails to fit over the top cross dowels as shown

Through dowels are 1170mm long 32mm diameter hardwood dowels

450

450

360

700

532

532

Outer bottom and top rails 1995mm long from 75×25mm PAR softwood.

Drilling the uprights

After cutting, mark each upright with a key letter so you can identify its position on the plan. Mark out each of the drilling holes at the correct height and on the correct side. Note whether the dowel runs through the upright or stops. If it stops, stop the hole at 30mm deep so that the end of the dowel does not project. Also mark out and drill each upright for the bolt holes for the top and bottom rails.

Finish

You can paint or lacquer the frame, but if this wears through, the timber underneath will be unprotected. A better alternative is to use timber preservative but make sure that you can use a non-toxic formulation.

Left: *For a small child, the design includes plans for a simple cradle seat in plywood. The component parts are dowel-jointed together, ready to receive a drop-in seat which is padded with foam and then covered with vinyl*

Below left: *More proficient swingers are certain to prefer a simple bench seat like this. Both types of seat are hung from eyebolts on heavy-duty galvanized steel welded-link chain*

A garden swing is one of the most traditional—and enjoyable—outdoor activities for children of all ages. This design uses a sturdy softwood frame and includes two types of seat to suit both toddlers and older children.

The frame is based on a strong crossbeam and four legs. Cut shouldered tenons on each end of the crossbeam, angling them as shown. All four legs are cut to an angle at the ends and housed to accept the tenons. The joints are secured with bolts. Make sure that you fit locking nuts on all bolts, either by using self-locking nuts with a nylon insert or adding a second nut to lock the first.

The lower ends of the legs are also cut to an angle. They are braced by being bolted to long boards which lie on the ground. If extra bracing is required, you can fix these to the ground, or add extra bracing between them.

Treat all timber thoroughly with timber preservative—or use pressure treated timber—to avoid problems with rot. Assemble the frame and erect it on a firm, level surface. If extra bracing is needed, fix the ground boards as described above. You can also add side guy ropes, fixed to the crossbeam and pegged to the ground.

Both seat designs are hung on chains hooked over swing hooks bolted to the crossbeam. Make sure you use a sturdy welded-link steel chain, and be sure to use locking nuts on the hooks.

The simpler seat is based on a softwood board. This is padded along its edges to prevent accidents, and covered in a waterproof fabric. You should still treat the timber, however, to resist damp. Fit eye bolts and attach it to the chain using shackles. You can adjust the height of the seat by raising or lowering the chain a few links on the swing hooks.

The cradle seat also has a foam and fabric covered seat, supported in a sturdy plywood frame. Additional safety can be ensured for very small children if you add a strap between the two side panels to prevent the child from slipping forward off the seat. Hang the strap on a double chain arranged as shown, and fix these to the ends of the chains attached to the swing hooks.

Ray Duns

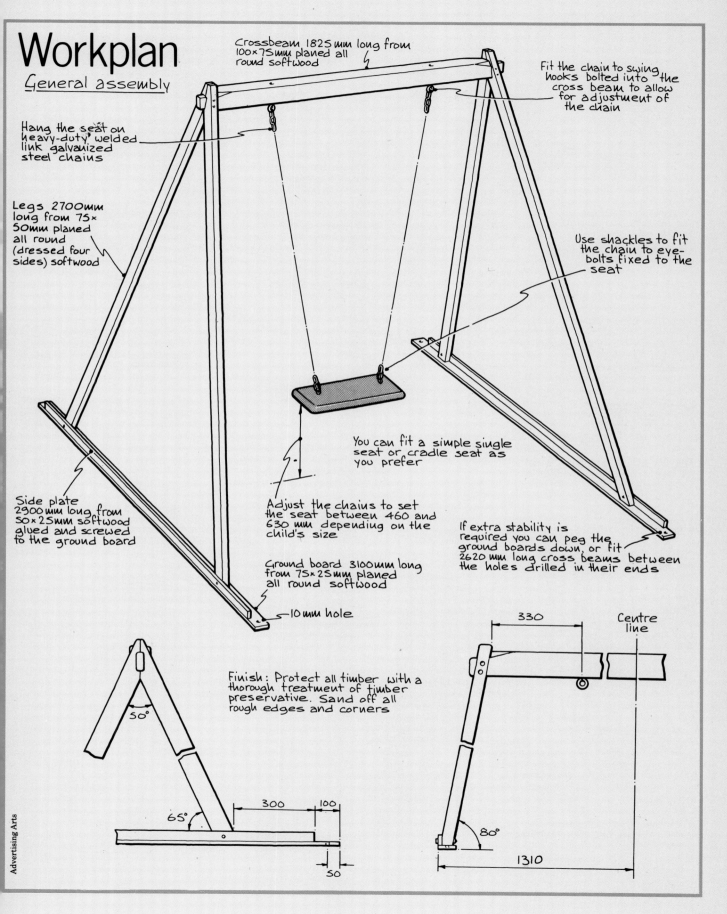

Workplan
General assembly

Crossbeam 1825mm long from 100×75mm planed all round softwood

Fit the chain to swing hooks bolted into the cross beam to allow for adjustment of the chain

Hang the seat on heavy-duty welded link galvanized steel chains

Legs 2700mm long from 75× 50mm planed all round (dressed four sides) softwood

Use shackles to fit the chain to eye-bolts fixed to the seat

Side plate 2900mm long from 50×25mm softwood glued and screwed to the ground board

You can fit a simple single seat or cradle seat as you prefer

Adjust the chains to set the seat between 460 and 630 mm depending on the child's size

If extra stability is required you can peg the ground boards down, or fit 2620 mm long cross beams between the holes drilled in their ends

Ground board 3100mm long from 75×25mm planed all round softwood

10mm hole

330

Centre line

50°

Finish: Protect all timber with a thorough treatment of timber preservative. Sand off all rough edges and corners

65°

300   100

80°

50

1310

Advertising Arts

123

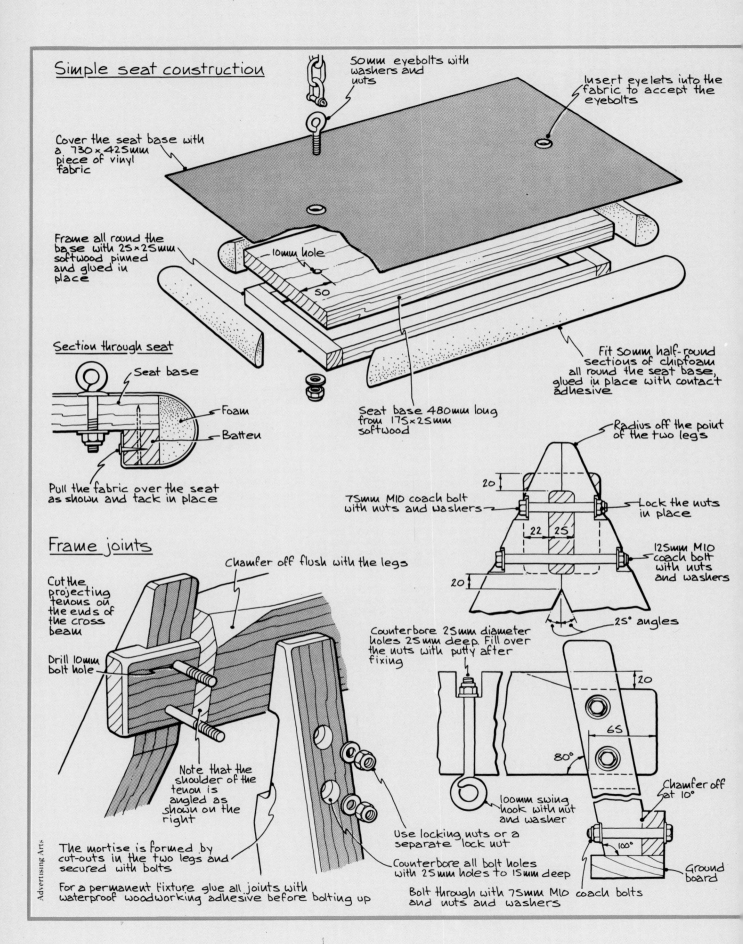

Simple seat construction

50mm eyebolts with washers and nuts

Insert eyelets into the fabric to accept the eyebolts

Cover the seat base with a 730 × 425mm piece of vinyl fabric

Frame all round the base with 25×25mm softwood pinned and glued in place

10mm hole

50

Section through seat

Seat base

Foam

Batten

Pull the fabric over the seat as shown and tack in place

Seat base 480mm long from 175×25mm softwood

Fit 50mm half-round sections of chipfoam all round the seat base, glued in place with contact adhesive

Radius off the point of the two legs

20

75mm M10 coach bolt with nuts and washers

Lock the nuts in place

22   25

125mm M10 coach bolt with nuts and washers

20

25° angles

Frame joints

Chamfer off flush with the legs

Cut the projecting tenons on the ends of the cross beam

Drill 10mm bolt hole

Note that the shoulder of the tenon is angled as shown on the right

The mortise is formed by cut-outs in the two legs and secured with bolts

For a permanent fixture glue all joints with waterproof woodworking adhesive before bolting up

Counterbore 25mm diameter holes 25mm deep. Fill over the nuts with putty after fixing

Use locking nuts or a separate lock nut

Counterbore all bolt holes with 25mm holes to 15mm deep

Bolt through with 75mm M10 coach bolts and nuts and washers

100mm swing hook with nut and washer

20

65

80°

Chamfer off at 10°

100°

100°

Ground board

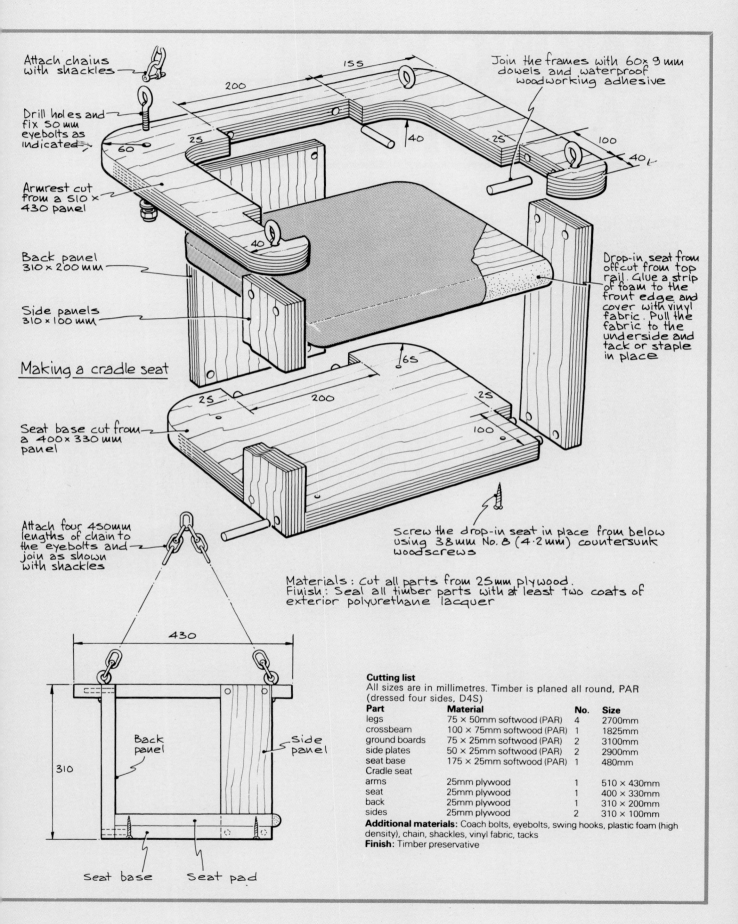

Attach chains with shackles

Drill holes and fix 50 mm eyebolts as indicated

Armrest cut from a 510 × 430 panel

Back panel 310 × 200 mm

Side panels 310 × 100 mm

Making a cradle seat

Seat base cut from a 400 × 330 mm panel

Attach four 450mm lengths of chain to the eyebolts and join as shown with shackles

Join the frames with 60 × 9 mm dowels and waterproof woodworking adhesive

Drop-in seat from offcut from top rail. Glue a strip of foam to the front edge and cover with vinyl fabric. Pull the fabric to the underside and tack or staple in place

Screw the drop-in seat in place from below using 38 mm No. 8 (4·2 mm) countersunk woodscrews

Materials: Cut all parts from 25mm plywood.
Finish: Seal all timber parts with at least two coats of exterior polyurethane lacquer

155
200
25
40
25
100
40
60
25
40
65
200
25
25
100
430
310

Back panel

Side panel

Seat base   Seat pad

Cutting list
All sizes are in millimetres. Timber is planed all round, PAR (dressed four sides, D4S)

Part	Material	No.	Size
legs	75 × 50mm softwood (PAR)	4	2700mm
crossbeam	100 × 75mm softwood (PAR)	1	1825mm
ground boards	75 × 25mm softwood (PAR)	2	3100mm
side plates	50 × 25mm softwood (PAR)	2	2900mm
seat base	175 × 25mm softwood (PAR)	1	480mm
Cradle seat			
arms	25mm plywood	1	510 × 430mm
seat	25mm plywood	1	400 × 330mm
back	25mm plywood	1	310 × 200mm
sides	25mm plywood	2	310 × 100mm

Additional materials: Coach bolts, eyebolts, swing hooks, plastic foam (high density), chain, shackles, vinyl fabric, tacks
Finish: Timber preservative

MAKING YOUR OWN FURNITURE

Make a studio bed

A studio bed which will double as a couch is a useful piece of furniture, particularly where space is limited or you want an occasional guest bed. This design makes the most of the space it occupies by providing storage inside the divan base and in the large trunk at the head of the bed.

Make it from strong, veneered chipboard (particleboard) panels. There is very little wastage, as most of the panels are standard sizes. Smaller sections can be made from the offcuts. See the cutting list for details.

Start with the softwood frame which supports the main bed section. You can join this with dowels, block joints or screws as preferred. Add the hardboard base panelling before you fit the top cross members. When the frame is complete, frame up the inside of the head and footboards and screw these to the frame. Fit the storage compartment dividers, which are made of hardboard held by a quadrant moulding. Fit the bed base shelving and the front

Whether you use it as a couch or a bed, you will appreciate the useful bedside shelves. There are four storage compartments in the frame

This studio bed is ideal for a small flat, bedsit or spare room. The frame incorporates plenty of storage space and some handy bedside shelves. Construction is easy using convenient veneered chipboard panels.

plinth strip across the frames using screws or block joints.

Now make up the softwood frame for the head trunk and screw this to the outside of the headboard. Panel in as shown. Hinge the lid in place and add the drop flaps to the storage compartments under the bed.

Panel in the back of the entire unit with hardboard, pinned and glued in place. Finish all cut edges with iron-on veneer edging strip. Sand lightly and finish with wax, teak oil or lacquer with polyurethane or melamine lacquer.

Frederick Mancini

Workplan

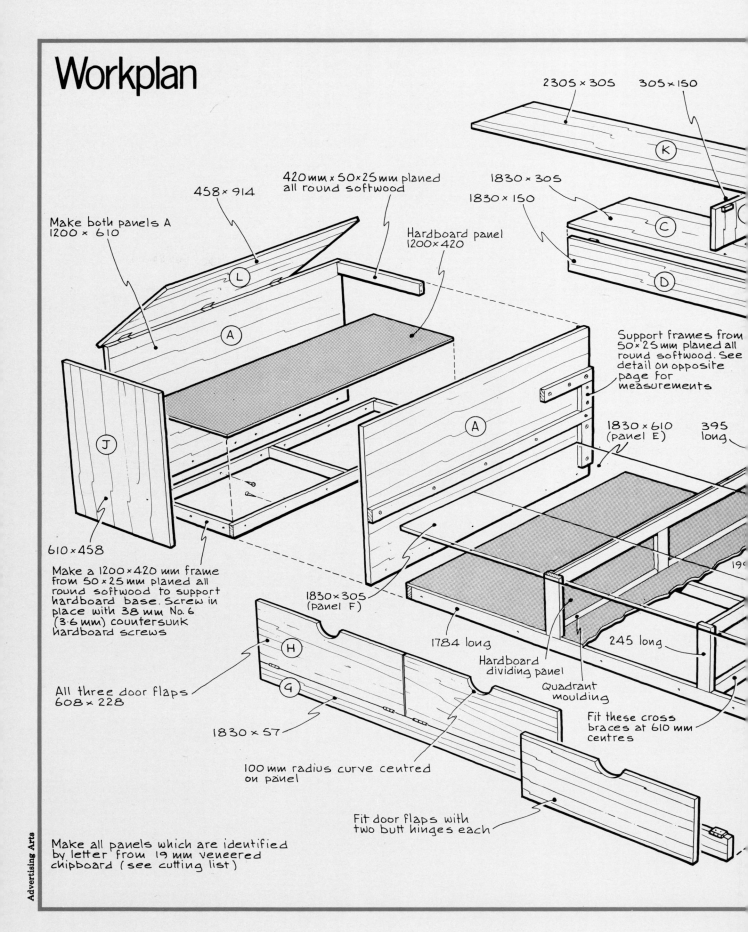

2305 × 305   305 × 150

458 × 914

420mm × 50×25mm planed all round softwood

1830 × 305

1830 × 150

Make both panels A 1200 × 610

Hardboard panel 1200 × 420

Support frames from 50 × 25 mm planed all round softwood. See detail on opposite page for measurements

1830 × 610 (panel E)

395 long

610 × 458

Make a 1200 × 420 mm frame from 50 × 25 mm planed all round softwood to support hardboard base. Screw in place with 38 mm No. 6 (3·6 mm) countersunk hardboard screws

1830 × 305 (panel F)

1784 long

Hardboard dividing panel

245 long

Quadrant moulding

All three door flaps 608 × 228

1830 × 57

Fit these cross braces at 610 mm centres

100 mm radius curve centred on panel

Fit door flaps with two butt hinges each

Make all panels which are identified by letter from 19 mm veneered chipboard (see cutting list)

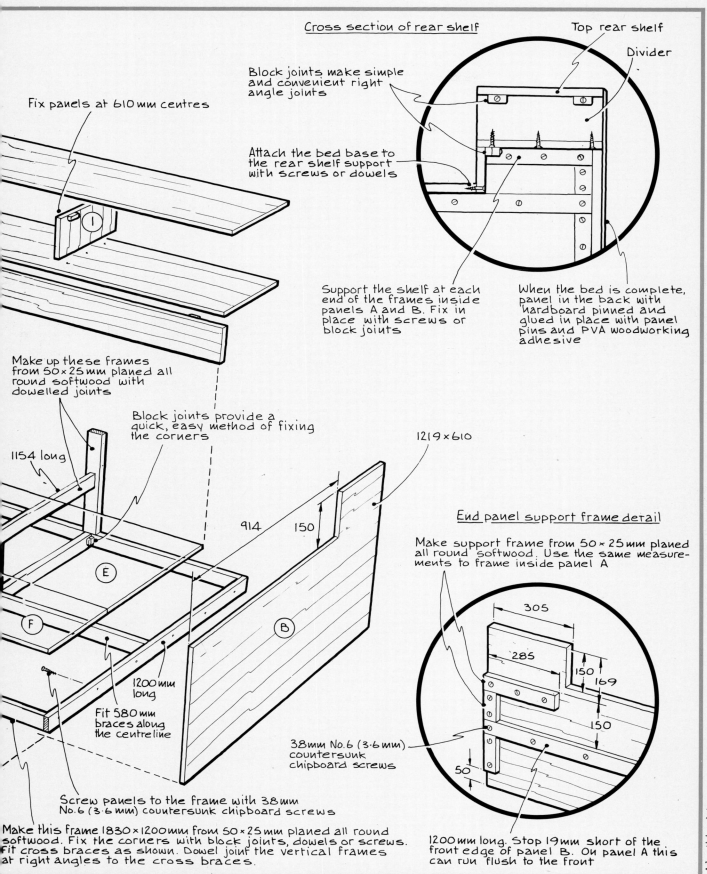

Cross section of rear shelf

Top rear shelf

Divider

Fix panels at 610 mm centres

Block joints make simple and convenient right angle joints

Attach the bed base to the rear shelf support with screws or dowels

Make up these frames from 50×25 mm planed all round softwood with dowelled joints

Block joints provide a quick, easy method of fixing the corners

1154 long

Support the shelf at each end of the frames inside panels A and B. Fix in place with screws or block joints

When the bed is complete, panel in the back with hardboard pinned and glued in place with panel pins and PVA woodworking adhesive

1219×610

End panel support frame detail

914   150

Make support frame from 50×25 mm planed all round softwood. Use the same measurements to frame inside panel A

305

285

150

169

150

50

38 mm No.6 (3·6 mm) countersunk chipboard screws

E

F

1200 mm long

Fit 580 mm braces along the centreline

Screw panels to the frame with 38 mm No.6 (3·6 mm) countersunk chipboard screws

Make this frame 1830×1200 mm from 50×25 mm planed all round softwood. Fix the corners with block joints, dowels or screws. Fit cross braces as shown. Dowel joint the vertical frames at right angles to the cross braces.

1200 mm long. Stop 19 mm short of the front edge of panel B. On panel A this can run flush to the front

Cutting list

All sizes are in millimetres. Capital letters identify the panels on the working drawings. Timber is planed all round, PAR (dressed four sides, D4S).

Part	Material	No.	Size
Headboard (A)	1220mm × 610mm × 19mm veneered chipboard	2	1200mm × 610mm
Footboard (B)	1220mm × 610mm × 19mm veneered chipboard	1	1219mm × 610mm
Shelf (C)	1830mm × 305mm 19mm veneered chipboard	1	1830mm × 305mm
Shelf support (D)	1830mm × 150mm × 19mm veneered chipboard	1	1830mm × 150mm
Bed base (E)	1830mm × 610mm × 19mm veneered chipboard	1	1830mm × 610mm
Bed base (F)	1830mm × 305mm × 19mm veneered chipboard	1	1830mm × 305mm
Plinth strip (G)	1830mm × 305mm × 19mm veneered chipboard	1	1830mm × 57mm
Doors (H)	(make from the board above)	3	608mm × 228mm
Shelf dividers (I)	(make from the offcut from the footboard)	2	305mm × 150mm
Front board (J)	610mm × 458mm × 19mm veneered chipboard	1	610mm × 458mm
Top shelf (K)	2440mm × 305mm × 19mm veneered chipboard	1	2305mm × 305mm
Trunk lid (L)	915mm × 458mm × 19mm veneered chipboard	1	914mm × 458mm

Additional materials: Framing from 50mm × 25mm PAR softwood (approx. 23 metres total). Panelling from 4mm hardboard (2 sheets 2440mm × 1220mm), 10mm quadrant moulding (approx. 3 metres total). Block joints, screws, hinges, panel pins, PVA woodworking adhesive.
Finish: Wax, oil or polyurethane or melamine lacquer.

Trunk lid detail

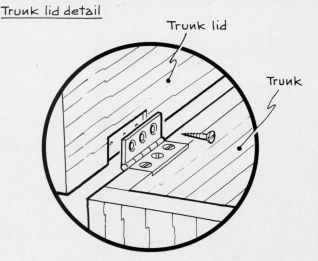

Trunk lid

Trunk

Fit the trunk lid with three butt hinges, rebated as shown. The storage compartment flaps in the base are fitted with two hinges each, rebated into the edge of the door and the edge of the base strip

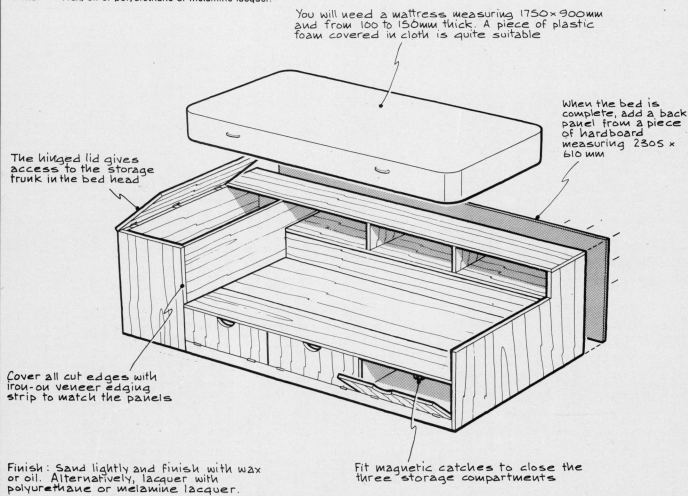

You will need a mattress measuring 1750 × 900mm and from 100 to 150mm thick. A piece of plastic foam covered in cloth is quite suitable

When the bed is complete, add a back panel from a piece of hardboard measuring 2305 × 610 mm

The hinged lid gives access to the storage trunk in the bed head

Cover all cut edges with iron-on veneer edging strip to match the panels

Fit magnetic catches to close the three storage compartments

Finish: Sand lightly and finish with wax or oil. Alternatively, lacquer with polyurethane or melamine lacquer.

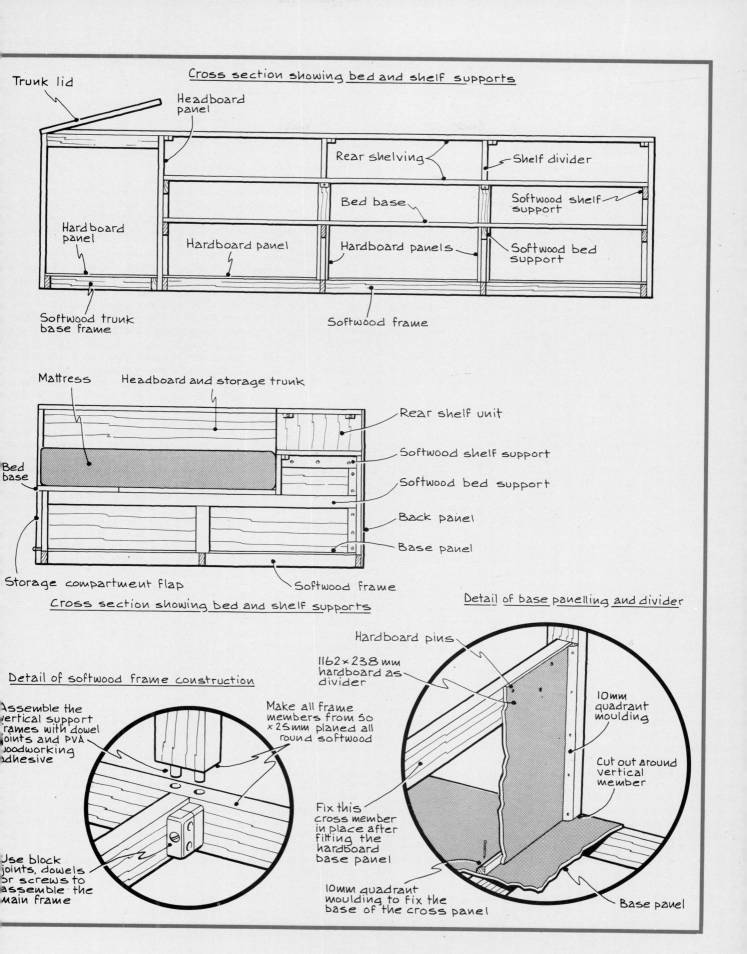

Cross section showing bed and shelf supports

Trunk lid

Headboard panel

Rear shelving

Shelf divider

Hardboard panel

Bed base

Softwood shelf support

Hardboard panel

Hardboard panels

Softwood bed support

Softwood trunk base frame

Softwood frame

Mattress

Headboard and storage trunk

Rear shelf unit

Softwood shelf support

Softwood bed support

Bed base

Back panel

Base panel

Storage compartment flap

Softwood frame

Cross section showing bed and shelf supports

Detail of base panelling and divider

Hardboard pins

1162 × 238 mm hardboard as divider

10mm quadrant moulding

Cut out around vertical member

Detail of softwood frame construction

Assemble the vertical support frames with dowel joints and PVA woodworking adhesive

Make all frame members from 50 × 25mm planed all round softwood

Fix this cross member in place after fitting the hardboard base panel

Use block joints, dowels or screws to assemble the main frame

10mm quadrant moulding to fix the base of the cross panel

Base panel

Elegant built-in wardrobe

This wardrobe has plenty of hanging space, a drawer unit and two storage compartments—yet you can build it into any spare corner so it takes up very little room. Decorative mouldings add style to the door panels

David Jordan

Built-in furniture is a classic way to save space and on construction. This wardrobe is designed to fill the dead space beside an old fireplace, giving you the maximum of storage space for the minimum intrusion into the room. If you have no convenient alcove, you can use the same construction to build a wardrobe in a corner of the room.

The main material for the carcase and doors is veneered chipboard (particleboard), but faced plywood might be a suitable alternative. The wardrobe shown here uses pine-effect board, and the opposite page shows some of the many alternatives possible.

Support the chipboard panels on softwood frames. You can screw these directly to the walls, eliminating the need for complicated support framing. One of the most important points about building-in furniture is that the space you are filling will very rarely be exactly square. This means that you should be careful to take your measurements from the walls, and be prepared to adjust your framing to compensate for variations.

When you come to panelling, these variations may mean that you have to shape some of the panels as well. The design shows one solution; using infill panels made from plywood to fit round complicated mouldings. You can also use infill panels to adjust the width. Chipboard comes in standard width panels, and you may find that, for example, the doors would have to be too wide to cut from a standard board and uneconomic to cut from a large sheet.

One other solution to the problems of non-standard sizes is shown here, where the ceiling is too high for a standard length board. Join two boards as shown, and cover the crack with a decorative moulding.

Use mouldings again to give an interesting finish to doors and hinged flaps. Choose a matching timber, or even a contrasting colour for a really striking effect.

Melamine needs no surface treatment—you should lacquer wood veneer and any wood mouldings you fit.

Alternative ideas

It is easy to adapt this type of framed and panelled construction to almost any style — simply by choosing a different material for the panels. This page shows just a few of many possibilities.

An obvious choice, particularly for bedroom furniture is white melamine-faced chipboard. This too can be trimmed with decorative mouldings and you can buy these in plastic to match the melamine.

Mirrors can make a small room look larger, and they can help to make a wardrobe really unobtrusive. If you just want the mirror for dressing, or do not want the expense, simply fit a smaller mirror inside one of the doors using mirror clips.

One way to give a different look to chipboard is to cover it. Here, hessian gives an interesting and unusual texture to the surface. You can fix the edges under a moulding.

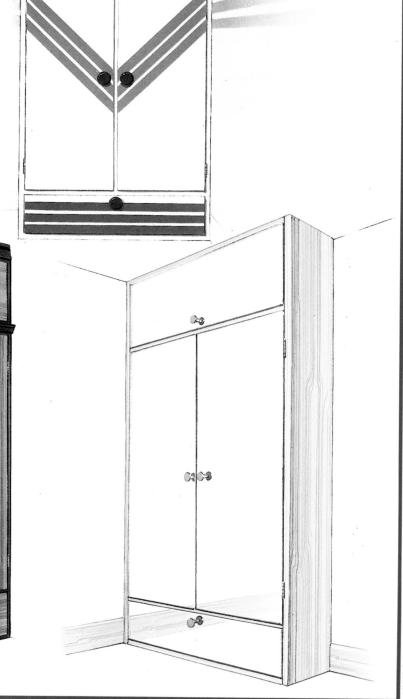

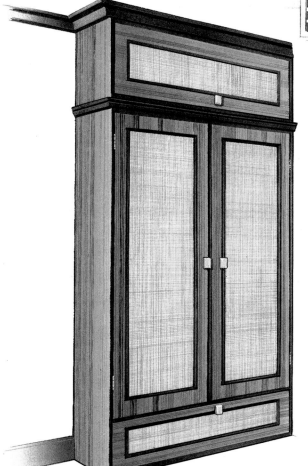

Nigel Osborne

Workplan

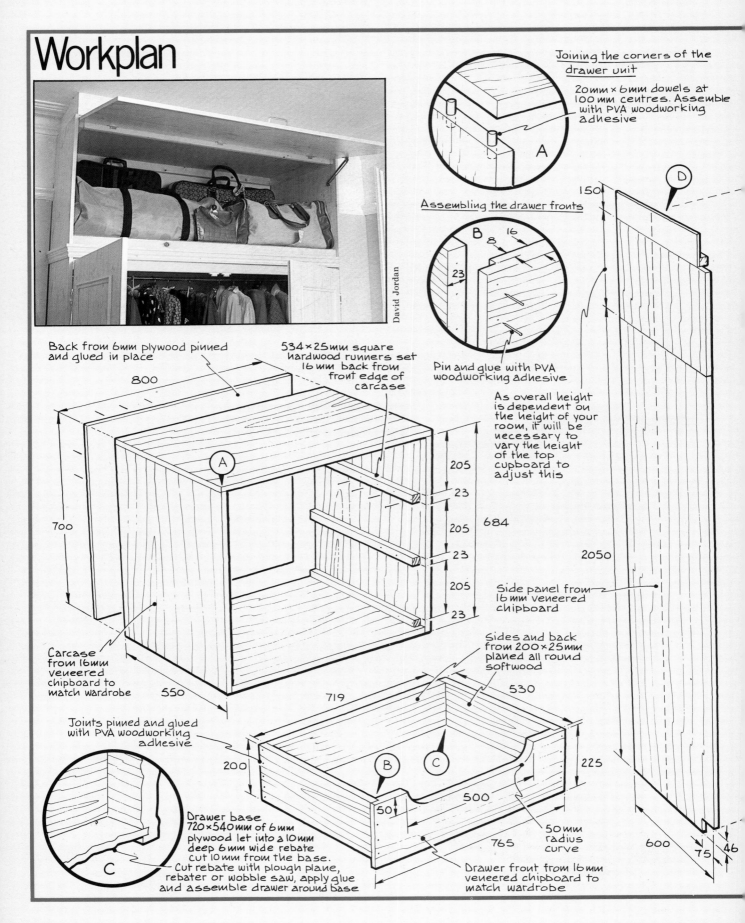

David Jordan

Joining the corners of the drawer unit

20mm × 6mm dowels at 100mm centres. Assemble with PVA woodworking adhesive

A

Assembling the drawer fronts

B

16

8

23

Pin and glue with PVA woodworking adhesive

D

150

As overall height is dependent on the height of your room, it will be necessary to vary the height of the top cupboard to adjust this

Back from 6mm plywood pinned and glued in place

800

534×25mm square hardwood runners set 16mm back from front edge of carcase

2050

205

23

205

23

205

23

684

700

A

Side panel from 16mm veneered chipboard

Carcase from 16mm veneered chipboard to match wardrobe

550

Joints pinned and glued with PVA woodworking adhesive

Sides and back from 200×25mm planed all round softwood

530

719

200

B

C

225

C

50

500

50mm radius curve

Drawer base 720×540mm of 6mm plywood let into a 10mm deep 6mm wide rebate cut 10mm from the base. Cut rebate with plough plane, rebater or wobble saw, apply glue and assemble drawer around base

765

Drawer front from 16mm veneered chipboard to match wardrobe

600

75

46

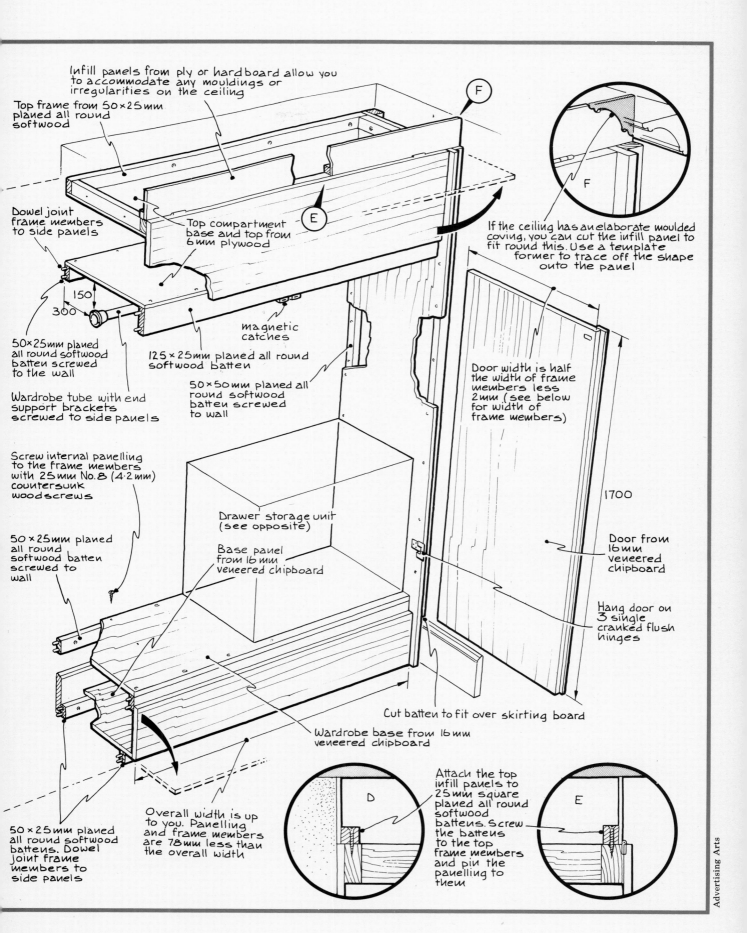

Infill panels from ply or hardboard allow you to accommodate any mouldings or irregularities on the ceiling

Top frame from 50×25mm planed all round softwood

Dowel joint frame members to side panels

150

300

50×25mm planed all round softwood batten screwed to the wall

Wardrobe tube with end support brackets screwed to side panels

Screw internal panelling to the frame members with 25mm No.8 (4·2mm) countersunk woodscrews

50×25mm planed all round softwood batten screwed to wall

50×25mm planed all round softwood battens. Dowel joint frame members to side panels

Top compartment base and top from 6mm plywood

magnetic catches

125×25mm planed all round softwood batten

50×50mm planed all round softwood batten screwed to wall

Drawer storage unit (see opposite)

Base panel from 16mm veneered chipboard

Overall width is up to you. Panelling and frame members are 78mm less than the overall width

Wardrobe base from 16mm veneered chipboard

F

E

If the ceiling has an elaborate moulded coving, you can cut the infill panel to fit round this. Use a template former to trace off the shape onto the panel

Door width is half the width of frame members less 2mm (see below for width of frame members)

1700

Door from 16mm veneered chipboard

Hang door on 3 single cranked flush hinges

Cut batten to fit over skirting board

D

Attach the top infill panels to 25mm square planed all round softwood battens. Screw the battens to the top frame members and pin the panelling to them

E

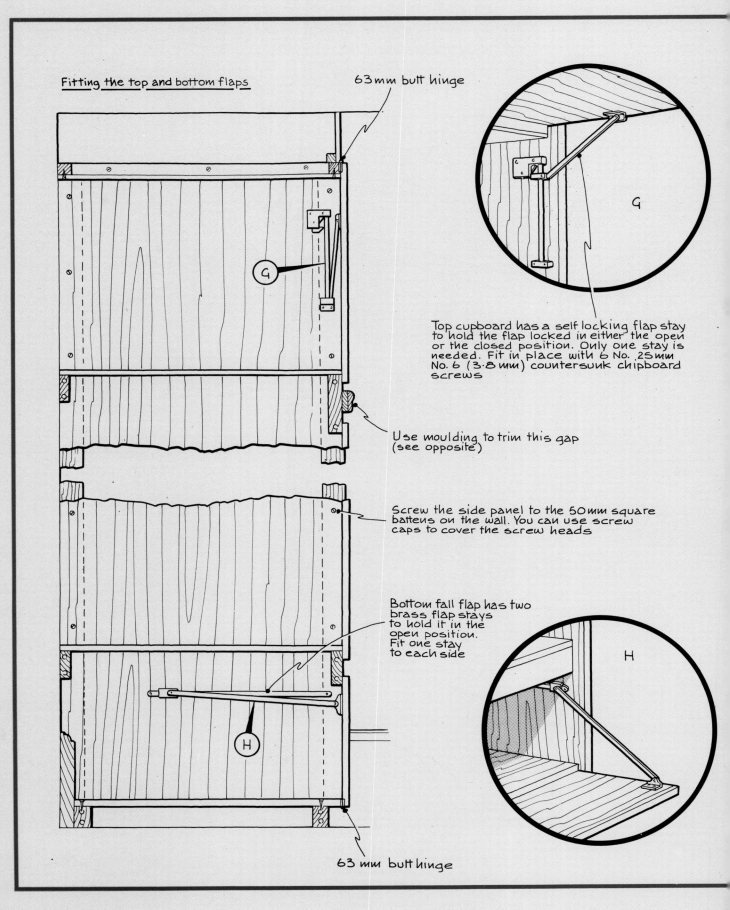

Fitting the top and bottom flaps

63 mm butt hinge

G

Top cupboard has a self locking flap stay to hold the flap locked in either the open or the closed position. Only one stay is needed. Fit in place with 6 No. 25 mm No. 6 (3·8 mm) countersunk chipboard screws

Use moulding to trim this gap (see opposite)

Screw the side panel to the 50 mm square battens on the wall. You can use screw caps to cover the screw heads

Bottom fall flap has two brass flap stays to hold it in the open position. Fit one stay to each side

H

63 mm butt hinge

Finishing details

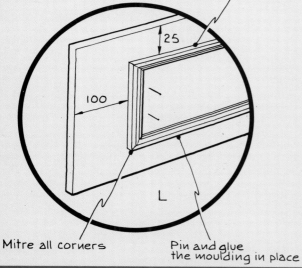

J

K

L

To trim the panel between the top lift-up flap and the doors, use a wooden moulding. Fit a batten as shown to bring this up to the level of the doors, then pin and glue the moulding in place

J

If you have a very tall room, you may not be able to make the side panels of the wardrobe out of one standard length board. If you have to make a join, you can cover this with moulding pinned and glued in place.

K

You should make the join align with the moulding on the front of the wardrobe

Decorative wood or plastic moulding

25

100

L

Mitre all corners

Pin and glue the moulding in place

Advertising Arts

Space-saving hi-fi unit

Finding space for the components of a hi-fi system can be a problem. This simple unit uses corner space that is often wasted to house record and tape decks, a tuner/amp and a collection of records and tapes

This unit is constructed using only the simplest techniques. The joints, for example, are made using wooden battens or plastic joint fittings.

The main material is veneered chipboard (particle board). This is easy to work with, and requires very little work to achieve a high standard of finish. The sawn edges of the chipboard are covered by using a matching iron-on veneer edging strip. The finished unit is stylish in mahogany veneer, which complements the decor of just about any room and matches the cabinets of most speaker units.

A hardboard back is fitted to give

the construction extra strength and keep dust away from the contents.

The unit is supported on a recessed plinth to protect the base from accidental knocks and to give a light appearance. This is made from planed softwood and finished matt black.

The top of the unit is large enough for most standard decks and provides a sturdy vibration-free support at a convenient height. Although designed **as free-standing furniture, you can fix** it to the wall for firmer support. Screw through the back—into studs on a timber-framed wall, or drilled and plugged holes otherwise.

The upper half of the unit is divided into space for a cassette deck and a tuner/amplifier(receiver). Those shown are of a typical size, but it is easy to modify the design to accommodate your own hi-fi equipment.

Below these, there is storage space for a sizeable record collection. The records are stored upright to prevent warping, so the titles are easily read on their spines. Space for cassettes is provided by the two small additional units which can also be used for accessories such as record cleaners.

Connections between the components of the hi-fi system are led through the back of the unit. This gives a neat, uncluttered appearance and protects the leads themselves from accidental pulls. The connections to external speakers can also be led out at the back of the unit and concealed at ground level by feeding them under a carpet or rug.

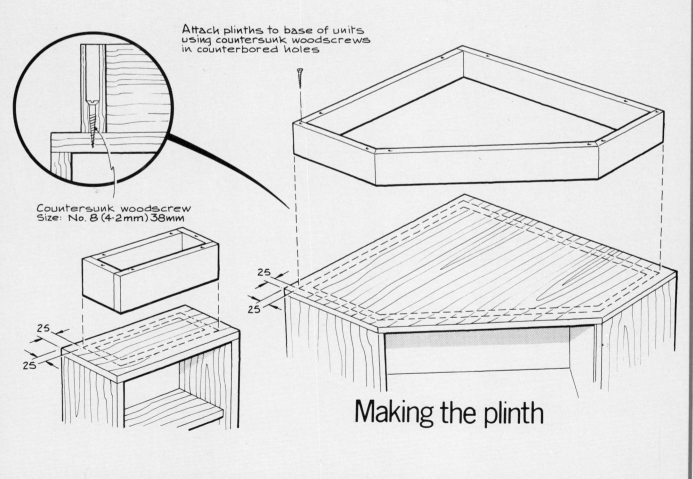

Attach plinths to base of units
using countersunk woodscrews
in counterbored holes

Countersunk woodscrew
Size: No. 8 (4·2mm) 38mm

25
25

25
25

Making the plinth

Workplan

Cutting list

Main unit

Top and base: 2 No. 610mm x 610mm x 16mm mahogany veneered chipboard
Side panels: 2 No. 688mm x 273mm x 16mm mahogany veneered chipboard
Shelves: 2 No. 594mm x 594mm x 16mm mahogany veneered chipboard
Backboards: 2 No. 714mm x 604mm x 3mm hardboard
Plinth: 2 No. 237mm x 70mm x 20mm planed softwood, 1 No. 540mm x 70mm x 20mm planed softwood, 1 No. 520mm x 70mm x 20mm planed softwood, 1 No. 457mm x 70mm x 20mm planed softwood, 10 No. 8 38mm steel screws (sizes given are those *after* planing)
Record compartment: 2 No. 372mm x 332mm x 3mm hardboard, 1 No. 477mm x 338mm x 3mm hardboard
Shelf supports: 4 No. 250mm x 25mm x 25mm planed softwood, 8 No. 8 38mm steel countersunk screws (or 8 No. plastic joint fittings)
Corner blocks: 4 No. 250mm x 25mm planed softwood, 8 No. 8 38mm steel countersunk screws (or 8 No. plastic joint fittings)
Record compartment supports: 4 No. 250mm x 25mm x 25mm planed softwood, 2 No. 400mm x 25mm x 25mm planed softwood, 12 No. 8 38mm steel screws
Edgings: about 3m of 16mm self-adhesive mahogany veneer edging strip, 20mm panel pins (common brads) and PVA woodworking adhesive as required

Side units (each)

Top and base: 2 No. 305mm x 153mm x 16mm mahogany veneered chipboard
Side panels: 2 No. 370mm x 153mm x 16mm mahogany veneered chipboard
Shelf: 273mm x 142mm x 16mm mahogany veneered chipboard
Backboard: 396mm x 299mm x 3mm hardboard
Plinth: 2 No. 83mm x 70mm x 20mm planed softwood, 1 No. 255mm x 70mm x 20mm planed softwood, 1 No. 215mm x 70mm x 20mm planed softwood, 8 No. 8 38mm steel countersunk woodscrews (sizes given are those *after* planing)
Shelf supports: 2 No. 120mm x 25mm x 25mm planed softwood, 4 No. 8 38mm steel countersunk woodscrews (or 4 No. plastic joint fittings)
Corner blocks: 4 No. 130mm x 25mm x 25mm planed softwood, 8 No. 8 38mm steel countersunk woodscrews (or 4 No. plastic joint fittings)
Edgings: about 2.3m of 16mm self-adhesive mahogany veneer edging strip, 20mm panel pins (common brads) and PVA woodworking adhesive

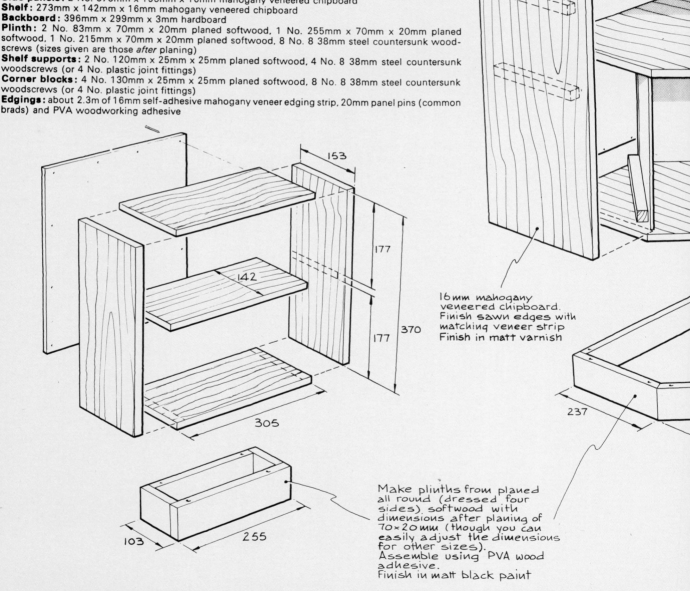

16mm mahogany veneered chipboard. Finish sawn edges with matching veneer strip Finish in matt varnish

Make plinths from planed all round (dressed four sides) softwood with dimensions after planing of 70×20mm (though you can easily adjust the dimensions for other sizes). Assemble using PVA wood adhesive. Finish in matt black paint

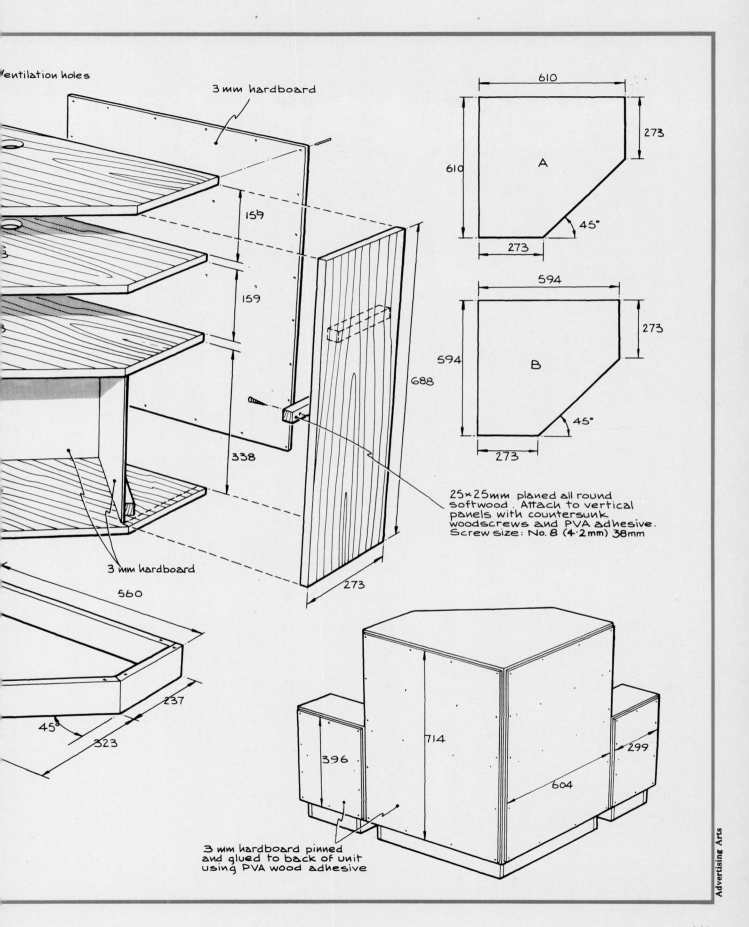

Ventilation holes

3 mm hardboard

159

159

338

3 mm hardboard

688

273

560

237

45°

323

610

610

273

A

273

45°

594

594

273

B

273

45°

25×25mm planed all round softwood. Attach to vertical panels with countersunk woodscrews and PVA adhesive. Screw size: No. 8 (4·2 mm) 38 mm

714

396

299

604

3 mm hardboard pinned and glued to back of unit using PVA wood adhesive

Making the record compartment

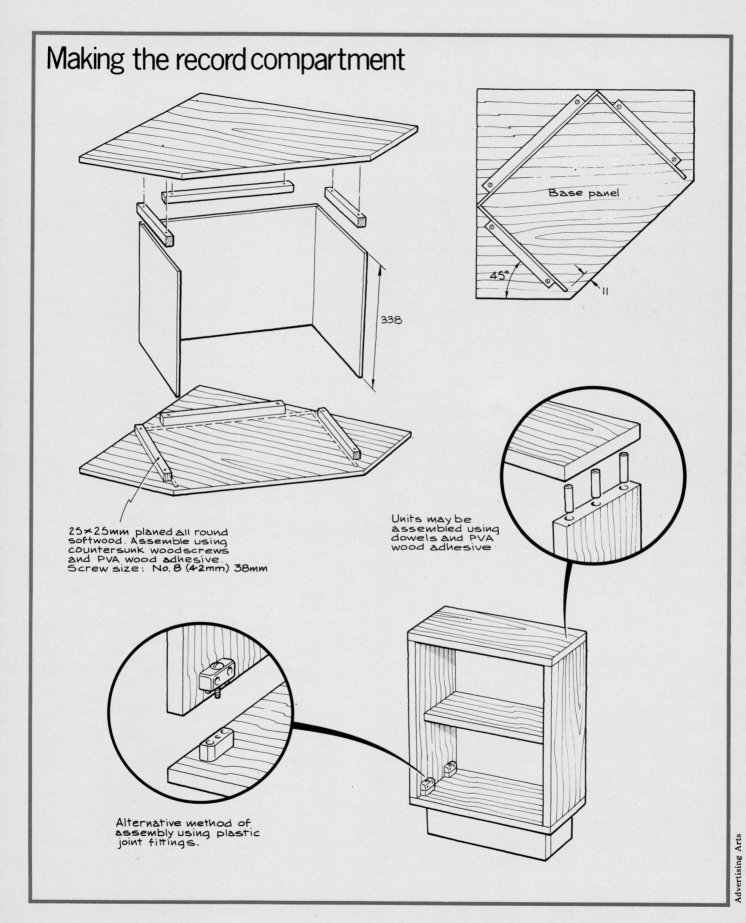

Base panel

45°

11

338

25×25mm planed all round softwood. Assemble using countersunk woodscrews and PVA wood adhesive. Screw size: No. 8 (4·2mm) 38mm

Units may be assembled using dowels and PVA wood adhesive.

Alternative method of assembly using plastic joint fittings.

Multi-purpose storage chest

This three-in-one storage chest is also a table and a bench seat. You can make this attractive and versatile piece at low cost from tongued-and-grooved pine boards

This traditional monk's chest is designed to be versatile. A simple sliding mechanism allows you to turn the top of the table into the back of a seat, and the base of the seat forms a storage chest providing three pieces of furniture in one. In a modern setting, where space is often limited, this traditional idea proves very useful.

The design retains its traditional character by using low cost tongued-and-grooved boards for a natural pine look. If you prefer, you can easily adapt the design by using plywood for the panelling and blockboard or chipboard for the top.

Construction is quite simple. The chest is based on a sturdy frame held together with mortise and tenon joints. First, shape the legs and the rebates in the frame rails, then assemble the frame together.

Panel the completed frame with tongued-and-grooved boards cut to fit the space. Assemble the chest lid and hinge it in place.

Then assemble the top boards and finish the edges. Cut the two sliding pivots which must be made in hardwood as shown overleaf. The groove in these rails runs on a metal pin set into the arm, and must fit accurately. Fit the two rails on to the pins and then fit the top. It is much easier if you have an assistant for this part of the job, and if you pre-drill the top.

Sand all the surfaces and edges thoroughly. You can finish the wood with oil and wax, or with a polyurethane or melamine lacquer.

Clive Helm

143

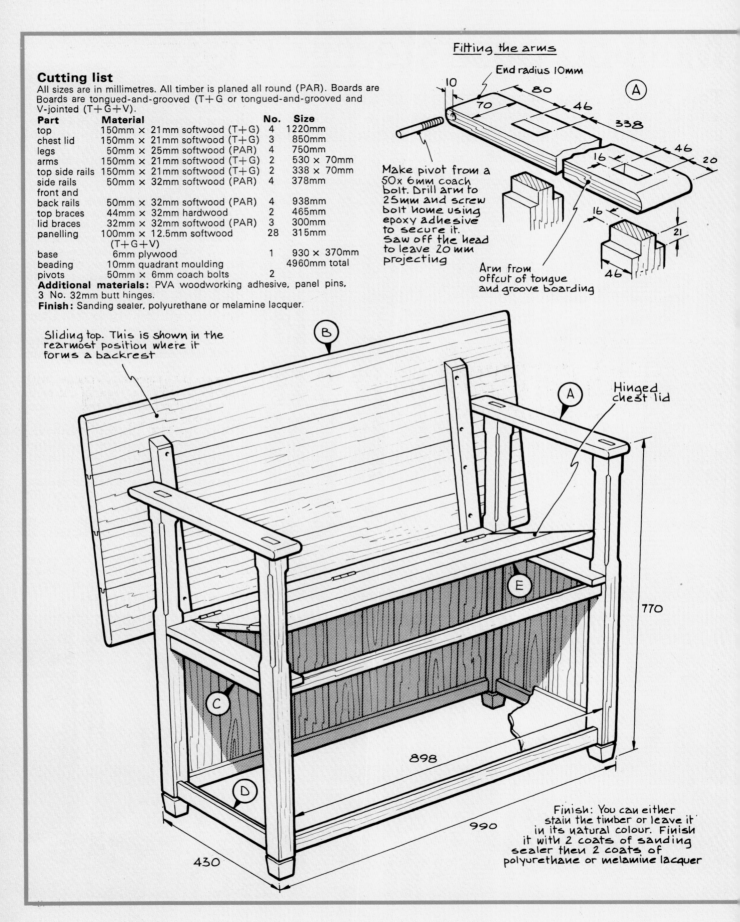

Cutting list

All sizes are in millimetres. All timber is planed all round (PAR). Boards are
Boards are tongued-and-grooved (T+G or tongued-and-grooved and
V-jointed (T+G+V).

Part	Material	No.	Size
top	150mm × 21mm softwood (T+G)	4	1220mm
chest lid	150mm × 21mm softwood (T+G)	3	850mm
legs	50mm × 25mm softwood (PAR)	4	750mm
arms	150mm × 21mm softwood (T+G)	2	530 × 70mm
top side rails	150mm × 21mm softwood (T+G)	2	338 × 70mm
side rails	50mm × 32mm softwood (PAR)	4	378mm
front and			
back rails	50mm × 32mm softwood (PAR)	4	938mm
top braces	44mm × 32mm hardwood	2	465mm
lid braces	32mm × 32mm softwood (PAR)	3	300mm
panelling	100mm × 12.5mm softwood	28	315mm
	(T+G+V)		
base	6mm plywood	1	930 × 370mm
beading	10mm quadrant moulding		4960mm total
pivots	50mm × 6mm coach bolts	2	

Additional materials: PVA woodworking adhesive, panel pins,
3 No. 32mm butt hinges.
Finish: Sanding sealer, polyurethane or melamine lacquer.

Fitting the arms

End radius 10mm

10
80
70
46
338
46
16
20
16
21
46

(A)

Make pivot from a
50 x 6mm coach
bolt. Drill arm to
25mm and screw
bolt home using
epoxy adhesive
to secure it.
Saw off the head
to leave 20 mm
projecting

Arm from
offcut of tongue
and groove boarding

Sliding top. This is shown in the
rearmost position where it
forms a backrest

(B)

(A)

Hinged
chest lid

(E)

(C)

(D)

770

898

990

430

Finish: You can either
stain the timber or leave it
in its natural colour. Finish
it with 2 coats of sanding
sealer then 2 coats of
polyurethane or melamine lacquer

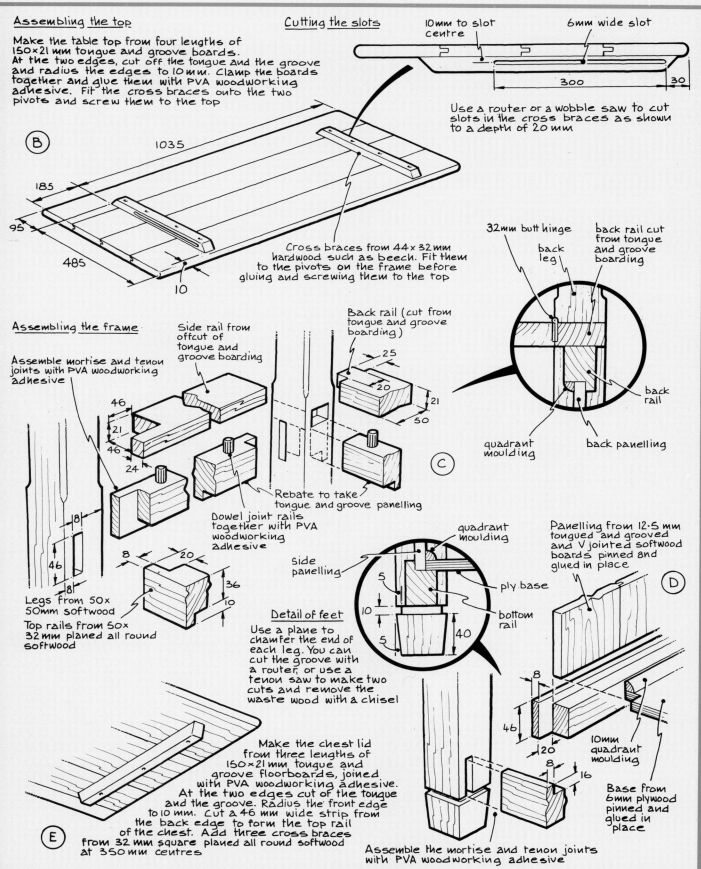

Assembling the top

Make the table top from four lengths of
150×21 mm tongue and groove boards.
At the two edges, cut off the tongue and the groove
and radius the edges to 10 mm. Clamp the boards
together and glue them with PVA woodworking
adhesive. Fit the cross braces onto the two
pivots and screw them to the top

B

1035

185

95

485

10

Cross braces from 44 x 32 mm
hardwood such as beech. Fit them
to the pivots on the frame before
gluing and screwing them to the top

Cutting the slots

10mm to slot
centre

6mm wide slot

300

30

Use a router or a wobble saw to cut
slots in the cross braces as shown
to a depth of 20 mm

32mm butt hinge

back rail cut
from tongue
and groove
boarding

back
leg

quadrant
moulding

back
rail

back panelling

Assembling the frame

Assemble mortise and tenon joints with PVA woodworking
adhesive

Side rail from
offcut of
tongue and
groove boarding

Back rail (cut from
tongue and groove
boarding)

25

20

21

50

C

46

21

46

24

Rebate to take
tongue and groove panelling

Dowel joint rails
together with PVA
woodworking
adhesive

8

46

8

8

20

36

10

Legs from 50 x
50mm softwood

Top rails from 50 x
32 mm planed all round
softwood

quadrant
moulding

side
panelling

5

10

5

ply base

bottom
rail

40

Panelling from 12.5 mm
tongued and grooved
and V jointed softwood
boards pinned and
glued in place

D

Detail of feet

Use a plane to
chamfer the end of
each leg. You can
cut the groove with
a router, or use a
tenon saw to make two
cuts and remove the
waste wood with a chisel

8

46

20

8

16

10mm
quadrant
moulding

Base from
6mm plywood
pinned and
glued in
place

Make the chest lid
from three lengths of
150×21 mm tongue and
groove floorboards, joined
with PVA woodworking adhesive.
At the two edges cut of the tongue
and the groove. Radius the front edge
to 10 mm. Cut a 46 mm wide strip from
the back edge to form the top rail
of the chest. Add three cross braces
from 32 mm square planed all round softwood
at 350 mm centres

E

Assemble the mortise and tenon joints
with PVA woodworking adhesive

Advertising Arts

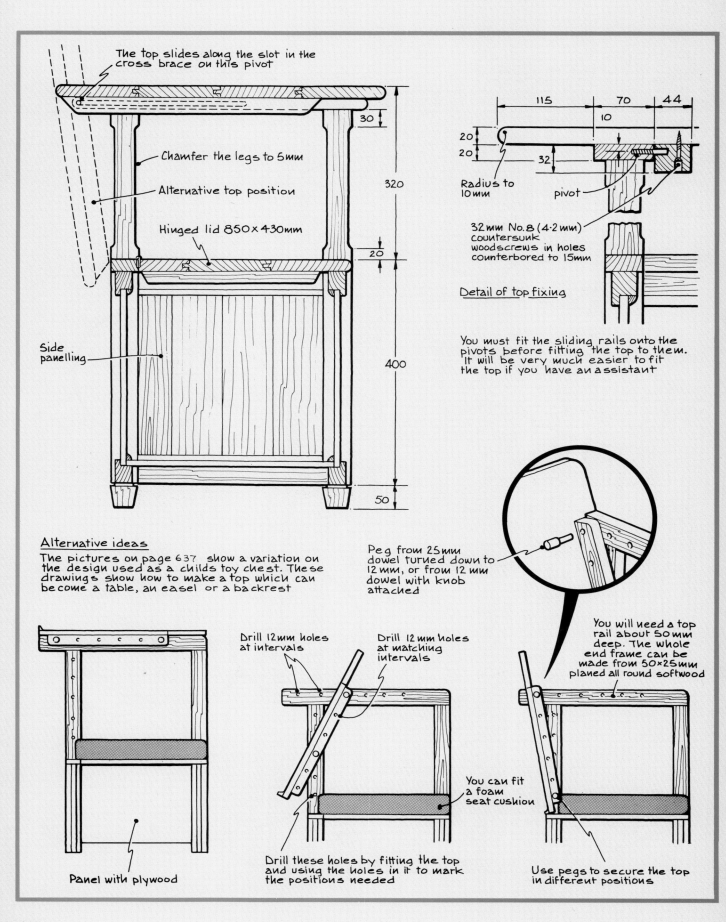

The top slides along the slot in the cross brace on this pivot

Chamfer the legs to 5mm

Alternative top position

Hinged lid 850 × 430mm

Side panelling

30

320

20

400

50

115   70   44

10

20
20

32

Radius to 10mm   pivot

32mm No.8 (4·2mm) countersunk woodscrews in holes counterbored to 15mm

<u>Detail of top fixing</u>

You must fit the sliding rails onto the pivots before fitting the top to them. It will be very much easier to fit the top if you have an assistant

Alternative ideas

The pictures on page 637 show a variation on the design used as a childs toy chest. These drawings show how to make a top which can become a table, an easel or a backrest

Peg from 25mm dowel turned down to 12mm, or from 12mm dowel with knob attached

You will need a top rail about 50mm deep. The whole end frame can be made from 50×25mm planed all round softwood

Drill 12mm holes at intervals

Drill 12mm holes at matching intervals

Panel with plywood

You can fit a foam seat cushion

Drill these holes by fitting the top and using the holes in it to mark the positions needed

Use pegs to secure the top in different positions

Alternative idea

Versatility is an important asset in furniture for childrens' rooms, where space is often at a premium and the childrens' needs change frequently. This budget variation on the monk's chest is a toybox, a table, a seat and a drawing board.

You can make it quite simply using a batten frame panelled with plywood. But remember to scale down the dimensions to suit the children concerned.

The top works in a similar way to that on the monk's chest. Instead of using the sliding pivot, however fix the top in position with dowel pins. This allows you to fix the top at several different angles so it can be used as an easel. Make the top itself from a solid piece of plywood or blockboard.

Cover the top with cork tiles so it can be used as a pinboard and protect the rest of the wood with paint or lacquer. Make sure that you sand off all edges thoroughly to prevent injuries from splinters.

Versatile storage trunk

Frederick Mancini

As a trunk or a seat or an occasional table this multi-purpose storage unit is sure to become indispensable. It is both simple and cheap to build and can be attractively finished

This versatile storage trunk has a hundred and one uses in and around the home. It is based on a system of interlocking trays, so you can increase the height very simply to store bulky or awkward objects. Alternatively, you can fit bottoms to each of the trays to store smaller objects. This means you can instantly go to any level to find stored objects, simply by lifting the appropriate tray.

The base section is fitted with castors, so you can easily move it around or even use it as a mobile trolley. Otherwise, rope handles can be fitted to make it easily portable.

The top section has a removable tray base, so you can use it as an occasional table. You can even paint it with board game designs so it can be used as a games table—ideal for a children's room. The pieces for the games can, of course, be stored in the tray below.

Alternatively, you can fit one or more seat cushions so the unit can be

used as a seat.

Just a few of the many possible uses are illustrated in the surrounding pictures—both outside and inside of your house.

The trunk is extremely simple to build, with no complicated joints. All the trays are held together by corner blocks which are glued and screwed in place. Make them from hardwood or softwood as you prefer—depending on the intended use. Hardwood gives a richer look—and is more durable—but it is more expensive.

You can make as many trays as you like, but in practice, it is not advisable to exceed a total height of about 900mm. You can finish the trays in clear lacquer, or paint or stain them.

The bottom section is double and should be fitted with handles and castors. Make up cushions for the top in any fabric you wish.

For even greater versatility, you could scale the given dimensions up or down to suit your requirements.

Workplan

Cutting list

Timber is planed all round, PAR (dressed four sides, D4S).
Use hardwood or softwood as preferred for the tray frames.

Part	Material	No.	Size
Base section			
sides	90mm × 12mm timber	4	890mm
ends	90mm × 12mm timber	4	450mm
base	6mm plywood	1	875mm × 425mm
corner angles	75mm × 19mm PAR softwood	4	75mm × 75mm
side tray supports	19mm × 19mm PAR softwood	2	819mm
end tray supports	19mm × 19mm PAR softwood	2	369mm
corner blocks	19mm × 19mm PAR softwood	4	180mm

Part	Material	No.	Size
Top section			
sides	90mm × 12mm timber	2	890mm
ends	90mm × 12mm timber	2	450mm
base	8mm birch or melamine faced plywood	1	875mm × 42
corner angles	75mm × 19mm PAR softwood	4	75mm × 75m
side tray supports	19mm × 19mm PAR softwood	2	819mm
end tray supports	19mm × 19mm PAR softwood	2	369mm
Additional trays			
sides	90mm × 12mm timber	2	890mm
ends	90mm × 12mm timber	2	450mm
bases	6mm plywood	1	875mm × 42
corner blocks	19mm × 19mm PAR softwood	4	90mm

Additional materials: Woodscrews, panel pins, castors, PVA adhesive, rope
Finish: Gloss paint, stain or lacquer as preferred

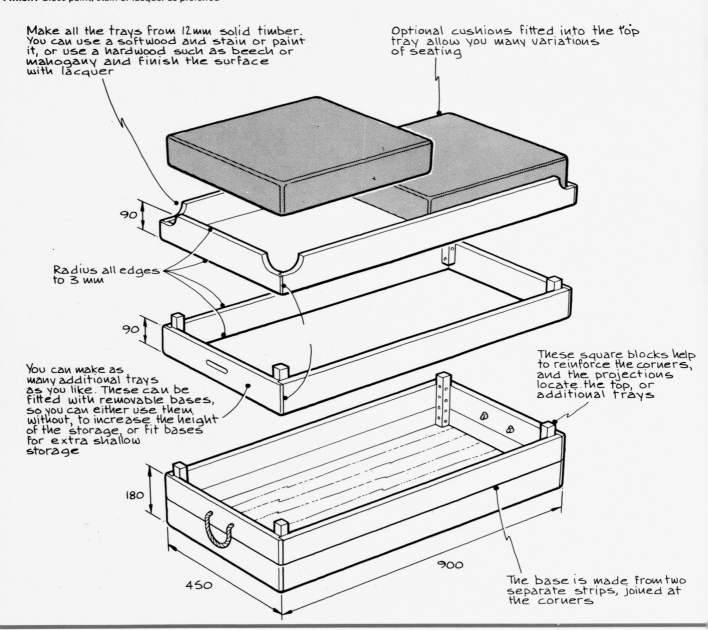

Make all the trays from 12mm solid timber.
You can use a softwood and stain or paint
it, or use a hardwood such as beech or
mahogany and finish the surface
with lacquer

Optional cushions fitted into the top
tray allow you many variations
of seating

Radius all edges
to 3 mm

You can make as
many additional trays
as you like. These can be
fitted with removable bases,
so you can either use them
without, to increase the height
of the storage, or fit bases
for extra shallow
storage

These square blocks help
to reinforce the corners,
and the projections
locate the top, or
additional trays

The base is made from two
separate strips, joined at
the corners

90

90

180

450

900

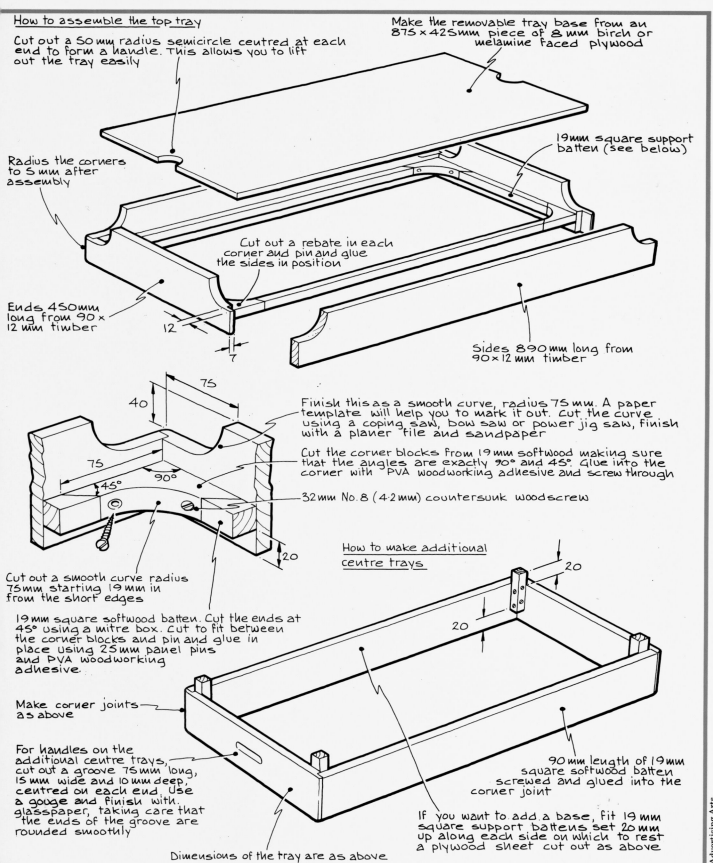

How to assemble the top tray

Cut out a 50mm radius semicircle centred at each end to form a handle. This allows you to lift out the tray easily

Make the removable tray base from an 875 × 425mm piece of 8mm birch or melamine faced plywood

19mm square support batten (see below)

Radius the corners to 5mm after assembly

Cut out a rebate in each corner and pin and glue the sides in position

Ends 450mm long from 90 × 12mm timber

12

7

Sides 890mm long from 90×12mm timber

75

40

75

90°

45°

Finish this as a smooth curve, radius 75mm. A paper template will help you to mark it out. Cut the curve using a coping saw, bow saw or power jig saw, finish with a planer file and sandpaper

Cut the corner blocks from 19mm softwood making sure that the angles are exactly 90° and 45°. Glue into the corner with PVA woodworking adhesive and screw through

32mm No.8 (4.2mm) countersunk woodscrew

20

Cut out a smooth curve radius 75mm starting 19mm in from the short edges

19mm square softwood batten. Cut the ends at 45° using a mitre box. Cut to fit between the corner blocks and pin and glue in place using 25mm panel pins and PVA woodworking adhesive.

How to make additional centre trays

20

20

Make corner joints as above

For handles on the additional centre trays, cut out a groove 75mm long, 15mm wide and 10mm deep, centred on each end. Use a gouge and finish with glasspaper, taking care that the ends of the groove are rounded smoothly

90mm length of 19mm square softwood batten screwed and glued into the corner joint

If you want to add a base, fit 19mm square support battens set 20mm up along each side on which to rest a plywood sheet cut out as above

Dimensions of the tray are as above

151

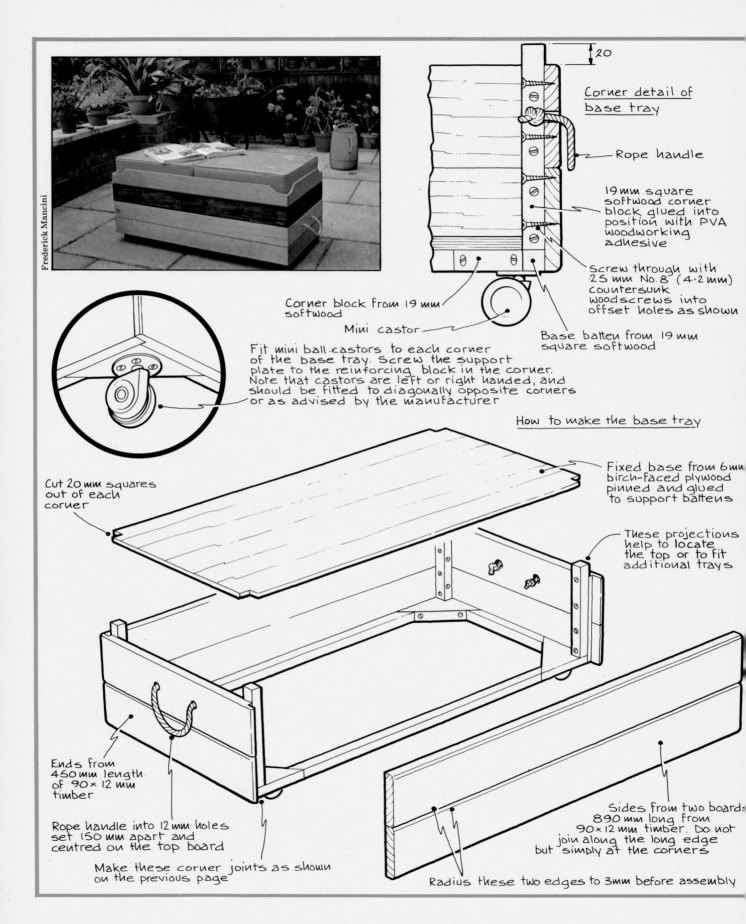

Frederick Mancini

↕ 20

Rope handle

19 mm square softwood corner block glued into position with PVA woodworking adhesive

Screw through with 25 mm No.8 (4·2 mm) countersunk woodscrews into offset holes as shown

Base batten from 19 mm square softwood

Corner block from 19 mm softwood

Mini castor

Fit mini ball castors to each corner of the base tray. Screw the support plate to the reinforcing block in the corner. Note that castors are left or right handed, and should be fitted to diagonally opposite corners or as advised by the manufacturer

How to make the base tray

Fixed base from 6 mm birch-faced plywood pinned and glued to support battens

Cut 20 mm squares out of each corner

These projections help to locate the top or to fit additional trays

Ends from 450 mm length of 90 × 12 mm timber

Rope handle into 12 mm holes set 150 mm apart and centred on the top board

Make these corner joints as shown on the previous page

Sides from two boards 890 mm long from 90 × 12 mm timber. Do not join along the long edge but simply at the corners

Radius these two edges to 3mm before assembly

152

Making the cushions

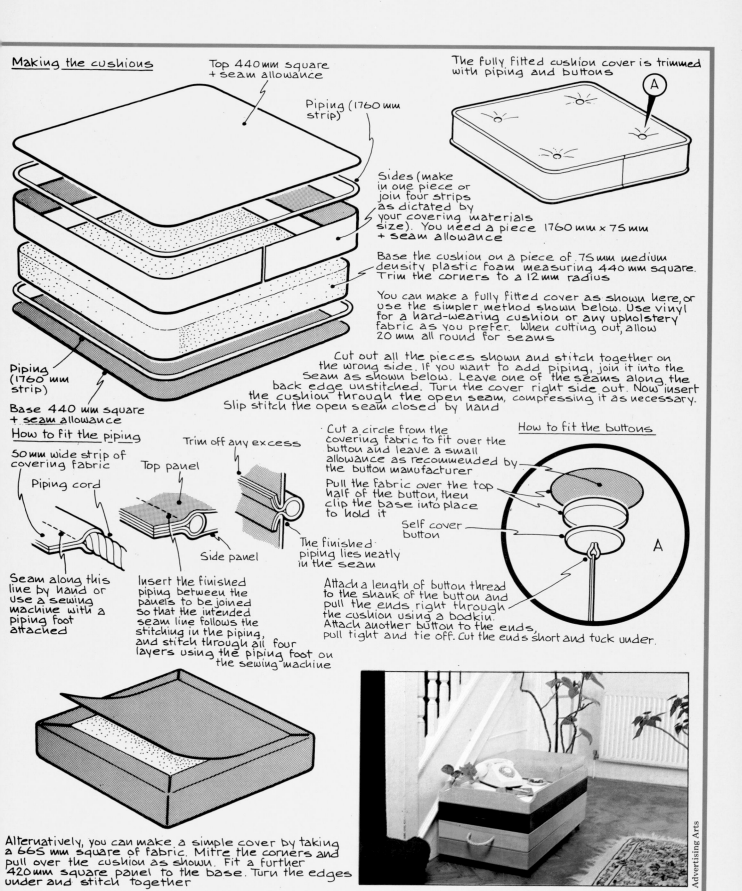

Top 440mm square + seam allowance

Piping (1760mm strip)

The fully fitted cushion cover is trimmed with piping and buttons

A

Sides (make in one piece or join four strips as dictated by your covering materials size). You need a piece 1760mm × 75mm + seam allowance

Base the cushion on a piece of 75mm medium density plastic foam measuring 440mm square. Trim the corners to a 12mm radius

You can make a fully fitted cover as shown here, or use the simpler method shown below. Use vinyl for a hard-wearing cushion or any upholstery fabric as you prefer. When cutting out, allow 20mm all round for seams

Cut out all the pieces shown and stitch together on the wrong side. If you want to add piping, join it into the seam as shown below. Leave one of the seams along the back edge unstitched. Turn the cover right side out. Now insert the cushion through the open seam, compressing it as necessary. Slip stitch the open seam closed by hand

Piping (1760mm strip)

Base 440mm square + seam allowance

How to fit the piping

50mm wide strip of covering fabric

Piping cord

Seam along this line by hand or use a sewing machine with a piping foot attached

Trim off any excess

Top panel

Side panel

Insert the finished piping between the panels to be joined so that the intended seam line follows the stitching in the piping, and stitch through all four layers using the piping foot on the sewing machine

Cut a circle from the covering fabric to fit over the button and leave a small allowance as recommended by the button manufacturer

Pull the fabric over the top half of the button, then clip the base into place to hold it

The finished piping lies neatly in the seam

How to fit the buttons

Self cover button

A

Attach a length of button thread to the shank of the button and pull the ends right through the cushion using a bodkin. Attach another button to the ends, pull tight and tie off. Cut the ends short and tuck under.

Alternatively, you can make a simple cover by taking a 665mm square of fabric. Mitre the corners and pull over the cushion as shown. Fit a further 420mm square panel to the base. Turn the edges under and stitch together

Advertising Arts

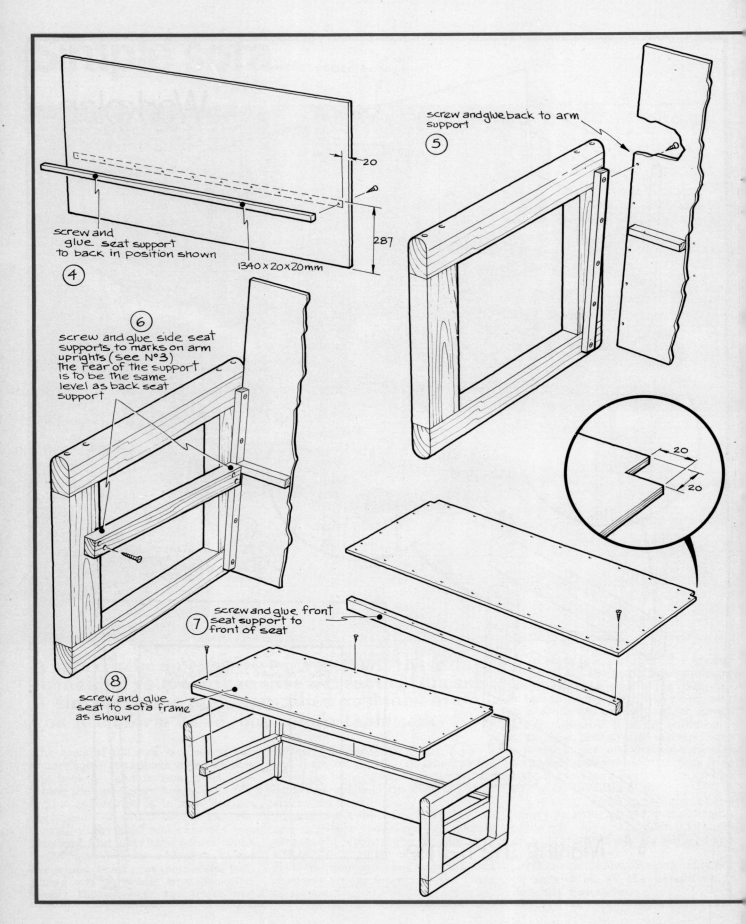

screw and glue back to arm
support

⑤

screw and
glue seat support
to back in position shown

④

20

287

1340 x 20 x 20mm

⑥ screw and glue side seat
supports to marks on arm
uprights (see N°3)
the rear of the support
is to be the same
level as back seat
support

20

20

screw and glue front
seat support to
front of seat

⑦

⑧ screw and glue
seat to sofa frame
as shown

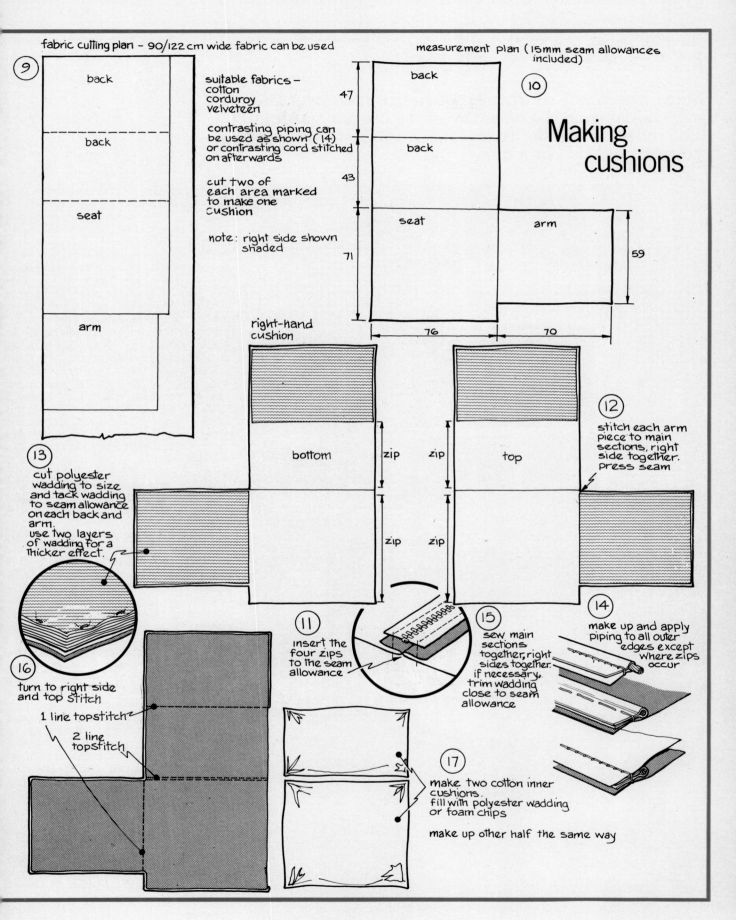

fabric cutting plan - 90/122 cm wide fabric can be used

⑨

back

back

seat

arm

suitable fabrics –
cotton
corduroy
velveteen

contrasting piping can
be used as shown (14)
or contrasting cord stitched
on afterwards

cut two of
each area marked
to make one
cushion

note: right side shown
shaded

measurement plan (15mm seam allowances
included)

back

⑩

back

seat

arm

47

43

71

59

76

70

Making
cushions

right-hand
cushion

bottom

zip

zip

zip

zip

top

⑫ stitch each arm
piece to main
sections, right
side together.
press seam

⑬ cut polyester
wadding to size
and tack wadding
to seam allowance
on each back and
arm.
use two layers
of wadding for a
thicker effect.

⑯ turn to right side
and top stitch

1 line topstitch

2 line
topstitch

⑪ insert the
four zips
to the seam
allowance

⑮ sew main
sections
together, right
sides together.
if necessary.
trim wadding
close to seam
allowance

⑭ make up and apply
piping to all outer
edges except
where zips
occur

⑰ make two cotton inner
cushions.
fill with polyester wadding
or foam chips

make up other half the same way

A corner cabinet

Make the most of unused corner space by building this attractive country-style corner cabinet. The case is made from softwood boards, and you can build it in a day

Martin Palmer

This attractive corner cabinet has a real country cottage air and fits in perfectly with a pine decor. It fits neatly into corner spaces which so often remain unused.

The carcase is made from softwood boards which are easy to obtain, and the sides are panelled with tongued-and-grooved pine for a really authentic look. The front has a glazed door with a diamond paned 'leaded-light' effect which looks complicated to achieve but is simplicity itself using self-adhesive lead strip.

This type of lead strip comes in rolls, with a removable backing paper, and can be cut with scissors or a sharp knife. To set out the design, you cut a sheet of paper to the same size as the glass, less the area covered by the rebates. Start your design at the middle —either with a point or a 'V'—and work outwards. With the design drawn in pencil, stick the paper to the back of the glass with flour-and-water paste while you set out the lead strip on the front.

Start by making up the main panels and the shelving. All of these are made by butt-jointing narrow boards along their edges to form the large sections needed. Note that the internal shelves and the base are smaller than the top by the thickness of the side panels to allow them to fit inside. Also, they do not fit right back into the corner in case this is uneven. The top shelf only has a point which makes contact with the back of the cupboard to prevent objects from falling down. Fit the parts together with glue and by screwing through the back, adding quadrant moulding to trim the joints.

Add the front subframe which is angled down the sides to fit the side panels. Add the two valances to top and bottom after cutting them to a neat profile. Make up the door to fit and glaze it, adding the lead strip to form a pattern. If you prefer a solid front, you could panel it with wood.

Finish the timber as you prefer, and fix the cabinet to the wall by screwing through the side panels or brass plates fitted to top and bottom.

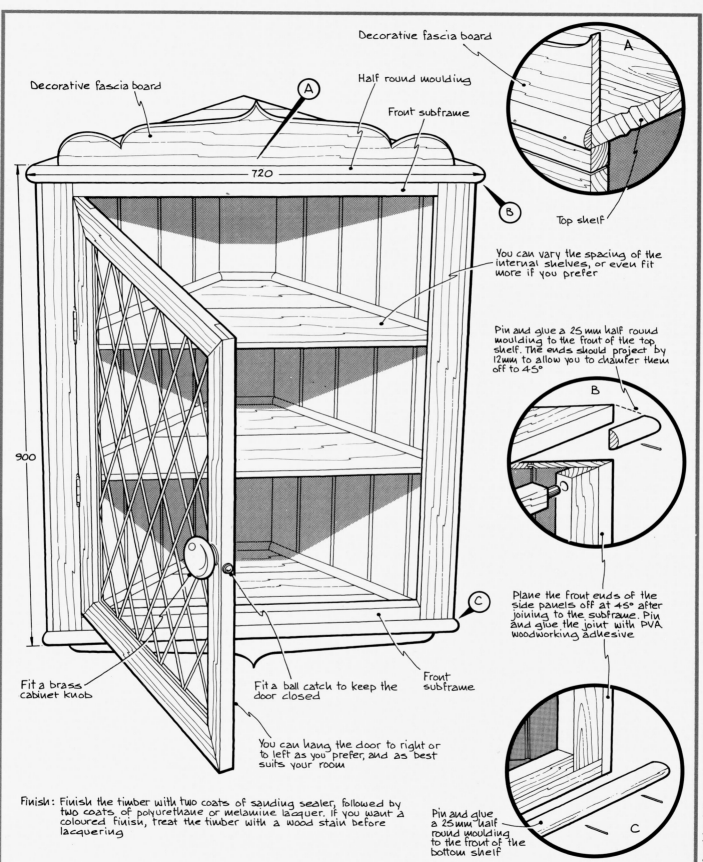

Decorative fascia board

Decorative fascia board

Half round moulding

Front subframe

A

720

900

B

Top shelf

A

You can vary the spacing of the internal shelves, or even fit more if you prefer

Pin and glue a 25 mm half round moulding to the front of the top shelf. The ends should project by 12mm to allow you to chamfer them off to 45°

B

C

Plane the front ends of the side panels off at 45° after joining to the subframe. Pin and glue the joint with PVA woodworking adhesive

Fit a brass cabinet knob

Fit a ball catch to keep the door closed

Front subframe

You can hang the door to right or to left as you prefer, and as best suits your room

Pin and glue a 25mm half round moulding to the front of the bottom shelf

C

Finish: Finish the timber with two coats of sanding sealer, followed by two coats of polyurethane or melamine lacquer. If you want a coloured finish, treat the timber with a wood stain before lacquering

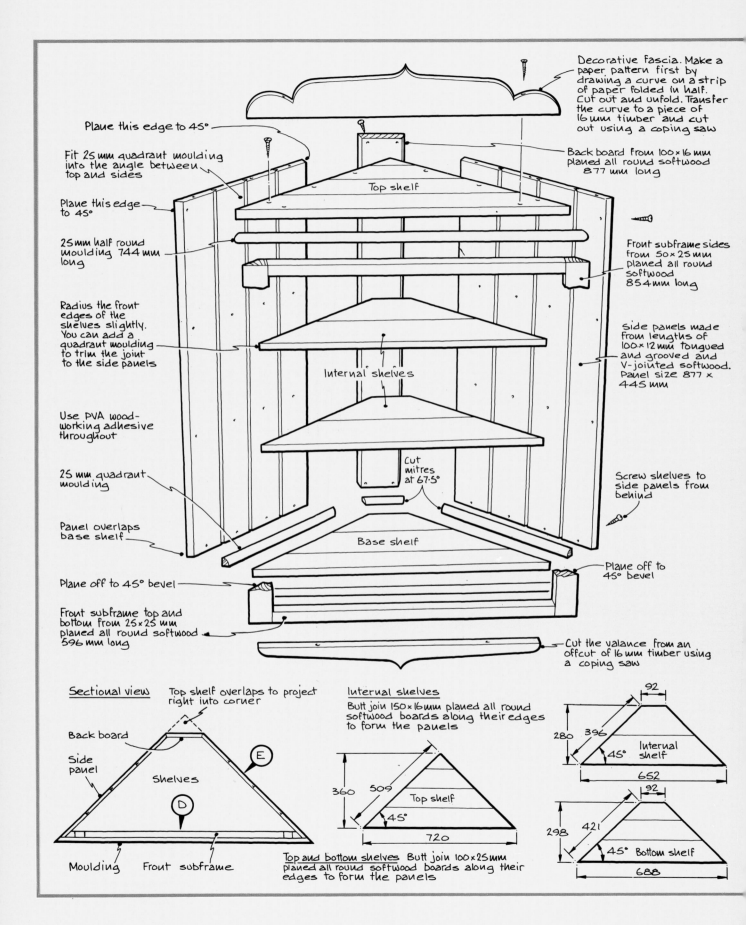

Decorative fascia. Make a paper pattern first by drawing a curve on a strip of paper folded in half. Cut out and unfold. Transfer the curve to a piece of 16 mm timber and cut out using a coping saw

Plane this edge to 45°

Fit 25 mm quadrant moulding into the angle between top and sides

Plane this edge to 45°

25 mm half round moulding 744 mm long

Radius the front edges of the shelves slightly. You can add a quadrant moulding to trim the joint to the side panels

Use PVA wood-working adhesive throughout

25 mm quadrant moulding

Panel overlaps base shelf

Plane off to 45° bevel

Front subframe top and bottom from 25 x 25 mm planed all round softwood 596 mm long

Top shelf

Internal shelves

Cut mitres at 67·5°

Base shelf

Back board from 100 x 16 mm planed all round softwood 877 mm long

Front subframe sides from 50 x 25 mm planed all round softwood 854 mm long

Side panels made from lengths of 100 x 12 mm tongued and grooved and V-jointed softwood. Panel size 877 x 445 mm

Screw shelves to side panels from behind

Plane off to 45° bevel

Cut the valance from an offcut of 16 mm timber using a coping saw

Sectional view

Top shelf overlaps to project right into corner

Back board

Side panel

Shelves

E

D

Moulding   Front subframe

Internal shelves

Butt join 150 x 16 mm planed all round softwood boards along their edges to form the panels

360   509   Top shelf

720   45°

Top and bottom shelves Butt join 100 x 25 mm planed all round softwood boards along their edges to form the panels

92
280   396
45°   Internal shelf
652

92
298   421
45°   Bottom shelf
688

160

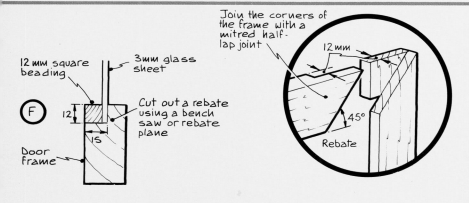

12 mm square beading

3mm glass sheet

F

12

15

Cut out a rebate using a bench saw or rebate plane

Door frame

Join the corners of the frame with a mitred half-lap joint

12 mm

45°

Rebate

Assembling the door

Cut the glass to fit the rebate less 2mm on each side. Approximate size is 740 × 532 mm

Retain the glass with a 12 mm square beading pinned into the rebate in the frame

Fit brass decorative flush hinges

Frame from 50 × 25mm planed all round softwood

F

Make up the door frame to fit snugly inside the subframe (approximately 808 × 600 mm)

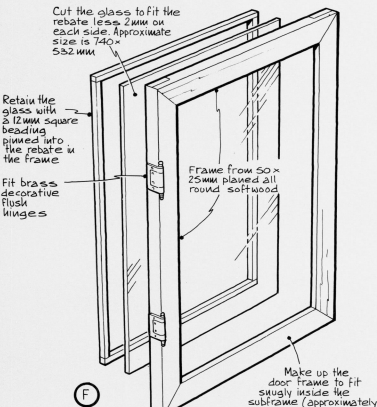

Leaded lights

You can give a leaded-light effect to the glazing pane by using self-adhesive lead strip. Start by cutting a piece of paper to the size of your glass. Rule lines on it to the pattern shown below to give you the diamond pane effect

Ruled lines

Paper cut to the same size as the glass

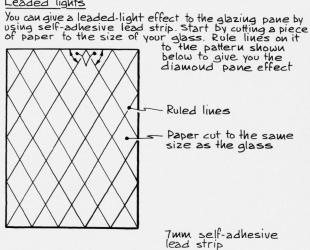

7mm self-adhesive lead strip

Door frame

Then lay the door over the paper so you can see the pattern through the glass. Using 7mm self-adhesive lead strip, stick this to the glass following the lines on the paper. Lay down all the lines in one direction first, then lay down the cross lines, overlapping the lead strip at the joints. Trim into the door frame and finish with a strip laid all around the inside of the frame

Paper pattern

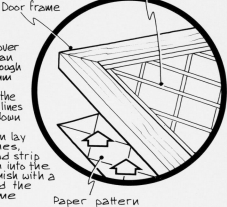

Cutting list
All sizes are set in millimetres. Timber is planed all round, PAR (dressed four sides, D4S).

Part	Material	No.	Size
side panels	100mm × 12mm softwood (T&G)	2	approx 9m
top & bottom	100mm × 25mm softwood (PAR)	2	approx 3m
shelves	150mm × 16mm softwood (PAR)	2	approx 2m
back	100mm × 16mm softwood (PAR)	1	877mm
subframe sides	50mm × 25mm softwood (PAR)	2	854mm
subframe ends	25mm × 25mm softwood (PAR)	2	596mm
door sides	50mm × 25mm softwood (PAR)	2	808mm
door top & bottom	50mm × 25mm softwood (PAR)	2	600mm
valances	100mm × 16mm softwood (PAR)	2	approx 1.4m

Additional materials: 25mm quadrant moulding, 25mm half round moulding, 12mm square moulding, 3mm sheet glass, self-adhesive lead strip, PVA woodworking adhesive, chipboard screws, panel pins.
Finish: Sanding sealer, polyurethane or melamine lacquer.

A sideboard with style

Frederick Mancini

This highly practical sideboard is finished in black with a solid hardwood frame to lend a touch of real style. Construction is much simpler than it looks, and the result will be a satisfying addition to your furnishings

The basis of this sideboard is a strong, box construction carcase, made from veneered chipboard or plywood to keep the job of building it simple. But in style it looks like a very much more complicated framed structure. This is achieved by giving the chipboard a solid hardwood edging, which also strengthens it and gives a neat finish to the sideboard.

Begin by cutting all the chipboard or plywood panels to the size specified in the drawings. Use a board veneered in a fine-grained timber, free of knots, to which you can give an attractive finish with wood stain. Edge the panels with strips of ramin or a similar hardwood, joined with a loose tongue or dowels.

Assemble the two drawer frames and fit them between the middle panels.

Now fit all the other vertical panels to the base and top using dowel joints or plastic corner blocks. Add the drawer runners and the back panel to complete the carcase.

Hang the doors at each side, and fit the optional shelf in each cupboard if desired. Make up the drawers, checking each for fit in its slot. Assemble the hardwood end frames and screw them to the carcase.

Use a black wood stain to bring out the 'frame'. You can prevent the stain affecting the hardwood by lacquering it first. Stain all the veneered boards, then add door pulls and finish throughout with lacquer or semi-gloss polyurethane varnish.

Workplan

Although the sideboard has a framed furniture appearance, the carcase is actually a simple box construction using veneered chipboard panels. These are edged in solid hardwood to give strength and provide the framed look.

The carcase is supported by two sturdy frames fixed on each end. Use 16 mm pine veneered chipboard for the basic construction and edge it with ramin as shown in the drawings. Cover the remaining cut ends of the chipboard panels, such as on the doors, with iron-on edging strip to match the veneer.

You can emphasize the framing by staining the veneer a dark colour using woodstain. Finish the entire piece by lacquering with polyurethane or melamine lacquer

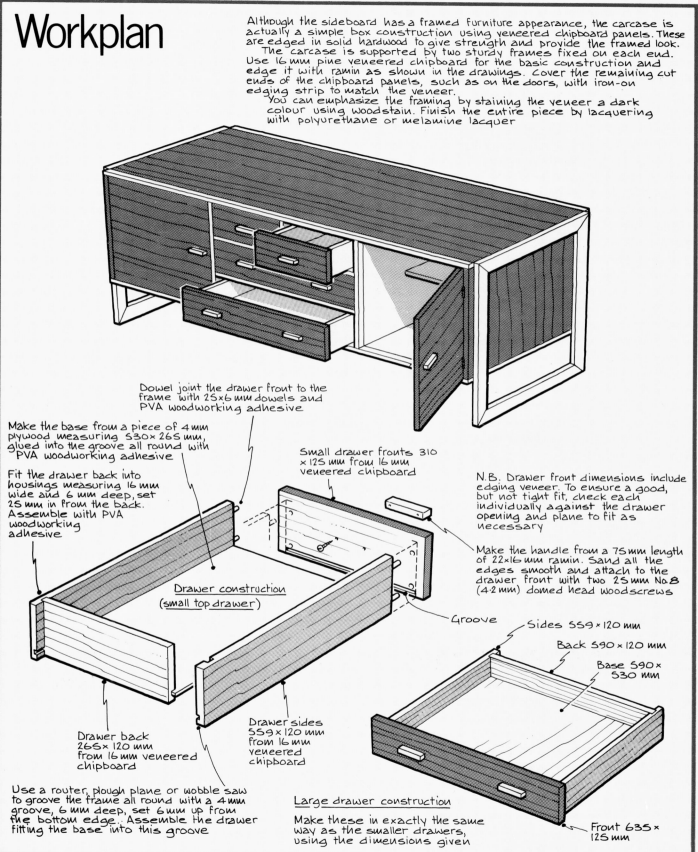

Dowel joint the drawer front to the frame with 25×6 mm dowels and PVA woodworking adhesive

Make the base from a piece of 4 mm plywood measuring 530×265 mm, glued into the groove all round with PVA woodworking adhesive

Fit the drawer back into housings measuring 16 mm wide and 6 mm deep, set 25 mm in from the back. Assemble with PVA woodworking adhesive

Small drawer fronts 310 ×125 mm from 16 mm veneered chipboard

N.B. Drawer front dimensions include edging veneer. To ensure a good, but not tight fit, check each individually against the drawer opening and plane to fit as necessary

Make the handle from a 75 mm length of 22×16 mm ramin. Sand all the edges smooth and attach to the drawer front with two 25 mm No.8 (4·2 mm) domed head woodscrews

Drawer construction
(small top drawer)

Groove

Drawer back 265 × 120 mm from 16 mm veneered chipboard

Drawer sides 559 × 120 mm from 16 mm veneered chipboard

Sides 559 × 120 mm

Back 590 × 120 mm

Base 590 × 530 mm

Use a router, plough plane or wobble saw to groove the frame all round with a 4 mm groove, 6 mm deep, set 6 mm up from the bottom edge. Assemble the drawer fitting the base into this groove

Large drawer construction

Make these in exactly the same way as the smaller drawers, using the dimensions given

Front 635 × 125 mm

Advertising Arts

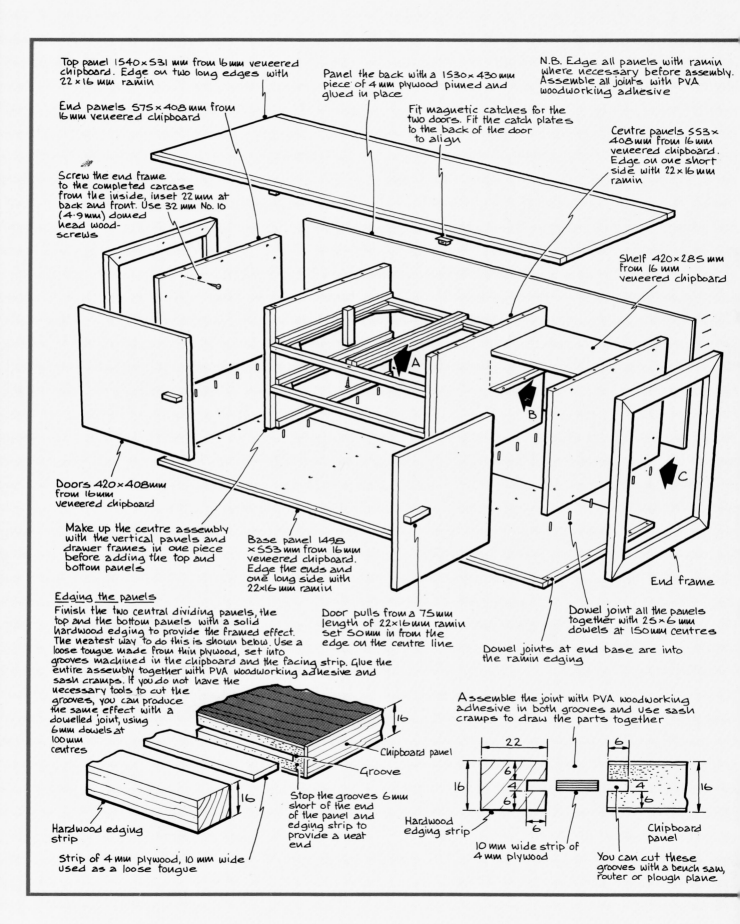

Top panel 1540×531 mm from 16mm veneered chipboard. Edge on two long edges with 22×16 mm ramin

End panels 575×408 mm from 16 mm veneered chipboard

Screw the end frame to the completed carcase from the inside, inset 22mm at back and front. Use 32 mm No. 10 (4·9mm) domed head wood-screws

Panel the back with a 1530×430 mm piece of 4 mm plywood pinned and glued in place

Fit magnetic catches for the two doors. Fit the catch plates to the back of the door to align

N.B. Edge all panels with ramin where necessary before assembly. Assemble all joints with PVA woodworking adhesive

Centre panels 553× 408mm from 16mm veneered chipboard. Edge on one short side with 22×16 mm ramin

Shelf 420×285 mm from 16 mm veneered chipboard

Doors 420×408mm from 16mm veneered chipboard

Make up the centre assembly with the vertical panels and drawer frames in one piece before adding the top and bottom panels

Base panel 1498 ×553 mm from 16 mm veneered chipboard. Edge the ends and one long side with 22×16 mm ramin

Door pulls from a 75mm length of 22×16mm ramin set 50mm in from the edge on the centre line

End frame

Dowel joint all the panels together with 25×6 mm dowels at 150mm centres

Dowel joints at end base are into the ramin edging

Edging the panels

Finish the two central dividing panels, the top and the bottom panels with a solid hardwood edging to provide the framed effect. The neatest way to do this is shown below. Use a loose tongue made from thin plywood, set into grooves machined in the chipboard and the facing strip. Glue the entire assembly together with PVA woodworking adhesive and sash cramps. If you do not have the necessary tools to cut the grooves, you can produce the same effect with a dowelled joint, using 6mm dowels at 100mm centres

Chipboard panel

Groove

Hardwood edging strip

Strip of 4 mm plywood, 10 mm wide used as a loose tongue

Stop the grooves 6mm short of the end of the panel and edging strip to provide a neat end

Assemble the joint with PVA woodworking adhesive in both grooves and use sash cramps to draw the parts together

22   6

16   6 4 6   16   4 6

Hardwood edging strip

10 mm wide strip of 4 mm plywood

Chipboard panel

You can cut these grooves with a bench saw, router or plough plane

<u>Section of drawer fittings looking on arrow 'A'</u>

Back panel

126

Runners

126

Drawer support frames

126

Runner

1 drawer fronts
5 mm deep

<u>Cross section of shelf fixing looking on arrow 'B'</u>

Internal shelf panel. Rest loosely on the bearers or fix if preferred

D

Back panel

Shelf bearer from 19×12 mm hardwood 285 mm long glued and screwed in place with PVA woodworking adhesive and 25 mm No.6 (3·6 mm) countersunk chipboard screws

<u>View on arrow 'C'</u>

E

531

case
d

560

d frame sides 560 mm
g from 50×25 mm ramin

End frame base and top 531 mm
long from 50×25 mm ramin

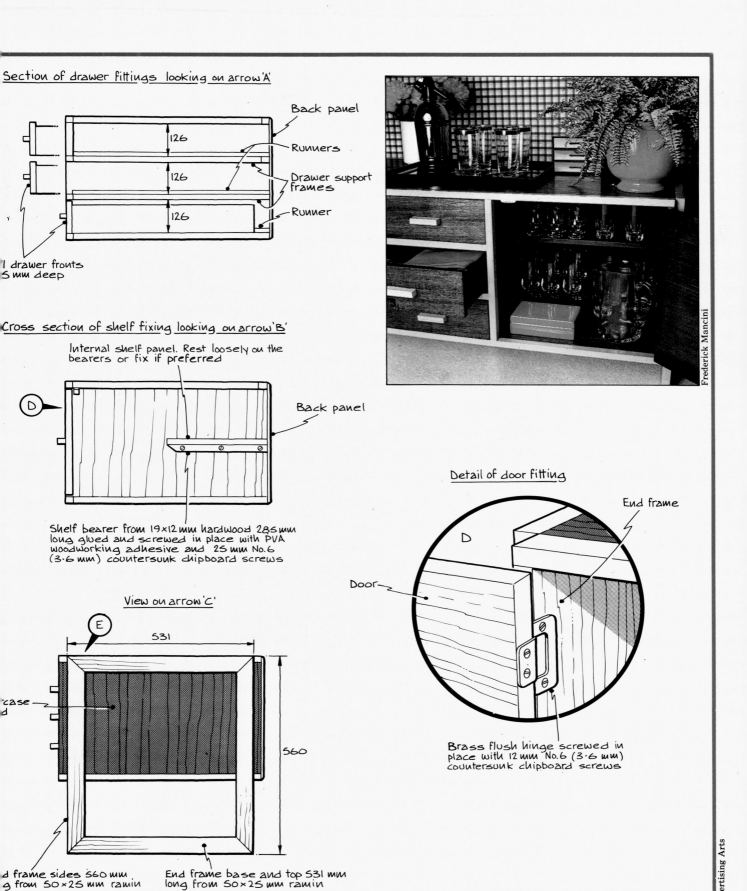

Frederick Mancini

Detail of door fitting

End frame

D

Door

Brass flush hinge screwed in place with 12 mm No.6 (3·6 mm) countersunk chipboard screws

Make triangular corner braces by dividing a 75 mm square of 4mm plywood in half diagonally. Fit into grooves with PVA woodworking adhesive

Back rail 635 mm long 22×16 mm ramin

Centre runners (see below)

4mm groove for corner braces. Cut with router, plough plane or wobble saw

Side rails 531 mm long from 22×16 mm ramin

Top rail

Make up the complete frames and dowel joint them between the vertical panels before adding the top and bottom panels

Front rail 635mm long from 22×16 mm ramin

All drawer runners 553 mm long from 19×12 mm hardwood screwed inside panels

Base panel

Side runner from 19×12 mm hardwood 553 mm long screwed to panel with 25 mm No.6 (3·6 mm) countersunk chipboard screws

Dowel joint the complete frame between the panels using 25×6 mm dowels and PVA woodworking adhesive

Side rail

4mm groove, 6mm deep to accept the corner brace

Triangular corner brace from 4mm plywood

Front rail (back rail is identical)

Two drawer runners from 22×12 mm hardwood 553 mm long

Screw to central brace with 25 mm No.6 (3·6 mm) countersunk woodscrews

Detail of top drawer frame
Make the lower frame in the same way, omitting the centre runners

Centre brace 531 mm long from 75×16 mm softwood dowel jointed to front and back rails

Secret dowel to the top panel with one 25×6 mm dowel and PVA woodworking adhesive

Detail of front vertical drawer divider

Divider 120 mm long from 22×16 mm ramin

Screw through from below with a 32 mm No.6 (3·6 mm) countersunk chipboard screw and PVA woodworking adhesive

Top panel

Drawer frame

Cutting list
All sizes are in millimetres. Hardwood sizes are for finished timber.
Chipboard is finished in whitewood veneer.

Part	Material	No.	Size
top panel	16mm chipboard	1	1540mm × 531mm
bottom panel	16mm chipboard	1	1498mm × 553mm
end panels	16mm chipboard	2	575mm × 408mm
centre panels	16mm chipboard	2	553mm × 408mm
doors	16mm chipboard	2	420mm × 408mm
drawer fronts (top)	16mm chipboard	2	310mm × 125mm
drawer fronts (bottom)	16mm chipboard	2	635mm × 125mm
drawer sides	16mm chipboard	8	559mm × 120mm
drawer backs (top)	16mm chipboard	2	265mm × 120mm
drawer backs (bottom)	16mm chipboard	2	590mm × 120mm
shelf	16mm chipboard	1	420mm × 285mm
drawer bases and back	4mm plywood		1 full sheet
end frame top & bottom	50mm × 25mm ramin	4	431mm approx.
end frame sides	50mm × 25mm ramin	4	560mm
hardwood edging	22mm × 16mm ramin		approx. 10.1 metres
drawer runners	19mm × 12mm ramin		approx. 3 metres
drawer runners	25mm × 12mm ramin		approx. 1.2 metres

Additional materials: 4 No. brass flush hinges, 12mm No. 6 (3.6mm) countersunk chipboard screws, 25mm No. 6 (3.6mm) countersunk chipboard screws, plywood offcuts for tongues, dowels, ramin offcuts for handles, door catches, PVA adhesive
Finish: Black woodstain, polyurethane or melamine lacquer

A coffee/games table

Although it is handy for coffee or occasional use, this versatile table has a hidden extra in the form of movable tops which turn it into a ready-made playing surface for cards, backgammon, chess or draughts

This attractive and versatile piece of furniture makes a very useful coffee table. And with its pine veneered surface and curving lines it looks unusual yet blends in well with many furnishing styles.

Its versatility is extended by the removable tops, which you can simply lift out and refit to give you interchangeable boards for playing all kinds of different games. There is plenty of space below the top for storing all the playing pieces, cards and counters.

Most of the construction is in pine veneered chipboard. You can buy this in large sheets and cut out all the pieces, or use narrow standard width boards, large enough to cut each piece you need.

Unusually for a chipboard construction, some of the parts have a curved shape. These are not difficult to cut, but you will need to use care when finishing the cut edges with an iron-on veneer, to avoid splitting the veneer as you bend it.

Mark out the curved sections by using the squared up diagrams to scale up to full size. The rectangular parts can be cut quite simply.

Begin your assembly with the end rails and legs. Then fit these together with the two side rails and the stretcher rail. You can add the pegs to the rail after assembly, as they are mainly decorative. Check that the frame is square and leave to dry.

Add the two fixed tops and then the top supports, which hold the movable tops flush. The two pivoting supports are for use with the chessboard, since the thickness of the backgammon board underneath precludes fitting both tops together. Panel in the underside of the frame.

Make up the two movable tops. The first has pine veneer on one side and felt on the other. On the second, draw out your playing surfaces, score the lines and fill in with different coloured wood stains and a small paintbrush. You can of course adapt the design for any favourite games or even glue a paper games board in place on the top.

To finish the table, sand and seal the entire surface thoroughly. You can use lacquer or wax, but make sure you seal the tops or they will mark. It is a good idea to seal before fitting the felt.

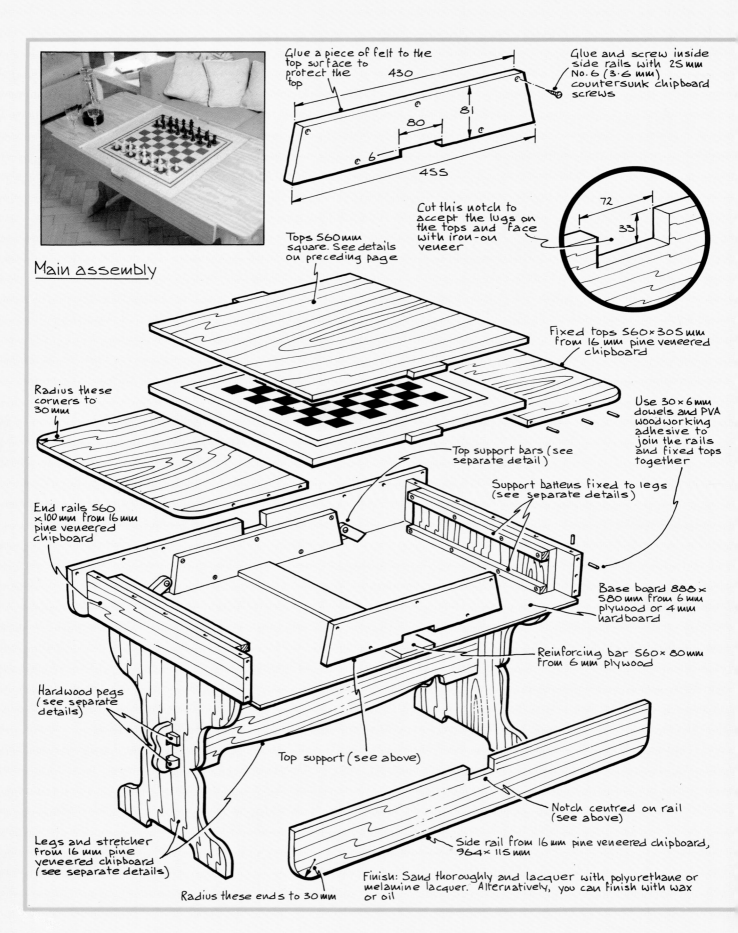

Glue a piece of felt to the top surface to protect the top

430

80

81

6

455

Glue and screw inside side rails with 25 mm No. 6 (3.6 mm) countersunk chipboard screws

Cut this notch to accept the lugs on the tops and face with iron-on veneer

72

33

Main assembly

Tops 560 mm square. See details on preceding page

Fixed tops 560 × 305 mm from 16 mm pine veneered chipboard

Radius these corners to 30 mm

Use 30 × 6 mm dowels and PVA woodworking adhesive to join the rails and fixed tops together

Top support bars (see separate detail)

Support battens fixed to legs (see separate details)

End rails 560 × 100 mm from 16 mm pine veneered chipboard

Base board 888 × 580 mm from 6 mm plywood or 4 mm hardboard

Reinforcing bar 560 × 80 mm from 6 mm plywood

Hardwood pegs (see separate details)

Top support (see above)

Legs and stretcher from 16 mm pine veneered chipboard (see separate details)

Notch centred on rail (see above)

Side rail from 16 mm pine veneered chipboard, 964 × 115 mm

Radius these ends to 30 mm

Finish: Sand thoroughly and lacquer with polyurethane or melamine lacquer. Alternatively, you can finish with wax or oil

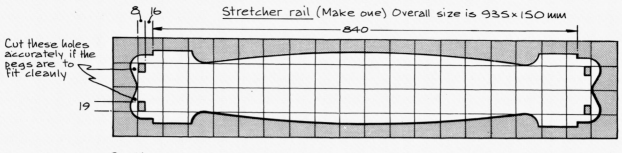

Stretcher rail (Make one) Overall size is 935 x 150 mm

8 16

840

Cut these holes
accurately if the
pegs are to
fit cleanly

19

Cutting out the stretcher rail and legs

Use these diagrams to mark out sheets of 16mm pine veneered chipboard for the curved sections of the table. Each square on the grid represents 50mm on the finished part so square up your boards and copy the curve on each square. Use a jig saw, coping saw or bow saw to cut out the curves, keeping square to the work. Cover the cut edges with an iron-on pine veneer

Hardwood fixing pegs

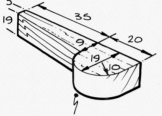

5
19
35
9
20
19
10

Make four pegs from 55mm lengths of 19mm square hardwood, such as beech. Push through the tusk of the tenons at each end after assembly and glue in place

Leg (Make two)

Overall size is
570 x 460 mm.
Mark both legs
together

Check the dimensions of this
mortise slot against the
tenons of the stretcher to
allow for any inaccuracy in
cutting

Leg fixing detail

16mm square support battens, 460mm long

Glue the upper part of the leg to
the end rail. Glue and screw
the support battens in place with
38mm No. 6 (3·6mm) countersunk
chipboard screws. A deep countersink
in the battens will ensure that the screws
lock all three timbers together

End rail

Side rail

Base board

Cut out 460mm long
and 24mm deep

Leg

Pin and glue the
base in position,
fitting it 'round'
the legs as
shown

Di Lewis

169

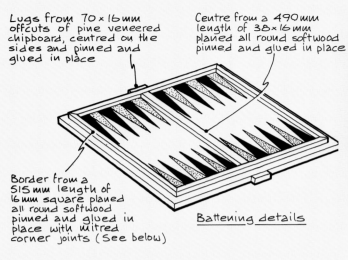

Lugs from 70 × 16mm offcuts of pine veneered chipboard, centred on the sides and pinned and glued in place

Centre from a 490mm length of 38×16mm planed all round softwood pinned and glued in place

Border from a 515mm length of 16mm square planed all round softwood pinned and glued in place with mitred corner joints (See below)

Battening details

Use PVA woodworking adhesive and 19mm panel pins to fix the battening

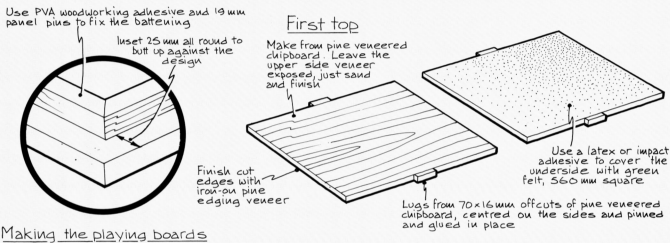

Inset 25mm all round to butt up against the design

First top

Make from pine veneered chipboard. Leave the upper side veneer exposed, just sand and finish

Finish cut edges with iron-on pine edging veneer

Use a latex or impact adhesive to cover the underside with green felt, 560mm square

Lugs from 70×16mm offcuts of pine veneered chipboard, centred on the sides and pinned and glued in place

Making the playing boards

The table has two removable tops. Each is 560mm square, but make one from 16mm pine veneered chipboard, and the other from 16mm high density chipboard. Follow these diagrams to finish each side of the second top

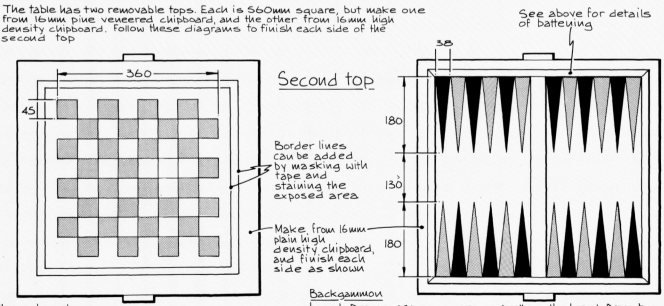

See above for details of battening

Border lines can be added by masking with tape and staining the exposed area

Make from 16mm plain high density chipboard, and finish each side as shown

Second top

Chessboard

Draw up a 360mm square and divide into eight 45mm squares each way. Score the lines with a ruler and a sharp knife, then stain each alternate square

Backgammon board

Draw a 490mm square centrally on the board. Draw two parallel lines across the centre, 180mm from each side. Draw the points from each side to meet these lines. Each has a base 38mm. Score the lines and stain with two colours

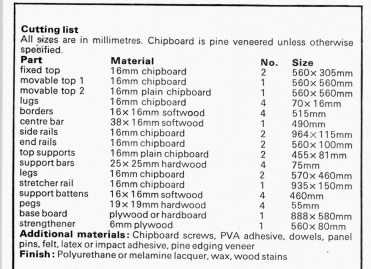

Cutting list

All sizes are in millimetres. Chipboard is pine veneered unless otherwise specified.

Part	Material	No.	Size
fixed top	16mm chipboard	2	560×305mm
movable top 1	16mm chipboard	1	560×560mm
movable top 2	16mm plain chipboard	1	560×560mm
lugs	16mm chipboard	4	70×16mm
borders	16×16mm softwood	4	515mm
centre bar	38×16mm softwood	1	490mm
side rails	16mm chipboard	2	964×115mm
end rails	16mm chipboard	2	560×100mm
top supports	16mm plain chipboard	2	455×81mm
support bars	25×25mm hardwood	4	75mm
legs	16mm chipboard	2	570×460mm
stretcher rail	16mm chipboard	1	935×150mm
support battens	16×16mm softwood	4	460mm
pegs	19×19mm hardwood	4	55mm
base board	plywood or hardboard	1	888×580mm
strengthener	6mm plywood	1	560×80mm

Additional materials: Chipboard screws, PVA adhesive, panel pins, felt, latex or impact adhesive, pine edging veneer
Finish: Polyurethane or melamine lacquer, wax, wood stains

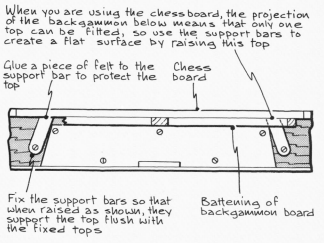

When you are using the chessboard, the projection of the backgammon below means that only one top can be fitted, so use the support bars to create a flat surface by raising this top

Glue a piece of felt to the support bar to protect the top

Chess board

Fix the support bars so that when raised as shown, they support the top flush with the fixed tops

Battening of backgammon board

Cross sections

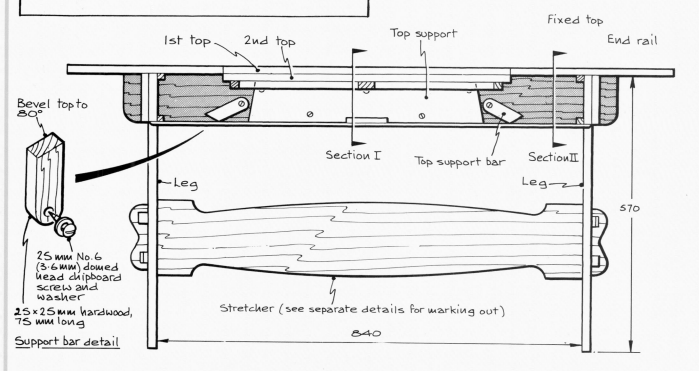

1st top   2nd top   Top support   Fixed top   End rail

Bevel top to 80°

Section I   Top support bar   Section II

Leg   Leg   570

25 mm No.6 (3.6mm) domed head chipboard screw and washer

25×25 mm hardwood, 75 mm long

Stretcher (see separate details for marking out)

840

Support bar detail

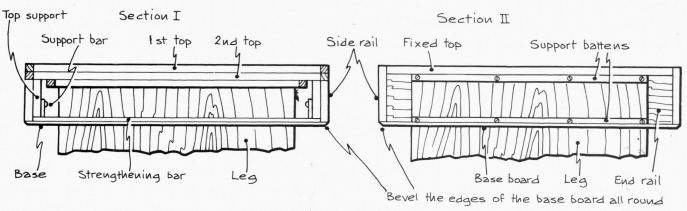

Top support   Section I   Section II

Support bar   1st top   2nd top   Side rail   Fixed top   Support battens

Base   Strengthening bar   Leg   Base board   Leg   End rail

Bevel the edges of the base board all round

171

CONVERSIONS AND EXTENSIONS

Converting the roof space

● **Making use of space overhead** ● **Simple conversions** ● **Surveying your loft** ● **Rules and regulations—headroom, floor joists, stairs** ● **Planning a loft conversion in detail** ● **How to overcome the problems—some examples**

A. Below: *What was once an untidy area used only as a general store and dumping ground for odds and ends has been transformed into two fair-sized loft rooms – one a study, the other an extra bedroom. The conversion was carried out using two large dormer windows*

A loft conversion is an ideal method of creating additional space in your home, space that can be used for an extra bedroom, a workroom or a children's play-room. But even if you are fairly experienced in constructional work this is not a project to rush into without a great deal of thought. Remember that many loft conversions can totally transform the external appearance of your home and significantly alter its internal layout. Only careful planning can produce a loft conversion that blends in with, and complements, your home, rather than a haphazard construction that looks as if it has just been tacked on as an afterthought.

Quite obviously your first task is to make a thorough inspection of your roof space with a view to deciding whether or not it is suitable for conversion. Take a sketch book with you and note down how the roof is constructed—this has by far the greatest bearing on the type of conversion possible (see below). At the same time —and assuming that space is not hopelessly cramped—start thinking about how the area naturally divides itself up.

Simon Butcher

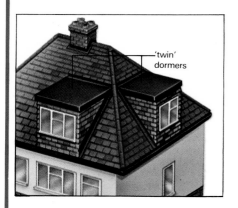

B. *Twin or through dormers give plenty of headroom but are inclined to look rather bulky on the roof*

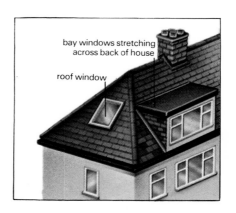

bay windows stretching across back of house

roof window

C. *A far less obtrusive alternative is to use a roof window on the gable and a larger dormer at the back*

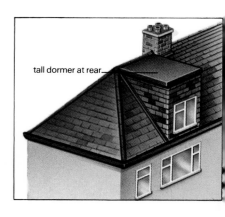

tall dormer at rear

D. *Maximum space created using the minimum of materials by installing a tall dormer at the rear*

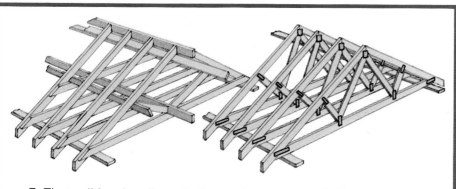

E. *The traditional purlin and rafter roof construction (left) is relatively easy to convert; the more modern trussed rafter construction (right) is very difficult*

Deciding on the use

While looking at your loft, think first about the use to which you want to put it. If you can, arrange for it to be used as a 'non-habitable' room (for example, a games room or workshop) even if this means reorganizing the existing accommodation. The reason for this is that the regulations for non-habitable rooms (especially within a loft space) are usually much easier to comply with than those for habitable rooms, for which you probably have to provide a fixed staircase, sufficient headroom and light and a strengthened floor. The only one of these that is essential for a non-habitable room is a strengthened floor.

Initial survey

Assuming you want a 'proper' habitable room, your initial survey is particularly important. Not all roofs are suitable—but the most unsuitable types can be ruled out very quickly.

First, check the height from the top of the existing ceiling joists to the bottom of the highest point of the rafters. If this is less than about 2.5m then you will not be able to meet the required planning regulations on headroom, except by actually raising the whole roof of the complete house.

Secondly, check the construction of the roof. If it is built of *trussed rafters* or something similar (see fig. F) then a loft conversion is difficult. All the timbers crossing from the rafters to the ceiling joists are interdependent, and you cannot remove any without the risk of the roof collapsing. Rebuilding the trusses so that the roof is safe and the loft area clear can be done, but is usually a professional job. The older purlin-rafter construction (fig E) is much more straightforward and easier to deal with.

The planning

Once you have decided that your loft is broadly suitable for conversion, you can set about the planning in detail. This is often a tricky job for a number of reasons: the project affects two floors; the inside of the loft is usually an odd shape; and both in the loft and on the floor below there will be a number of walls, water tanks, chimney stacks, joists and rafters, not all of which can be moved easily.

As well as measuring up and actually drawing the loft area itself, you will also need an accurate detailed drawing of the floor below. Do this in ink so that you can pin sheets of tracing paper over it while you experiment with different layouts for the loft. Vertical sections through both floors are also useful—especially around the proposed site of the stairs. A cardboard model may also help.

The point of drawing all these plans is to make sure that you can satisfy the three basics of a loft conversion: sufficient headroom; strengthened joists; and a suitable stairway.

Headroom

The regulations for headroom vary from country to country, but in general, you will need a head height of at least 2.3m over at least half of the floor area of each room in the loft. The 'floor area' is usually defined as that part of the floor where the head height is 1.5m (1.4m abroad) or more. In other countries, you may alternatively have a head height of 2.1m over the whole floor area.

Check the dimensions as you measure up the loft for your plans—but

174

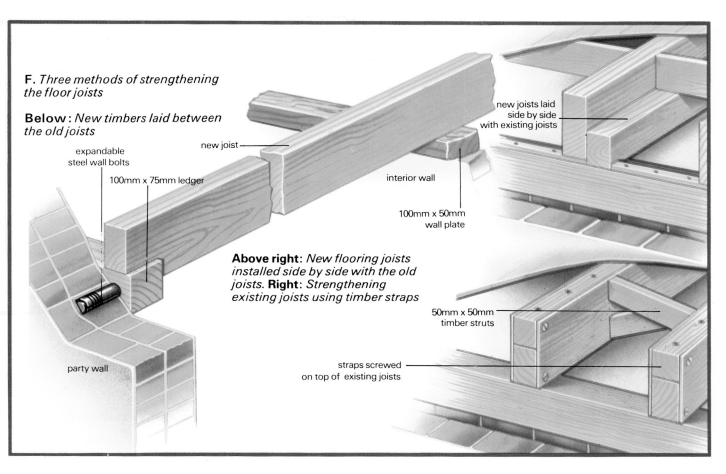

F. *Three methods of strengthening the floor joists*

Below: *New timbers laid between the old joists*

expandable steel wall bolts

100mm x 75mm ledger

new joist

interior wall

new joists laid side by side with existing joists

100mm x 50mm wall plate

Above right: *New flooring joists installed side by side with the old joists.* **Right**: *Strengthening existing joists using timber straps*

50mm x 50mm timber struts

party wall

straps screwed on top of existing joists

remember that the strengthened joists you will almost certainly need (see below), the floorboards, and the ceiling plaster will all reduce the available height: allow an extra 200mm to cover all this.

If you cannot provide this amount of space within the shape of the existing roof, then you will have to provide one or more dormer windows, which effectively increase the height of the roof. Installing a dormer window is dealt with in a later part of the Roofing course. If you do not need dormer windows to meet the headroom regulations, think about installing sloping roof windows, which involve much less work.

Strengthening the joists

The existing loft joists are rarely designed to carry the weight of a proper floor, and of furniture and people. So you will almost certainly have to strengthen them.

The correct size depends on the width that the joists span, and the distance apart they are; it may also depend on the species of timber used. The table on this page gives some typical joist sizes; for other sizes, consult your building regulations (local building code).

As an example, the first floor plan in fig. G shows that the maximum span for the existing loft joists is 2.8m, and the table shows that, in the UK, joists at 450mm centres would need to be of 50mm × 150mm timber—not the 50mm × 100mm that were probably originally fitted. Although other spans may be shorter, it is sensible to fit this depth of joist over the whole loft area, otherwise the new floor would be uneven.

Note that the span of a joist is calculated as the distance between *loadbearing* walls—and not all first floor walls are loadbearing: in the UK, for example, few timber stud walls are loadbearing.

There are two ways of strengthening joists in this situation. One method is to insert new joists between the existing ones. One end of each joist will rest on the existing wall plates, but at the party wall they will have to be supported either on individual joists hanger set into the brickwork or by being notched to fit over an existing ledger (fig. F). If the ceiling is at all uneven, it is a good plan to lift the joists about 10-12mm above it so that the weight of the new floor does not crack the old plaster. If you use packing pieces to gain this

Joist sizes
Maximum spans for joists of different sizes and spacings.

Joist size	Spacing (centre to centre)		
mm	mm		
	400	450	600
50 × 100	2.03m	1.85m	1.46m
50 × 125	2.70m	2.55m	2.10m
50 × 150	3.23m	3.05m	2.66m
50 × 175	3.75m	3.55m	3.09m
50 × 200	4.27m	4.04m	3.52m

These spans apply strictly only in the UK.

extra height, make them of plywood for extra strength and nail them to the wall plates—otherwise, vibration might cause them to move.

Another possible method is to increase the depth of the existing joists by screwing extra straps on top of them. These straps must be at least 75mm deep for spans less than 3.7m, and 100mm deep for spans up to 5.5m. This is more econmical than buying new joists but involves a lot of work: the straps must be screwed down at 150mm intervals with No. 12 screws which pass through the straps and about three-quarters of the way through the joists. And anyway, some local planning authorities do not permit this method, so check this point with your local building inspector before you start drawing up any plans.

Having established what depth your joists must be, add 38mm to allow for the flooring on top of them. Then measure the height of your first floor room, including the thickness of the ceiling plaster, and add it all up. Now you know the height your stairs must climb.

Planning the stairway

The next job is to plan your stairway.

Take great care over this, as any mistakes could turn out to be very costly. There are a number of points that you have to consider: first, a stairway takes a great bite out of the space on both floors; second, the regulations governing stairways are strict; third, you do not want to make the simple mistake of bringing the stairway out under the eaves where there is insufficient headroom. So it is best to think about the stairs and the dormer or dormers together, and keep experimenting until you have the best all-round solution.

There are defined regulations for straight stairs which must be checked, in addition note that:
● At the foot and (in the UK) at the head of a staircase, there must be a landing whose 'going' (ie, its length) is at least the width of the staircase.
● In the UK, the planning regulations are very clear and precise. They firmly stipulate that you cannot position a door across the top or bottom of the stairs unless there is a landing situated between the stairs and the actual door.
● The regulations for tapered steps, or winders, are complicated: they need

to be checked on fully before you start the work. In general, though, allow for no more than three or four symmetrically-arranged winders for each 90° of turn. The actual width of the top and bottom winder step must be the same as for the rest of the flight, but the total space taken up by the winder set will be a little more—at least 150mm on each side. (Abroad, you cannot have more than one set of winders, consisting of three steps turning through a total of 90°).
● In the UK, if the staircase is to serve only a single room, which is not a living room or a kitchen, or is to serve only a bathroom and a WC, then it need be only 600mm wide, not 800mm.

There are a number of other points that you have to consider when planning stairways to a loft room.
● Straight flights of stairs, which can be bought ex-stock from joinery manufacturers, are cheaper than turned flights, which have to be purpose-built. So use a straight flight if this is at all possible.
● Flights with one turn in them are best positioned so that the turned section cuts through and across an existing wall as in fig. G. This means

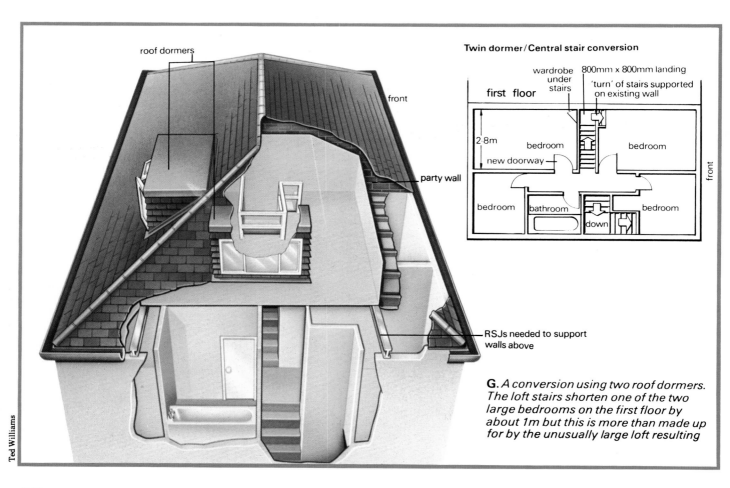

roof dormers

front

party wall

RSJs needed to support walls above

Twin dormer / Central stair conversion

wardrobe under stairs

800mm x 800mm landing

'turn' of stairs supported on existing wall

first floor

2·8m

bedroom

bedroom

new doorway

bedroom

bathroom

bedroom

down

front

G. A conversion using two roof dormers. The loft stairs shorten one of the two large bedrooms on the first floor by about 1m but this is more than made up for by the unusually large loft resulting

Ted Williams

the wall can be used to support the upper part of the stairs, obviating the need for a newel post standing in isolation in the room below.

● Double-turned flights—that is, those forming a U-shape—are best positioned in an existing stairwell, where support is already available on three sides.

● The most economical use of space—theoretically, anyway—is obtained by placing a new stairway directly over an existing one, since you need to 'steal' less space from adjoining rooms.

You cannot, however, plan your stairs in isolation. You also need to take into account the space they will take from both floors, and the nature of any dormer window you may be thinking of using.

Stairway/Dormer combinations

Figs G, H and I show three ways of installing stairways and dormers in identical (or 'mirror image') semidetached houses. All the schemes have different advantages and disadvantages, and illustrate how you will have to compromise in planning your own loft room and stairway.

In fig. G the stairs are of economical construction, supported where they

Gravity-Randall Ltd

1 *Simple conversions can be carried out using a retractable loft ladder. This folds down from your existing hatch when you want to get into the roof space*

2 *The ladder folds up neatly once you have finished with it and can be stowed away unobtrusively just inside the lip of the roof space*

turn by the wall between the larger bedrooms. They shorten one bedroom by about 1m, although some of this space is 'reclaimed' for a wardrobe, but leave the smaller bedrooms intact. In the loft room the roof line is altered

only by standard dormers, not the more obstrusive bays. The stairwell intrudes about half-way across the room—an arrangement which effectively divides it into 'territories' to suit two children, for either sleeping or playing, but

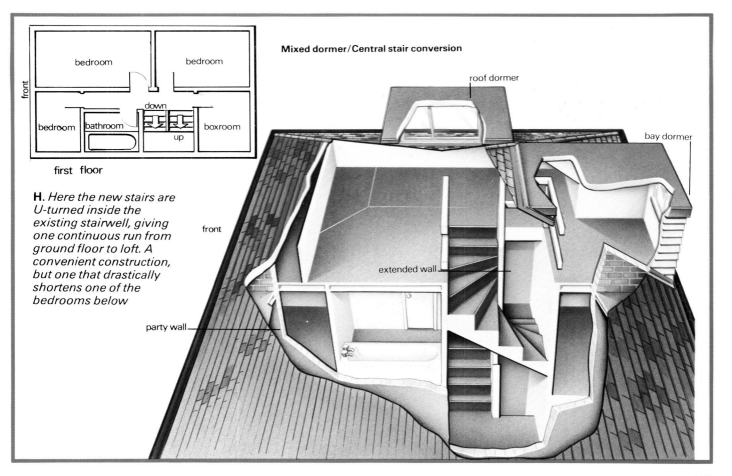

H. *Here the new stairs are U-turned inside the existing stairwell, giving one continuous run from ground floor to loft. A convenient construction, but one that drastically shortens one of the bedrooms below*

Mixed dormer/Central stair conversion

roof dormer

bay dormer

front

extended wall

party wall

first floor

bedroom

bedroom

bedroom | bathroom | down | up | boxroom

front

3 *Start your conversion by carrying out a thorough survey of the roof space. Place a number of boards across the joists to prevent you falling through*

4 *Using a 2.5m batten and a spirit level, work your way down both sides of the loft and mark out the areas with a height of 2.5m or more*

5 *Then using a shorter batten, mark those areas in which you have 1.7m of clearance in between the joists and the rafters*

would make it an awkward shape for one large single room.

In fig. H the new stairs are U-turned inside the existing stairwell. This means that the small bedroom has had to be shortened to a tiny box to provide access to the foot of the stairs. The stairwell's intrusion into the loft room is more compact, however, giving a

more 'unified' room for either living or sleeping. The roof line at the side of the house is altered only by a standard dormer, the big bulge of the bay dormer being round the back.

Fig. I shows probably the most economical construction—though not the most attractive from inside, since it provides no view. The stairs are on the

opposite side from the other houses— under the eaves instead of against the party wall. This 'loses' one bedroom on the first floor, but frees the head-height area in the loft room of any intrusion by the stairwell. Only one dormer is needed, giving headroom over the stairway. Although it is a bay dormer it is modest in size and, because it is 'blind'

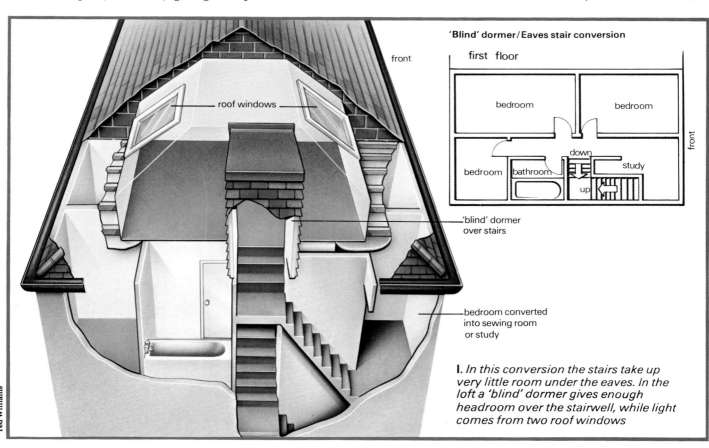

roof windows

front

'blind' dormer over stairs

bedroom converted into sewing room or study

'Blind' dormer/Eaves stair conversion

first floor

bedroom

bedroom

front

bedroom

bathroom

down

up

study

I. *In this conversion the stairs take up very little room under the eaves. In the loft a 'blind' dormer gives enough headroom over the stairwell, while light comes from two roof windows*

Simon Butcher

Ted Williams

6 *Using these marks, measure the floor area of the loft to see whether your planned conversion complies with local building regulations*

(windowless) it can be tile-hung to merge into the rest of the roof. Light in the loft room comes from two roof windows.

Loft rooms can, of course, be squeezed into far smaller houses than these. Fig. J shows a cottage—originally 'three up and two down', but with two of its box bedrooms since knocked into one—in which there was no bathroom and no space to build one. By stealing a small area from the bigger bedroom, however, it was possible to build a new stairway directly over the old one and instal a bathroom in the loft space. Should you confront a similar situation try to ensure that the

loft window starts half-way across the room so that it can be reached easily.

As well as studying the illustrations in this article, it is a good idea when planning your loft room to visit other houses in your street with reasonably new loft conversions (older ones may no longer comply with the building regulations) to see what has been done —and, if possible, what could be done to improve on it. Most people will not mind; in fact, they will quite like 'showing off' their new rooms.

Fire precautions
You should check whether converting your loft will mean having to take extra precaution against fire. For example, in the UK converting a loft would turn a two-storey house into a three-storey one, for which the fire regulations are stricter. In practice, it would be easier to apply for a *relaxation* (a dispensation from the additional regulations) than to make your house conform. Discuss the problem at an early stage with your building inspector.

Obstructions
In most cases, you can move obstructions—either in the loft or the floor below—that will impede a well-planned conversion.

Plumbing Water pipes, cisterns and so on are fairly easily re-routed. Take the opportunity to update any worn components. If you are planning 'wet' central heating for your loft conversion, remember that the feed and expansion tank will have to be positioned above the level of the radiators. If any taps (faucets) or WCs are to be fed from a cold water cistern, this too will have to be raised completely off the loft floor. **Chimneys and flues** You may be able to demolish any unused chimneys (check regulations carefully first). Remaining flues may need to be encased, to satisfy building regulations.

Walls Be careful when moving walls. either in the loft or the floor below. If you remove any part of a loadbearing wall, you will need to provide alternative support.

Regulations
As usual, your planned loft conversion will have to strictly comply with your local building regulations (building code).

The actual loft conversion is unlikely to require planning permission in the UK (unless your house is 'listed' or similar), but a dormer might.

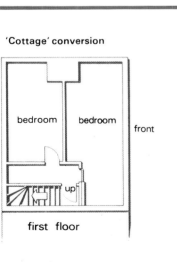

'Cottage' conversion

bedroom | bedroom | front

up

first floor

J. *A conversion suitable for a small house or cottage. A sliding door leads from the larger bedroom to the loft, which could be used as a bathroom*

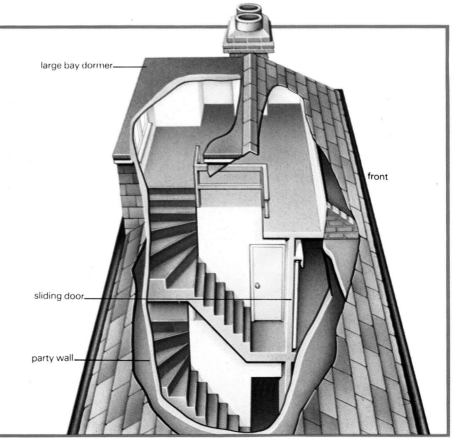

large bay dormer

front

sliding door

party wall

Planning the conversion work

● **The best order of work** ● **Running pipework and electric cable in the loft** ● **Building the perimeter walls** ● **What to do with existing components** ● **Internal finishes**

A. The layout and interior decoration of your loft will to a large extent be determined by the amount of light and ventilation available, and by whether you decide to install a dormer (below) or one or more windows (below right)

A loft conversion is an obvious and popular means of increasing the amount of space in your home, because it is neither as complicated as building an extension, nor as costly as moving to a bigger house. The work involved is well within the capabilities of an experienced do-it-yourselfer, but great care must be taken at all stages to ensure that the finished job complies with all the planning and safety regulations.

If you have taken time to plan out the loft conversion in detail (see the previous section) the actual construction work should be fairly straightforward–even if it does take you a few weeks or even months to complete. As with any large project, the key to success is to tackle the work one stage at a time, making sure that each stage is completed to your satisfaction before you start the next part of the conversion (see below).

Construction notes

The best order of work on a loft conversion will vary from job to job. But you can use this list of the main jobs as a basis, remembering that in practice some jobs must overlap.

● Install sub-joist RSJs, if any. Erect joists and trim around the stairway opening. If you plan to install any roof windows these should be actually fitted now.

● Erect the stairs, including any walls needed to support them and/or box them in.

● Do stage one of your services (plumbing and electricity).

● Erect the trimmer where the dormer roof meets the main roof and install its side supports.

● Erect the dormer walls and roof.

● Glaze the dormer and finish the exterior cheeks and front.

● Complete the ceiling joists and remove the existing collar ties.

● Erect any internal walls and remove the bracing on the lower purlins.

● Lay the floor and erect the stair rail (or walls around the landing).

● Insulate the joists in the area outside the floor. Insulate the loft walls, including sloping walls.

● Line the interior and complete the plumbing and electricity.

Camera Press

180

Before you begin, you may find it helpful to cut a long slot in the ceiling plaster—without disturbing the joists yet—where the stairwell is to go. This makes it easier to manoeuvre long components such as floor joists into the loft area.

B. Below: *Confined space under the eaves at the gable end of a loft can be put to good use—as this storage unit shows*

Services
It is best to begin running service pipes and cables after any new joists have been fitted, but before you begin any other construction. This will ensure that, for example, your bulky cold water storage tank does not have to be manoeuvred behind a newly-built wall. It also ensures that you have ample power and light while you do the conversion.

Your cold water cistern could be anywhere at all in the old loft space but you may wish to move it so that it does not intrude on the roof space. The best place to move it to, usually giving ample pressure, is under the eaves and immediately above the bathroom. Before you move it, lay a small area of 25mm boards to carry it, removing the insulation between these boards and the ceiling below so that the heat from the house can reach the tank. When the tank is in place, wrap it in 50mm glass fibre insulation. Also lag any hot or cold water pipes which run round the eaves above the insulation to protect them from frost damage.

If you intend to instal one or more central heating radiators in your new loft room you will need an expansion tank at a level higher than the highest radiator. This tank is quite light and can be carried on the new loft ceiling under the ridge board, with its overflow pipe running down the roof between the rafters to an outlet just below the eaves. Remember to instal this pipe, and the cold water feed to the expansion tank, before you insulate and plasterboard over your rafters—otherwise you will have an almost impossible job trying to fix it through the insulation. For access to the tank you will need to incorporate a tiny trapdoor—only about 500mm square—in your new ceiling (fig. C).

Alternatively, you could instal the expansion tank in a high cupboard inside the room, with both the cold water pipe and the overflow pipe entering through the back of the cupboard.

Electricity is usually no problem. In the UK, you can usually extend existing ring main power circuits and lighting circuits—providing this does not overload them. You should, however, plan how much power you will need carefully before you attempt to start work. Ensure wiring is in good condition.

Remember that at least one of your lights should be positioned squarely above the stairway, preferably over the landing or the turn in the stairs, for safe walking. If you are fitting a ceiling light, be sure to leave plenty of cable coiled up under the eaves ready to run up the side of your new walls, up the sloping part of the roof (through the insulation again) and across the ceiling. It is easy to be 'caught' here with a cable that is too short. Also remember to run the live cable from the light(s) to the wall switch(es) before you insulate your walls.

Dormer windows
If you are planning to install one or more dormer windows, you should **complete the construction work at this stage.**

Perimeter walls
The perimeter walls which enclose the new room at about 1.1m are built from 75mm × 50mm timber. Those running at right-angles to the floor joists will of course rest on a number of joists and thus be adequately supported. Where the wall runs parallel to the joists, however, the joists on which it rests should be doubled to give 100mm of support.

There are two ways of building such walls. If the existing rafters are straight, you can nail one wall stud to each rafter, using a builder's line to check the

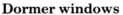

alignment of the studs along the length of the wall (fig. E). Alternatively, if the rafters are bowed or out of alignment, it is easier to assemble and erect a complete wall frame with top and bottom plates as well as studs. This will help give a straight line where the top of the wall meets the sloping wall above it—and this is important, because this particular joint will be near eye level and therefore very noticeable.

While you are building these walls, remember to include the noggins needed to carry the radiator brackets for your central heating, and the boxes to which your power sockets and light switches will be fixed.

Existing components
Some of the existing components in your roof space can be moved, but some should be left strictly alone.

Purlins: These are heavy timbers fixed below the rafters about 1.2m above the floor joist level. Rather than remove them, it is easier to hide them behind, or incorporate them into, your perimeter walls. If you do want to remove them because they are too high and therefore obtrusive, the frame of your perimeter walls may be able to take their place—but on no account do this without first consulting the building inspector.

In large lofts, another row of purlins may be found about halfway between the first row and the ridge board. If these are reasonably straight they can be sanded down and sealed or painted; otherwise they should be neatly boxed in with plywood, tongued-and-grooved pine boarding or some other material to match your ceiling finish. The long struts beneath these purlins should not be removed without building permission.

Trimmers: The trimmers around the chimney stack, and the struts that support them, should also be left in place unless the building inspector agrees otherwise. (Sometimes it is possible to transfer the load, by means of new struts, to part of your new construction outside the loft room).

Collar ties: These are essential to stop the rafters from splaying apart. If they are above the level of your loft room ceiling you can of course just leave them in place. But if they are too low for that you have three choices.

You could instal new ones above ceiling level and remove the old. If you have to do this, remember that the higher they are the less effective they become, so keep them just above the ceiling level.

Alternatively, you could 'clean up' the old ones and use them as an attractive visual feature (fig. H). A third solution to

C. Left: *If you have a cold water storage cistern, move this out of the middle of the loft into the eaves—preferably above the bathroom. If you want radiators in the loft, the small expansion tank could be placed under the ridge board, with a trapdoor for easy access*

expansion tank for radiators in loft

cold feed to central heating boiler

25mm boards

cold water storage tank moved under eaves above bathroom

cold water feed to tank

overflow pipes

25mm boards

Venner Artists

610mm sheets, makes a much less expensive floor covering than conventional tongued-and-grooved flooring. Since it is screwed down instead of nailed, its installation is also less likely to loosen the plaster in the ceilings below (though this will not be a problem if the new joists are lifted clear of the ceiling, as suggested on pages 173 to 179). Although the ends of chipboard sheets are tongued-and-grooved, each join should be directly over a joist, so your joist spacing will have to be thought out in advance. Noggins will also have to be installed between the joists to carry the joints at the ends of sheets.

Should you decide to use a chipboard floor, it is theoretically easier to reverse the order of work given above and lay the floor before you build the dormer walls. This obviates the problem of having to cut large sheets accurately to butt against the walls, and of having to cut the tongues off some sheets to allow them to be slipped into place. It also provides a smooth working surface on which other components – lengths of wall and so on – can be assembled with ease.

The 'catch' is that once a chipboard floor is down it is difficult to lift again should you find that, for example, you need an extra floor joist under a wall. So if you use this method you must think ahead to make sure that everything needed under the floor – including central heating pipes and electricity cables – is in place before the floor is laid.

D. Left: *The stairway to the loft should be soundly constructed with an adequate guard rail. The landing can be used as a display area for plants and flowers*

the problem might be to fit new ceiling joists so that they act as collar ties.

Chimneys: These require special attention. Where their bottom edges will be 'buried' by the new joists and floor, they must first be rendered with a 1:3 sand and cement mix to ensure that smoke or fire cannot emerge from the brickwork and set fire to your floor. An air space of 38mm must be allowed between a chimney and floor joists or wall framing to prevent heat from the flue reaching the timber.

Flooring and stairwell rail

Laying the floor and erecting the rail around the stairwell are best combined in one operation because the guard rail posts cannot simply stand on the floor, but must be carried down beside the joists and bolted to them. This means in turn that short extra lengths of noggin are needed to carry the floor around the posts.

Flooring-grade chipboard, in either 2440mm × 1220mm or 2440mm ×

E. Right: *The perimeter walls which enclose the new loft conversion at about 1.1m are built from 75mm × 50mm timber. Nail one wall stud to each rafter along the length of the wall*

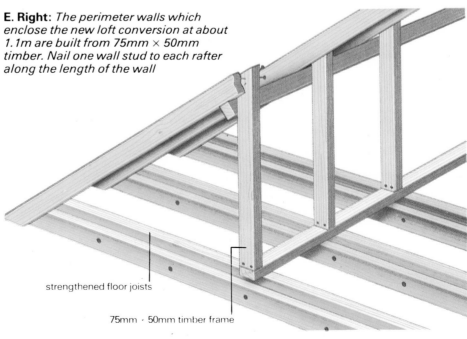

strengthened floor joists

75mm · 50mm timber frame

183

Insulation

Most modern houses are built with roofing felt between the tiles and the rafters. If your house has none, it is a wise precaution to install some before you insulate between the rafters; otherwise the insulation material could in time become damp and cause discolouring to your lining material.

There is no need to remove the tiles to do this. Instead, cut the roofing felt into strips about 100mm wider than the spaces between the rafters, fold it so that it fits, apply a little roofing mastic along the edges and fix it in place with flat-headed felt nails. Work from the top downwards, so that if any water does enter it will flow from one sheet to the next–not escape between them.

Good standards of insulation will be important, and fig. F shows where you should position insulating material.

The amount of insulation you need to provide depends on the severity of your climate: in the UK, 100mm of insulation is usually considered quite a sufficient amount.

Good ventilation on the 'cold' side of the insulation is vital to prevent condensation that could lead to rot—avoid at all costs. The sloping roof part is particularly difficult to ventilate well: treat it as a flat roof.

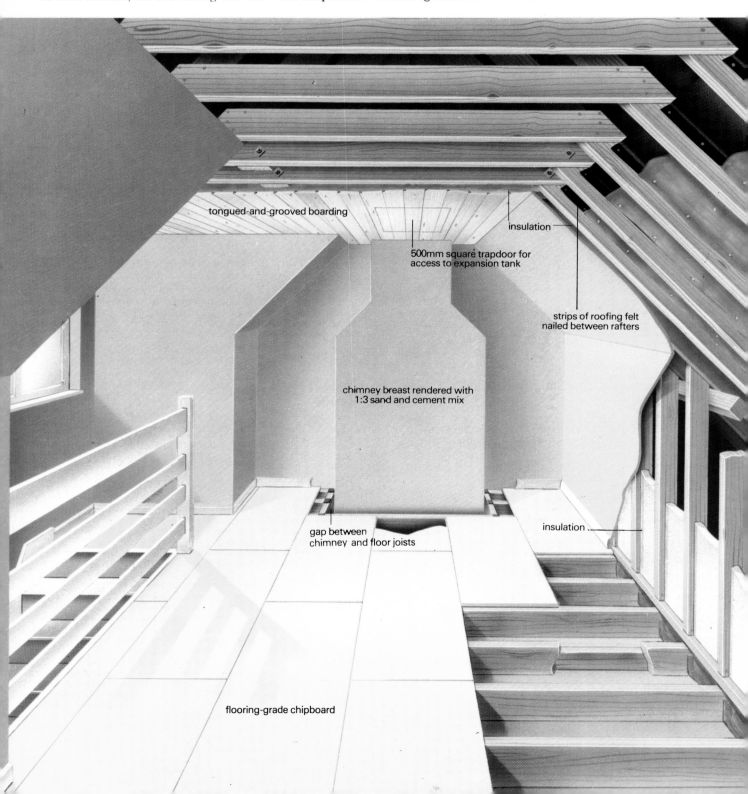

tongued-and-grooved boarding

insulation

500mm square trapdoor for access to expansion tank

strips of roofing felt nailed between rafters

chimney breast rendered with 1:3 sand and cement mix

gap between chimney and floor joists

insulation

flooring-grade chipboard

This may mean you need to increase the thickness of the roof joists; and you should take this into account right from the start, for it will affect your headroom calculations.

Internal finish
Plasterboard, either skimmed with 5mm of finish plaster or merely 'stopped' at the joins and nail holes, is the usual method of lining both the walls and ceiling. It does not, however, succeed in making a loft room look like an ordinary room because the sloping walls at the sides are a 'giveaway'. One way round this is to carry the plasterboard only as high as the 2m level (or to the height of the top purlins), raise the ceiling as high as possible, and finish the upper part of the walls and the ceiling in tongued-and-grooved pine. This makes the room obviously, and frankly, a loft—and also makes it more spacious and airy.

F. Left: *Pay special attention to the internal finish of walls, ceilings and floor and ensure that all air spaces are adequately insulated*

G. Right: *Tongued-and-grooved panelling on the ceiling and roof slope gives a loft room a spacious and airy feel*

H. Below: *Existing components—such as rafters and collar ties—can often be 'cleaned up' and used as visual features*

Crescourt Loft Conversions

Crescourt Loft Conversions

Studio window conversion

Add interest, light and space to your home by building this studio window conversion. Its sloping glazing panels admit plenty of light, and are double glazed to retain heat

A studio window is one of the best ways to make most use of available light. The sloping glazing panels in this design are upturned to the sun to present the largest possible heat collection area. Using this design, you can construct an attractive rear extension, which will really open up the view into the garden, and create an ideal environment for a conservatory housing indoor plants. Sealed double-glazing panels are used throughout, so there will be no problem with heat loss or insulation efficiency.

The drawings overleaf show the type of situation which is ideal for conversion and is common to many homes. The rear entrance is housed in

John Ward

a small lean-to extension with a sloping roof and existing small window. But there are many other ways to use the design. You can just as easily build on to a flat roofed extension, or, as shown below, directly on to the wall of the house. In each case, all you need do is provide a low retaining wall for the lower part of the window frame, and a secure fixing for the top bearer bar which can be bolted to the wall and covered with a flashing.

Before you begin work, you should plan your window carefully. The first thing to check is that your proposed alteration will not infringe building regulations or local planning restrictions. You should also consider the siting. Ideally, to admit the maximum light, it should face south. If this is not possible, aim to find the brightest location available avoiding obvious shady areas. You should not site it too near trees for this reason, and also because falling leaves will have to be cleaned off the glass in autumn.

The first thing you will need is a foundation for the new structure; set this out then lay a concrete slab to form a floor and provide footings for the retaining walls. How deep this slab must be will depend on local soil conditions; check this point with the building inspector. Build the retaining walls on to this, tying in to the existing brickwork where necessary. The sloping side walls can be extensions of existing walls as shown, or completely new structures tied in to the house. You can glaze the sides as shown below if you prefer.

Enlarge the wall opening as required to provide access to the new structure, supporting it with a lintel.

Build up the glazing frames on the brickwork, using the sections shown. If you are building up against a side wall, you can tie in to this as shown.

Fit flashings, bargeboards and soffits, and install sealed double-glazing units, which you can have made to measure. Paint or varnish all the timber for maximum protection, and make sure that you have sealed thoroughly around the edges of the frame to prevent leakages, using a waterproof mastic throughout.

Elizabeth Whiting

Alternative idea

You do not have to build a complete extension to take advantage of this design. The picture shows how you can adapt the idea by building directly on to the rear wall to form a glazed conservatory.

All you need is an opening in the walls, supported by a lintel, but you may be required to extend the house foundations under the new structure. Build the low retaining wall around the perimeter and erect the timber supports for the glazing. The details of this are much the same as those shown overleaf. Just fix the upper bearer to the lintel, and form a flashing to the wall to prevent rain from entering.

Workplan

You can make the conversion on any type of rear wall, possibly by knocking out an existing window or patio door, but a typical location is shown below, with an existing small rear addition. Before you begin work, you should check that the proposed extension does not contravene building regulations or local planning restrictions

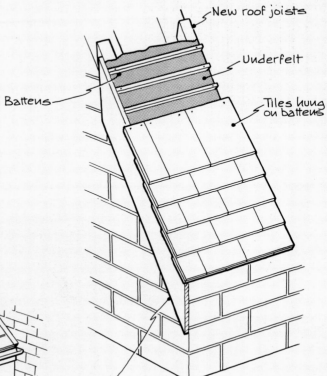

New roof joists

Underfelt

Tiles hung on battens

Battens

Barge board

Existing rear addition with pitched roof, back door and window. You can base your extension on this kind of structure, or build it as a lean-to on a flat wall

Detail of side wall

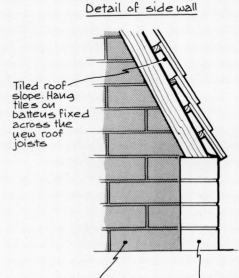

Tiled roof slope. Hang tiles on battens fixed across the new roof joists

Area of new brickwork extension tied into existing brickwork

Front retaining wall

This drawing shows the completed extension. Compare this with the drawing opposite to see how the original walls have been extended and the roof has been tied in to the sloping double glazing panels. Use double glazed sealed units for heat retention. You will need to extend the foundations to support the new structure and form a floor. If you are building against a flat wall, you can support the upper end of the glazing bars on a bearer batten fitted to the wall and build a small brickwork buttress and retaining wall on each side, tied into the original brickwork

Existing house wall. You can make a small access doorway if none exists, or enlarge the opening and fit a lintel to create a large through space as an extension of the room behind

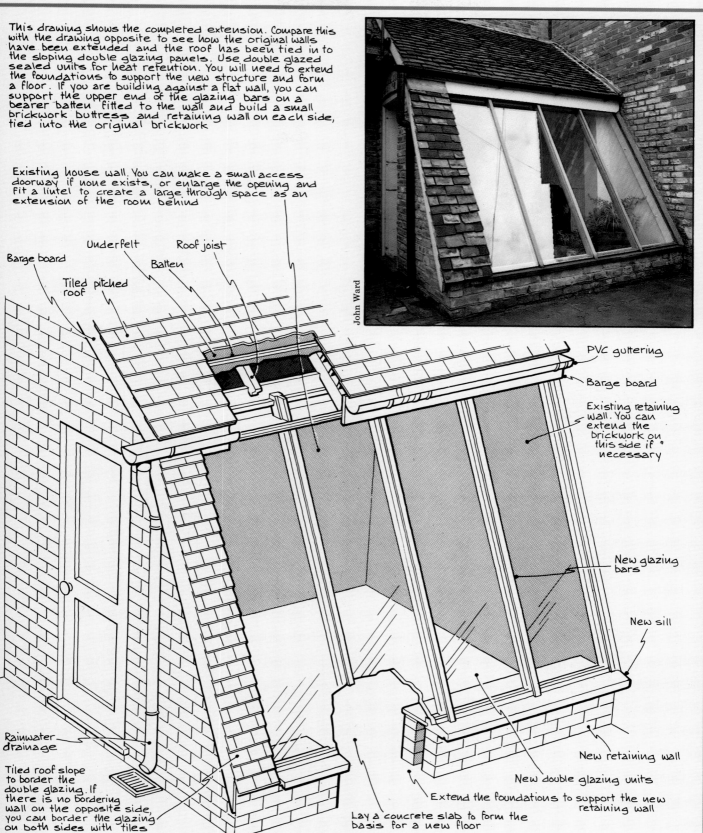

John Ward

Barge board

Tiled pitched roof

Underfelt

Batten

Roof joist

PVC guttering

Barge board

Existing retaining wall. You can extend the brickwork on this side if necessary

New glazing bars

New sill

New retaining wall

New double glazing units

Extend the foundations to support the new retaining wall

Rainwater drainage

Tiled roof slope to border the double glazing. If there is no bordering wall on the opposite side, you can border the glazing on both sides with tiles

Lay a concrete slab to form the basis for a new floor

Advertising Arts

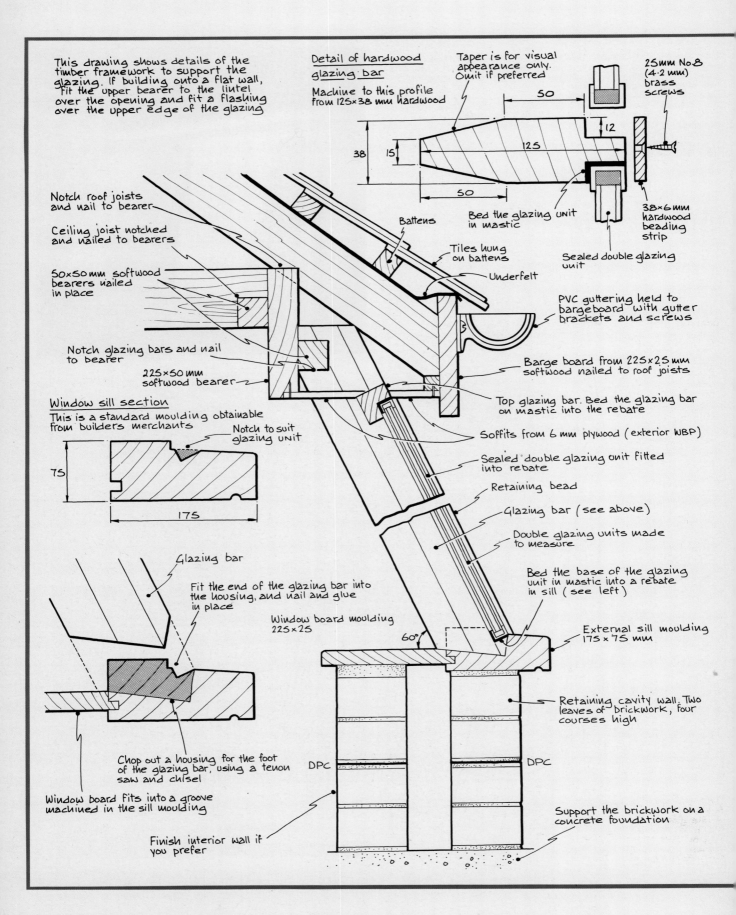

This drawing shows details of the timber framework to support the glazing. If building onto a flat wall, fit the upper bearer to the lintel over the opening and fit a flashing over the upper edge of the glazing

Detail of hardwood glazing bar

Machine to this profile from 125×38 mm hardwood

Taper is for visual appearance only. Omit if preferred

50

38   15   125   12

50

25mm No.8 (4·2 mm) brass screws

Bed the glazing unit in mastic

38×6mm hardwood beading strip

Sealed double glazing unit

Notch roof joists and nail to bearer

Ceiling joist notched and nailed to bearers

50×50 mm softwood bearers nailed in place

Notch glazing bars and nail to bearer

225×50 mm softwood bearer

Battens

Tiles hung on battens

Underfelt

PVC guttering held to bargeboard with gutter brackets and screws

Barge board from 225×25 mm softwood nailed to roof joists

Top glazing bar. Bed the glazing bar on mastic into the rebate

Soffits from 6 mm plywood (exterior WBP)

Sealed double glazing unit fitted into rebate

Retaining bead

Glazing bar (see above)

Double glazing units made to measure

Window sill section

This is a standard moulding obtainable from builders merchants

Notch to suit glazing unit

75

175

Glazing bar

Fit the end of the glazing bar into the housing, and nail and glue in place

Window board moulding 225×25

60°

Bed the base of the glazing unit in mastic into a rebate in sill (see left)

External sill moulding 175 × 75 mm

Retaining cavity wall. Two leaves of brickwork, four courses high

DPC   DPC

Chop out a housing for the foot of the glazing bar, using a tenon saw and chisel

Window board fits into a groove machined in the sill moulding

Finish interior wall if you prefer

Support the brickwork on a concrete foundation

190

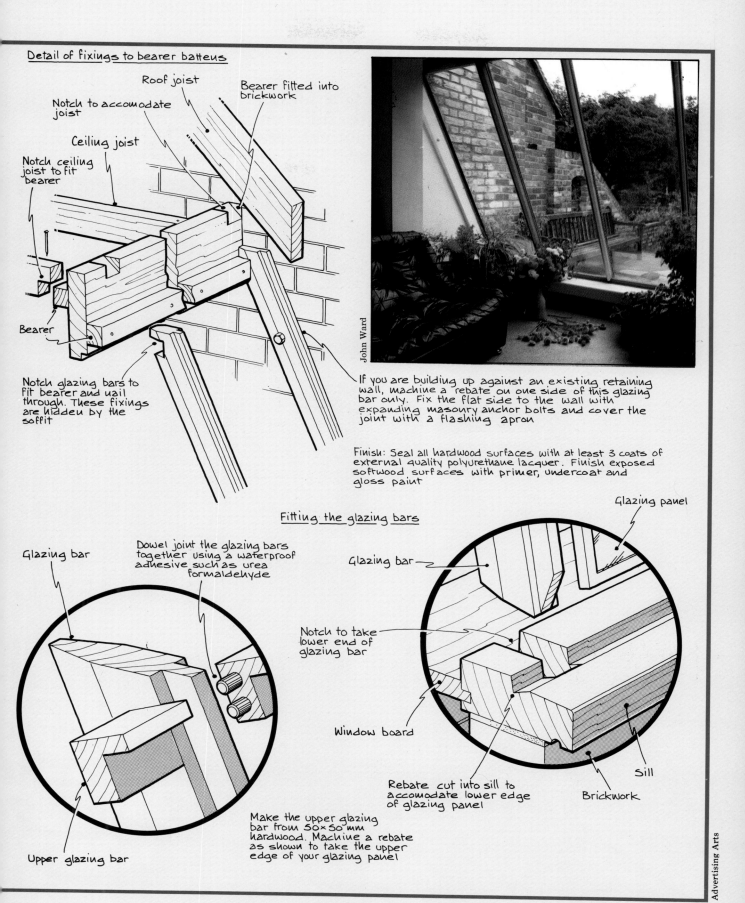

Detail of fixings to bearer battens

Roof joist

Notch to accomodate joist

Bearer fitted into brickwork

Ceiling joist

Notch ceiling joist to fit bearer

Bearer

Notch glazing bars to fit bearer and nail through. These fixings are hidden by the soffit

John Ward

If you are building up against an existing retaining wall, machine a rebate on one side of this glazing bar only. Fix the flat side to the wall with expanding masonry anchor bolts and cover the joint with a flashing apron

Finish: Seal all hardwood surfaces with at least 3 coats of external quality polyurethane lacquer. Finish exposed softwood surfaces with primer, undercoat and gloss paint

Fitting the glazing bars

Glazing bar

Dowel joint the glazing bars together using a waterproof adhesive such as urea formaldehyde

Upper glazing bar

Make the upper glazing bar from 50×50 mm hardwood. Machine a rebate as shown to take the upper edge of your glazing panel

Glazing panel

Glazing bar

Notch to take lower end of glazing bar

Window board

Rebate cut into sill to accomodate lower edge of glazing panel

Brickwork

Sill

Advertising Arts

Choosing a porch

A well-designed porch, whether it is a simple canopy construction or an elaborate fully enclosed design, can be both a practical and decorative improvment to your house

Below: *This simply constructed porch —painted in pale blue to match the front door and railings—provides a touch of colour for an otherwise plain and neutral facade*

A porch comes into its own in winter—it provides a shelter from the elements, a place in which to remove muddy boots or dry off a dripping dog and generally saves bringing too much of the outside world inside.

But it is not just a winter convenience, because all the year round a porch can provide the little bit of extra space that makes the world of difference. Properly designed and fitted out, it can be a place for storing anything from outdoor shoes to children's bicycles, from wine bottles to a dog basket. Add it all up and you may wonder why you never considered the possibility of having a porch before.

Right: *An excellent way to add a country flavour to the front of your house is to add a simple trellis and some climbing vines*

Below: *These semi-enclosed porches are not only decorative in their own right, but also give an attractive appearance to the entire row of houses. The tiled gable roofs blend well with the brickwork and the paint picks out the most decorative features*

The first thing to decide is what sort of porch you want. The larger it is, the more scope for storage it will give you. But even the smallest porch will provide extra amenities—an enclosed space between the house interior and the outside which, in winter, is invaluable for keeping in warmth. In fact, it need not even be enclosed, because just a canopy-style porch will offer some shelter. You might also consider building it in two stages to spread the cost; you start with the canopy and add the sides and front door later.

The next thing to think about is how the porch would look on the house. A plain exterior style is probably the easiest to handle since there will be few features with which the porch can clash. But whatever the style of your home, you can find a porch design to harmonize with it. Experimenting with different designs can be a pleasure in itself, since all you have to do is sketch the house exterior then draw on a variety of different designs. The one to choose is the one that looks as though it has been there all the time.

Begin by looking at your roof. If it has gables or dormer windows, this gives you your first design principle— a porch with a gable roof. If the roof has a slope to the front, this too can be matched in your porch design. Similarly if the roof slopes up from the sides to an apex, a porch can be built to match this. In each case, the porch will end up looking like part of the house rather than just an afterthought.

The same principle should also be followed when it comes to choosing the materials for building the porch. If you have red brick walls, you should search local builders' merchants until you find matching bricks for the porch walls. You should also try to match roofing materials and any decorative details that already exist on the house. And doors and windows should be chosen with care since these can so easily clash with those you have already. It is always worth looking at neighbouring houses with porches to see, in practice, what different styles already exist—particularly if you have an old house with its own distinctive character.

There are several common styles of porch. The first—and often the prettiest—is the kind found on old cottages where a simple gable-roofed canopy is supported at the front on two wooden posts, perhaps with half walls to either side and small benches inside. This type of porch can easily be altered so that it becomes fully

Above: *The clean lines of this arched porch and the neutral colours give the house a truly elegant appearance. Black paintwork and brass door furniture make for a beautiful contrast*
Below: *Well-established flowering climbers over this country style porch have a bright, welcoming appeal*

enclosed, building up the walls and adding windows, then finishing off with a new front door.

In many Victorian and Edwardian houses, open porches were incorporated into the front of the house by recessing the front door. This simple manoeuvre gave shelter from the rain, some space to store non-perishables like milk bottles, but also the opportunity for owners to add an enclosed front at a later date. Making this conversion nowadays is relatively easy and inexpensive—and you end up with a real porch as well as a tidier house frontage.

Many modern houses are built with simple canopy porches directly over the front or back door, or with flat box canopies. Either of these can be converted to the fully enclosed type of

Above: *Unusual cut-out designs turn a simple arch framework into an attractive porch which complements the pale wood panelled door perfectly*

porch with the minimum of constructional work. But as with older buildings, it is important to make sure that the conversion is in keeping with the style of the rest of the house. If the house has a rendered finish, this can actually make the work a great deal easier since building blocks can be used rather than bricks.

Whether you are converting an existing open canopy or starting from scratch, it is likely that you will have to consider local planning and/or building regulations. Although this may only involve drawing up rough sketches and outlining your plans, it is important that the structural changes are taken fully into account.

Any solid wall, even if it supports only a roof canopy, will require some kind of foundation. Similarly, the roof will need to be properly joined to the house wall—flashing is the simplest way—to prevent water creeping down behind the roof and causing penetrating damp into the house itself. You will have to consider also how to dispose of rainwater; if you do not, even the relatively small amount that falls off the porch roof may splash back and cause dampness in the walls. This means including some kind of guttering and water drainage in your design plans.

Apart from the traditional materials used for porch construction, there are alternatives like corrugated PVC sheeting which can serve a highly functional purpose without necessarily blending in with the existing house style. This approach will give you something that looks rather like a greenhouse—it does not blend, but it is obviously not intended to. Where two houses are close together and you have your entrance at the side, facing your neighbour's blank wall, you might think about bridging the gap between the houses in this way. Simple wooden supports work like roof rafters to which you attach the sheeting; the front and back can be left open, or filled in largely with glass. The amount of light in this sort of addition would make the porch ideal for growing plants—even grape vines can flourish in such locations.

Summing up, the kind of porch you choose should depend on two things: what you want to use it for, and what style fits in best. In bad weather a storm porch, providing shelter and a half-way zone between inside and outside, is invaluable. And in summer, although not every house needs a

barrier against insects coming in and cool air-conditioned air going out, there are still many ways in which a porch can add an extra amenity.

Facilities

The inside walls of a porch can be used for a variety of purposes. Shelves lining the walls can be used for plants, long-term storage, or displaying items such as pottery. When you choose the decoration for the inside of a fully enclosed porch you should aim to blend it as much as possible with the style of the inside of your house. Rough plastered or rendered walls are often the easiest to deal with and, as long as the colours match the inside, there will be no clash.

If you are going to fit a light, remember that this should be switched from inside the house. But otherwise there is no reason why you should not choose either ceiling or wall-mounted lamps. Both will cast an attractive glow at night and help light the way to the house.

Lastly, you should give careful

thought to the flooring. While quarry tiles might be the most suitable they are also rather expensive and difficult to lay properly. So, as an alternative, think about vinyl floor coverings which come in a wide variety of decorative patterns (including quarry tile patterns) and are almost as durable. A mat which can absorb some of the dust, rain or snow which finds its way in, is also a good idea. But remember that if you start laying carpet, you will end up being unable to use the porch for the original purpose—a place halfway between inside and out.

Below left: *This fully-enclosed porch houses the staircase. This leaves more space inside the house for more practical uses and also admits the optimum amount of light* **Below:** *Almost a room in itself, the design of this decorative porch uses eye-catching patterned and coloured glass panels.* **Right:** *A porch that blends perfectly with the house – made by bricking in the original open one*

Jessica Strang/Frank Linden

keeping window sills at the same height you still retain a feeling of continuity. The same applies to roof lines – it is often preferable to go for a broken roof line than to try to dovetail a new roof into the existing one.

Similarly, instead of erecting a living room extension parallel to the wall at the rear of the house, you might consider building it as a wing at right angles to the house for a more dramatic effect.

Construction of the extension can be anything from the prefabricated package kit type to an entirely new masonry project, depending on your requirements.

A playroom for the children or a utility room could be provided by adding the simplest form of prefabricated extension to the back, or possibly the side, of the house. Living rooms on the other hand will need to be of a more substantial structure although both types must comply with fire and other regulations.

The most ambitious home extensions are those on two storeys, providing extra rooms on both the ground and first floors. But unlike the typical 'sun lounge' extension, where access is easily provided through existing windows or French doors, a two-storey extension requires access through existing rooms. Therefore you will need to think about rearranging those rooms to take account of this, perhaps even to the extent of constructing lobbies and passageways leading to the new doors.

Below: *A simple 'kitchen' extension using bricks to match the quoins of the main building and glazed sliding doors to admit plenty of light*

The problem of access also arises if you have decided on a loft conversion to meet your space requirements. And if the area is to provide habitable rooms rather than just a playroom or storeroom, then again the conversion must comply with local building regulations and you must provide a proper staircase giving access.

Blending old with new

Your choice of building materials is vitally important if the extension is to blend perfectly with the existing house.

Matching brickwork is notoriously hard – unless your house is comparatively new – and it is well worth looking out for

Peter Summersgill Assoc.

Above: *A first floor timber extension at the rear of the house is painted white to match the door and window frames for a bright, clean-looking finish*

Tim Street-Porter

local demolition that could provide you with a supply of secondhand bricks that will match your brickwork far better than any new bricks could. Alternatively, ask your builders' merchant for details of regional bricks which might match yours more closely.

Another point worth bearing in mind when building on to very old houses is that new brick sizes are likely to be different and it might prove tricky getting a perfect match with courses.

Matching rendering styles is often easier, and even if the front and sides of your house are of facing brickwork, it may be worth having the rear wall and the new extension rendered to make the new work look part of the original.

Roofs, too, raise the problem of matching tile patterns and colours. One useful, if lengthy, solution is to strip the whole of, say, the rear face of the existing roof and use the tiles on the front face of your extension to match the front of the house roof. You can then use new tiles on the whole of the rear face.

Try to match windows and doors for the extension as closely as possible with existing ones. It should be possible to find

a good match, in style at least and preferably in height, from among the many standard window frames available from builder's merchants. Avoid mixing materials—aluminium frames in an extension look very uneasy beside small paned

Above: *An unused garage converted to form an excellent children's playroom*
Below left: *A fully glazed extension enclosing a swimming pool ensures hours of entertainment and exercise— even in the rain. If a suitable heating system is installed the pool can be used all the year round*

sliding sashes in the rest of the house.

It is far easier to blend the new room with the house on the inside. Access can be via arches if they form through rooms, or sliding doors can be fitted to separate the room while still allowing a visual link. By choosing the same style of doors for new openings off landings and halls, and by running carpet of the same colour or pattern through into the rooms, the feeling of continuity can be maintained.

It is worth remembering that attractive features can be created by clever use of the dividing walls between old and new work. Apart from the obvious idea of creating an arch, you could keep the low brick walls which housed windows at either side of an entrance once fitted with French doors, and use the space above them for shelving or display cabinets. Other unwanted window and door openings can also be put to similar use, creating attractive alcoves for storage.

When you are planning and building your new extension, do not miss the opportunity to include the sort of features you wished you had in the rest of the house—such as wall insulation, double glazing, labour-saving ideas like plastic fittings that do not need painting, ceilings with concealed lighting, plenty of power points, even a fireplace as the focal point of a new living room or washbasins in new bedrooms. All can be easily incorporated during the construction, but at the least can be a nuisance to add later.

Converting a flat roof

● **Planning the work** ● **Checking the present roof structure** ● **Erecting a safety rail** ● **Gaining access to the roof** ● **Patio doors** ● **Suitable floor coverings** ● **Brickwork planters** ● **Building a roof storage chest**

Roof-top patios and gardens are becoming increasingly popular in crowded urban areas where space at ground level is limited. And even if you already have a garden at ground level, a well-planned roof garden could make a welcome addition to your home. Not only will it allow you more space for relaxation and enjoyment, but it can also add a new dimension to upstairs rooms (see below).

Planning considerations

A single storey extension with a flat roof probably offers the ideal site for a roof garden as few houses are initially built with flat roofs. But before you start to plan and convert the area you should consider carefully whether or not the roof is suitable.

The most important consideration is whether the roof construction is strong enough to bear the weight—not just of people but of the many pots, planters and pieces of garden furniture you may want to put on it. On no account should you undertake the assessment yourself because of the complex and variable stresses involved. Instead, approach a reliable structural engineer, an architect or your local building inspector for advice. After considering your plans and the roof structure itself, they will be able to tell you if you can go ahead.

Your existing roof will be built using either timber joists or some type

A. Below: *Building work completed, this small roof garden just needs the addition of plants and furniture to bring about a total transformation*

Ray Duns

1 *Hardly ever used—except as a general storage area—this flat roof is wasted space crying out for renovation and repair*

2 *Start by preparing any areas which are to be painted. Remove loose, flaking paint and clinging moss with a wire brush*

3 *Completely dismantle any old timber trellis work. Unscrew the stanchions and then work them away from the wall with a crowbar*

of reinforced concrete slab construction. A well-built concrete slab should be capable of supporting almost any reasonable weight—although it should still be checked carefully by an expert. A timber roof, on the other hand, poses far greater problems since the joists may not be thick enough to bear the weight of a roof garden check this carefully before you start work. And if the roof is old, the timbers could be affected by rot, or fixings such as joists hangers may have worked themselves loose. Once again it is imperative to seek expert advice before starting on the work.

Drainage is another problem to consider when checking the present roof

structure. Bear in mind that—despite its name—a flat roof is never truly flat but always has a slight slope to ensure that rainwater runs off quickly. In order to improve waterproofing both timber and concrete roofs are often given an additional covering consisting of layers of bituminous felt held together with asphalt.

Before conversion check that the drainage pitch is adequate and that the roof covering is intact and undamaged. Also remember to check that gutters and downpipes (eavestroughs and downspouts) and gullies are free from blockages and that they are all in complete working order. Bear in mind at all times also that the pitch

of the roof and its ability to drain efficiently must not be interfered with when the roof garden has been completed.

If you discover that the pitch of the roof is too low and that drainage is poor, there is little you can do about it when the roof is of timber construction apart from rebuilding from scratch. But with a concrete slab roof, the pitch can be altered by laying a thin concrete screed over the top of the existing roof.

In this case, the new roof should have a pitch of 1:50. Lay a 50mm thick slab at the top end of the roof, gradually reducing this thickness as you progress downwards. The screed should not bridge any of the existing DPCs and these possibly may have to be relaid.

Guard rail and access
After you have thoroughly checked the suitability of the roof for the installation of a roof garden, you can begin to make detailed plans of its layout. Obviously the exact location of items such as flower beds and furniture are a matter of taste. But for safety, and to conform to regulations and codes, you will need a suitable guard rail and a proper means of access to the roof.

It is a good idea for the lower part of a guard rail to be solid—that is safer than an open barrier and also provides

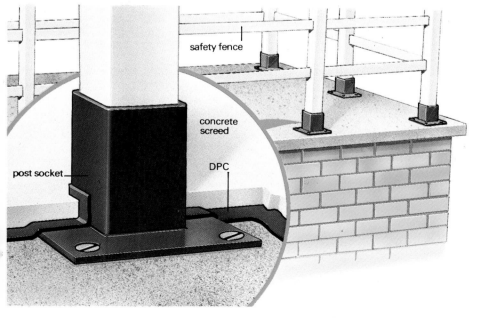

B. Left: *Ready-made steel fencing posts can be screwed directly to the roof. Try to ensure that the fixings are protected from corrosion*

203

4 Cut new stanchions and secure them in place with screws and wall plugs. Angle the top of each stanchion to aid waterproofing

5 Then give the prepared masonry surfaces at least two coats of paint. Leave the final coat to dry for 24 hours before continuing

6 Make up the trellis and nail it in position. Notice how the distance between horizontal battens gets greater as you work upwards

7 Once the trellis work is complete, apply two coats of wood preservative to prevent the new timber from rotting

8 Keep brickwork planters to a size which can be supported by the roof. Lay the first course of bricks on a thin bed of mortar

9 The bottom of the planter should consist of a complete course of bricks laid side by side. This helps to prevent water seeping through

some protection against the wind. The featured roof already has a low brick-built wall around it, and in a masonry-built house you could do something similar. Steel fencing posts could then form the basis of the guard rail: mortar these firmly into the brickwork of the parapet wall.

A brick parapet wall is not essential, of course, and may not be possible with some forms of house construction; one alternative is stout timber planks bolted to timber or metal posts. The posts in turn must be securely fixed to the roof or wall structure: if in doubt about how to do this consult an architect or surveyor. With a wooden roof decking, you might be able to take the posts through the roof decking and bolt

the posts to the roof joists. Another possibility is to use post sockets as for a concrete roof (see below).

On a concrete slab roof without parapet walls, a safety fence can be erected by bolting steel posts directly to the roof itself (fig. B). The posts—or stanchions—should be fixed to the top of the roof using expanding masonry bolts and rustproof screws. Coat the base plate of each stanchion with bitumen or other corrosion-preventative paint. Then cover the plate and the bottom few millimetres of the upright with small patches of felt held in place with hot bitumen (fig. B). This ensures that the fixings are fully protected from corrosion and that damp does not penetrate the roof

timbers or concrete slab below.

To comply with building regulations you must also provide a reasonable means of access to the roof. This can consist either of an outside staircase from ground level or a door or patio doors leading directly to the roof from the first floor of the house. The method you choose depends on the exact layout you want and the site of the roof in relation to the main house.

An outside staircase must comply with local building regulations and must also be fitted with a safety balustrade. It should be strong enough to take the weight of regular and occasional traffic, and be wide enough to allow bulky objects to be carried on to the roof without great problems.

10 Cover the bottom of the planter with a 25mm thick bed of concrete. This will provide a completely watertight seal

11 When you lay the second course of bricks, leave a number of occasional gaps between bricks to act as drain holes

12 The top course of bricks can be laid on end as an added decorative feature, and more elaborate patterns are perfectly possible

13 To help waterproof the inside of the planter, coat the adjoining brickwork on the parapet wall with one or more coats of bitumen paint

14 Once the mortar sets—usually in about two to three days—the brickwork inside the planter should also be coated with bitumen paint

15 Quarry tiles should be laid on top of a thin bed of 1:3 mortar. The mix should be capable of being flattened with a shovel

The staircase can be built in brick or even from wood—providing it is properly treated to protect it from weathering. It can be free-standing—depending for its support on brick pillars or timber stanchions—or bolted to an adjoining wall.

Alternatively, access can be provided from the first floor of the house, either by adapting a suitable window or by cutting a hole through the wall. A door or French window can then be inserted, allowing you to walk directly on to the roof from an upstairs room and adding a new dimension to the room in tne process.

If you decide to adapt an existing window for this purpose, it must be directly above the roof.

In brick-built houses, first remove the existing window and frame. Then run a plumbline down both sides of the opening and carefully mark out the bricks to be removed using a crayon, marking pencil or perhaps a piece of chalk.

Remove the sill and then chop away the bricks, one at a time, using a hammer and bolster. Try to cut a neat vertical line down both sides so that the new door frame can be inserted easily. Some of the brickwork may have to be mortared back into place—especially where a half brick width has been cut away from the existing wall on each side of the opening.

Remove just enough courses of brickwork to ensure a neat watertight

finish. Never cut below the level of the internal floor and try if you can to leave at least two full courses of bricks above the line of the roof on the outside. This will probably mean that the roof is below the level of the existing inside floor—or vice versa.

In timber-framed houses, enlarging an opening is easier—though brick veneer should be dealt with in much the same way as outlined above.

In both cases, ensure that the lintel over the existing window is sound enough to bear the reconstructed opening before starting work.

If there is a large difference between inside and outside levels, then provide steps on the appropriate side of the threshold (fig. E).

Make a sun lounger

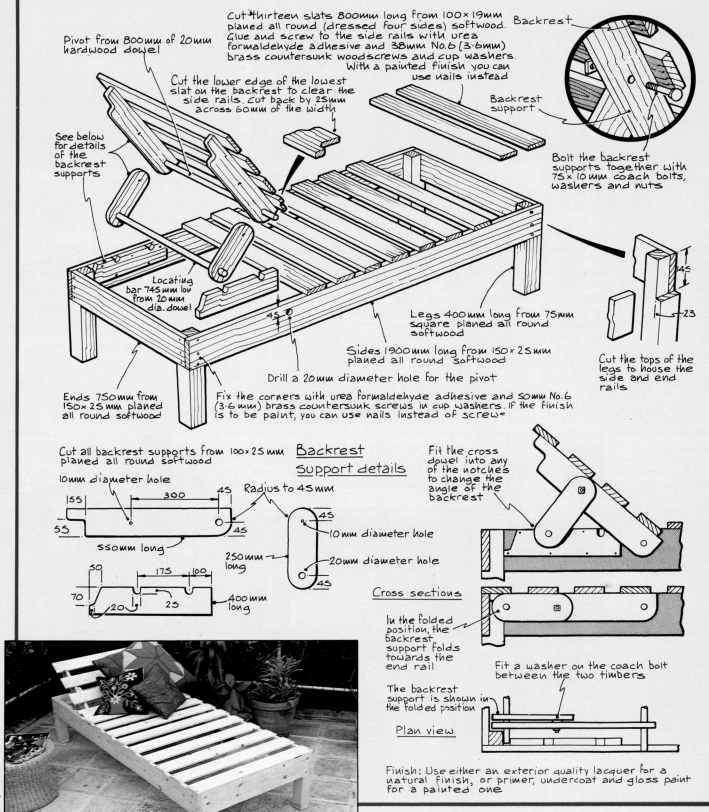

Pivot from 800mm of 20mm hardwood dowel

Cut thirteen slats 800mm long from 100×19mm planed all round (dressed four sides) softwood. Glue and screw to the side rails with urea formaldehyde adhesive and 38mm No.6 (3·6mm) brass countersunk woodscrews and cup washers. With a painted finish you can use nails instead

Backrest

Cut the lower edge of the lowest slat on the backrest to clear the side rails. Cut back by 25mm across 60mm of the width

Backrest support

See below for details of the backrest supports

Bolt the backrest supports together with 75×10mm coach bolts, washers and nuts

Locating bar 745mm long from 20mm dia. dowel

45

Legs 400mm long from 75mm square planed all round softwood

145

23

Sides 1900mm long from 150×25mm planed all round softwood

Drill a 20mm diameter hole for the pivot

Cut the tops of the legs to house the side and end rails

Ends 750mm from 150×25mm planed all round softwood

Fix the corners with urea formaldehyde adhesive and 50mm No.6 (3·6mm) brass countersunk screws in cup washers. If the finish is to be paint, you can use nails instead of screws

Cut all backrest supports from 100×25mm planed all round softwood

Backrest
Support details

10mm diameter hole

155

300

45

Radius to 45mm

55

45

45

550mm long

250mm long

10mm diameter hole

20mm diameter hole

45

50

175

100

70

20

25

400mm long

Fit the cross dowel into any of the notches to change the angle of the backrest

Cross sections

In the folded position, the backrest support folds towards the end rail

The backrest support is shown in the folded position

Fit a washer on the coach bolt between the two timbers

Plan view

Finish: Use either an exterior quality lacquer for a natural finish, or primer, undercoat and gloss paint for a painted one

Ray Duns

Advertising Arts

IMPROVING___ YOUR GARDEN

Planning your garden

Getting the right mix of flowers, shrubs and trees in a house garden is no easy task. It is important to know exactly what kind of atmosphere you want before you start and then build up a design to suit the area available

Below: *A little flair and ingenuity can turn a concrete terrace into a colourful, decorative area where you can sit in peace and comfort. Pots of all shapes and sizes are used to hold a selection of flowers with a wall trellis for climbing plants*

Michael Warren

Because a garden is a practical and visual extension of the house, it is logical to give its style and layout extremely careful consideration. The demands of a garden change with the family life cycle and at some time or another it will probably have to cater for a wide range of activities each requiring an allotted space and a particular design. If you want to include flowers, vegetables, shrubs, trees, a lawn, a terrace, and have privacy as well as children in your garden, achieving a balance is not entirely straightforward.

Of the various outside factors which affect the way you set about planning or replanning your garden, the most important is what exists there already. You may find you have to deal with a garden which has been totally neglected by former owners and you must decide how much effort you are willing to put in to changing it—a general overhaul is quite different from a new landscaping plan.

Another point to bear in mind is that climatic conditions, the location and the soil in your garden will influence the type and style of garden with which you end up. Certain flowers, plants and shrubs will be more suited to your particular conditions than others; if in doubt consult your local garden centre.

Finally there is the immediate environment of your garden. If you

Above: *This elegant leisure garden with its secluded pond has been given extra privacy with a border of tall shrubs.* **Below**: *A pergola with climbing plants provides a peaceful, shady nook for hot summer days*

live in a town and are surrounded by houses or ugly industrial buildings it will probably be important to establish privacy and to try and blot out the worst of the views—high hedges, trees, fences and plant screens being the principal ways of doing this. With all these factors in mind, you can move on to establish the basics of style and layout. After this, there is no end to the visual interest and ornamentation you can achieve; and no space, however small or irregular in shape, need be a restriction.

Determining the style

The visual and practical link between the house and outside is of great importance in determining the style of the garden.

Your first task is to recognize the style of your house. Take careful note of the building materials used: if concrete and bricks are the main elements, you can establish a sense of unity by incorporating these materials in the garden for walls, terraces and paths. On the other hand a cottage or rustic-styled house looks wrong with a predominance of brick or concrete in the garden, however cheap or available these materials may be. A house with a good deal of timber in the structure looks better with timber fences and a timber-framed greenhouse or shed.

The style of the garden depends

Michael Warren

211

also on its surroundings and in a residential area, it pays to blend in your garden to some extent with those around you. Shock-tactic contrasts are seldom successful.

The interior of the house is another major consideration: as the garden is a physical extension of the house, it should in some measure harmonize with it. An English country cottage with small rooms and picturesque furniture does not look right with large terraces and a geometric layout; instead it demands a more ornamental approach with natural stone and perhaps an area of rockery.

By the same rule, asbestos plant pots look out of place in the garden of a brick-faced house. And the more modern interior is better complemented by a streamlined type of garden with the architectural use of plant materials, terraces and paths.

But whatever the style, remember that it will be influenced also by any long-established features such as a break in the level of the plot or a group of trees. Such features tend to serve as indicators of the way a garden will be laid out. They point to whether it requires an open, spacious aspect with a sweeping lawn and herbaceous borders or whether it is more suited to intricacy, cobbles, shrubs and ornamentation. A heavily featured garden might even look in style completely paved over with raised beds and trees highlighted in the artificial surroundings.

Design and layout

Taking style and outside factors into account, the design and layout is going to depend on what you want your garden for—growing flowers, growing vegetables, relaxing, sunbathing, an outside dining area, a children's play area, or a combination of all these.

You must consider also how much terrace you need, how much of the garden you require for vegetables and herbs, how much lawn you want in relation to flower beds and where to site such service areas as sheds, greenhouses and water taps—not to mention special requirements like an enclosed play area, a sandpit, pond or colourful rockery.

Careful planning with the aid of squared paper is essential for roughing out your ideas to get a guideline for shaping and proportioning the plot. But before doing this consider the various possibilities that concern each type of garden and some of the many types of materials and plants you may **require to keep it at its best.**

Michael Warren

The front garden

This needs particular attention in terms of the overall style of the house. Front gardens tend to be showpieces or, at the very least, areas which introduce the visitor or passer-by to the individuality of the house. Most front gardens are too small to use as anything more than a decorative frontage. Nothing looks worse than a bare, shabby area or one that clashes in style with the house itself.

In small, terraced houses the front area often comprises a single brick wall hiding a place to keep dustbins. But even this can be made attractive: you can place window boxes on the front window sills, establish creepers such as clematis, ivy, virginia creeper and honeysuckle on the walls and set a run of flower boxes along the front wall. To increase the exterior greenery still further, plant hardy shrubs— many of which are colourful and need little attention—in one corner. Altogether, these effects give an urban terraced house a very pleasant cottage-like appeal.

Larger front gardens can be used as children's play areas if you want to use the main garden for your own purposes. In this case, you must pay particular attention to the safety factor of the enclosed area: make walls and hedges high enough to keep in children and fit a secure gate.

Another possibility is to pave the

Above: *Make the front garden a showpiece for your home with splashes of colourful flowers and let one colour dominate for extra effect. For instance, these brilliant red salvias provide a dramatic display*

area completely and use it as a place to tinker with cars and motorcycles, or for other practical outdoor activities such as carpentry or the odd painting job the handyman might embark upon.

On more conventional lines, the front garden can go a long way towards setting up the atmosphere of privacy—with high hedges or young saplings on the front border. And, for the green-fingered, the area can greatly enhance the look of the house if it includes a rose bed or two or a bed of colourful flowers.

The flower garden

The garden given over solely to attractive plants and flowers is not for those who dislike gardening. But is a good choice for the keen horticulturist who has only a small garden area; a restricted space does not deny the effect of a profusion of flowers if the garden is properly planned. A few beds assymetrically or geometrically arranged around a small lawn is both practical and attractive, because the flowers and plants themselves make the layout unique.

A flower garden should not normally have a large terraced area but there ought to be some hard surface—such as a path or a narrow terrace—at the back of the house next to an outside tap for use as a solid base on wet days. If there is room, a squared island terrace jutting out from the back of the house will give you a base to sit on warm summer days to enjoy the view of the flowers.

If the design of the garden is to be wholly successful the planting should be worked out as carefully as the layout. There are three basic levels for planting design. The first is the sculptured level with larger plants and shrubs taking up dominant positions; the second level provides the bulk of garden planting including grass and small shrubs against which the third level, the decorative element, is set.

It is particularly important in the flower garden to remember the background effect created by such plants as evergreen shrubs.

But try not to overburden the borders of the garden with high hedges and greenery, as this detracts from the decorative effect of the flowers and restricts the amount of light coming into the garden.

Try to find room for a garden tool shed and possibly a greenhouse within the design. Sheds are best tucked away into corners and made accessible by means of natural stone pathways, paved or even cobbled paths.

The site of the greenhouse will depend to some extent on what you use it for. If you intend growing attractive hot plants such as orchids you might want to bring the greenhouse forward into the visual scheme of things. But if you use it for raising seeds or keeping the odd garden tool in, then a site at the end of the garden might be more suitable.

The vegetable garden

Even in a small garden it is possible to be self-sufficient in flowers and fruit to a fairly large degree. The emphasis should be on practicality and accessibility: allowing yourself enough beds or plot space to work a seasonal rota of growing.

The traditional area for vegetables is at the end of the garden, screened off by a trellis. But nowadays the high price of fruit and vegetables often makes the vegetable garden the central part of the garden layout. In this case, their conspicuous position demands that you grow them in as neat and attractive a form as possible. Give the visual appearance of the garden

Michael Warren

as much consideration as the productivity of what you are growing.

In a small square, or average-sized rectangular garden, a good functional layout is to have three vegetable areas intersected by pathways with the fourth quarter given over to a terrace for a timber-frame garden shed housing essential tools.

You can then plant espaliered fruit trees such as plum, apple and pear around the borders and turn over spare areas at the back of the house to potted strawberries. In Britain, plants such as gooseberries and currants grown fan-like on walls take up little room and are both attractive and productive.

In terms of visual appeal, a combination of herbs and vegetables provides interest throughout the year. Remember that many of these can be grown intensively in containers or raised brick boxes which serve to

Above: *Shrubs and borders of varying heights give a most effective, sculptured look when used together.* **Overleaf**: *Small gardens come to life with short and tall plants in many colours*

ornament the garden. Fruit trees also double as decorative plants—especially if you consider the merits of apple and cherry blossom, or grape vines draped around a pergola.

As with flowers, light is important to the appearance and productivity of vegetables so keep their plot as much to the centre as possible.

The leisure garden

Designing purely for peace, privacy and leisure—with space to sunbathe, eat and give the children free rein—allows a great deal of scope. For a start, it is a good idea to incorporate a large area of terrace—which need not be in one block—especially now that the range of stone flooring, concrete paving and brickwork is so wide and varied.

A combination of terrace, lawn and herbaceous borders with a good deal of shrubbery and the odd tree, is ideal for the leisure garden. But the prime consideration should be the bordering hedges, fences or walls. For extra privacy you can build up small neighbouring walls, either with more of the same brick or by adding a stretch of louvred or interwoven wooden fence to the top of them.

Plenty of shrub and tree foliage is the natural way to increase the sense of isolation and privacy, but a wooden-framed pergola extending over the terrace at the back of the house goes even further. Such a framework should be distinct and simple, and the wood need not necessarily be of the highest quality to be adequate. With a profusion of climbing plants around it, blossoming overhead in spring, a pergola provides an attractive, shady sitting area, a place to eat out of doors or leave a pram on warm, sunny days.

If you are thinking in terms of a play area for the children, a terraced area surrounding a central lawn with a built-up sandpit situated accessibly on one side is a practical answer. This gives the children a circuit for riding tricycles while you have the lawn to yourself for sunbathing.

On more geometric lines, you could extend the terrace down one side of the garden and inset a shallow paddling pool and a sandpit with the rest made over to a lawn and attractive flower border.

The leisure and play garden tends to be one which requires little maintenance, but you could lessen the amount of work even more by concentrating less on flowers for decoration and more on shrubs and trees. There are several hardy, attractive shrubs—rhododendrons, camellias, azaleas, bush roses, lilacs and tree peonies, to mention but a few—which look ideal in eye-catching positions. And once planted, they can be left largely to themselves.

Likewise, trees are most obliging plants: they live longer and grow larger than other plants, they give shade, screen you from neighbours, provide fruit to eat, flowers for decoration and grow while you sleep—sometimes surprisingly quickly. Trees in a new plot, if you choose the right kind, can give the appearance of maturity within only a year or two.

The all-purpose garden

This type of garden, which incorporates something of all the other types, requires a very carefully worked-out balance. To start with, it is probably best to relegate the vegetable garden to its traditional place at the end of the garden and grow a small hedge or build a fence to screen it from the rest. Remember, too, that the garden lawn is usually the dominant feature and that it must be in proportion to the other areas: a small lawn will be incongruously overwhelmed by a large terrace—it is far better the other way round.

In long, narrow plots or awkward L-shaped gardens the shapes lend themselves to the division of the garden into separate areas—often a necessity in the all-purpose garden. It is even possible to accentuate the

garden are the materials used for partitioning and paving. Get these right and even the most varied garden can be prevented from looking too 'patchy' and untidy.

Terraces and fences

When you terrace an area it is best to use a stone, concrete slab or brick that suits your house and its location. Local stone in country areas is worth searching for despite its comparative expense. Brick houses can often take a warm-coloured local stone or brick placed side-on as a terrace and even rather bland concrete can sometimes look good.

Concrete for walls and paving is probably most suited to the garden of a modern house while for a house with delicate features, internal hedges and wooden fences are a good choice— and wooden fences are by far the easiest to erect yourself. You can even carry a bordering palisade fence into the garden to form a wrap-around compost heap.

Brick walls can be matched with brick paths and terraces, arranged in herringbone, diagonal or circular patterns. In the same way, concrete or stone slabs can unify an area if you inset them in the border of the lawn as a path or a pattern. All these materials should be used with three important purposes in mind: to establish the different sections, to lead the eye, and to give continuity of theme to the garden.

Making a plan

Once you have weighed up all the various factors and decided exactly where your needs lie, it is a good idea to make a scale plan of the proposed layout on graph paper.

Start by measuring up the garden and marking this in outline. Follow with the positions of all the immovable objects such as trees, humps, and depressions.

After this, you can start to plot in your proposed features—flower beds, the lawn, paths, terraces. As you make each addition, stop for a moment and think carefully whether it fits in with the rest of the house.

For example, a sunbathing patio will be of no use if it is overshadowed for most of the day. Nor will the children's play area be very safe if you cannot see it from the kitchen or living room window.

Finally, remember that if you try at every turn to make your garden both a physical and practical extension of your home, you can be sure of the very best results.

Above: *A monochrome garden using a variety of interesting shapes and textures is an effective alternative to the colourful flower garden.* **Below**: *Add charm and character to a town house entrance with a selection of plants in pots and window boxes to simulate a garden*

individual areas by dividing them off with hedges, bamboo thickets or saplings so that each can be given its own particular style.

But a more flowing layout could be adopted in a small square garden, perhaps by having a central lawn surrounded by flowers, shrubs, trees and vegetables with the vegetable area occupying a slightly elevated section.

If you have room for a lily pond or fish pond you will find the effects particularly worthwhile: plants and flowers grow in profusion around ponds because they benefit from the reflected sunlight. And like a sandpit, a statue or a tree, a pond provides a highlight for the garden and leads the eye in a particular direction.

Remember that the most important unifying factors in the all-purpose

215

Make a window box

Even a city outlook becomes rural when you bring the garden up to your window sill. Make this simple window box as the basis for a miniature garden.

The most durable timbers are cedar or oak. Ordinary softwood can be used but will need painting as protection against the elements. Do not omit the drainage holes as these are essential for healthy growth. If your sill slopes, fit wedges as shown. In all cases, you should fit safety chains to hold the box in place.

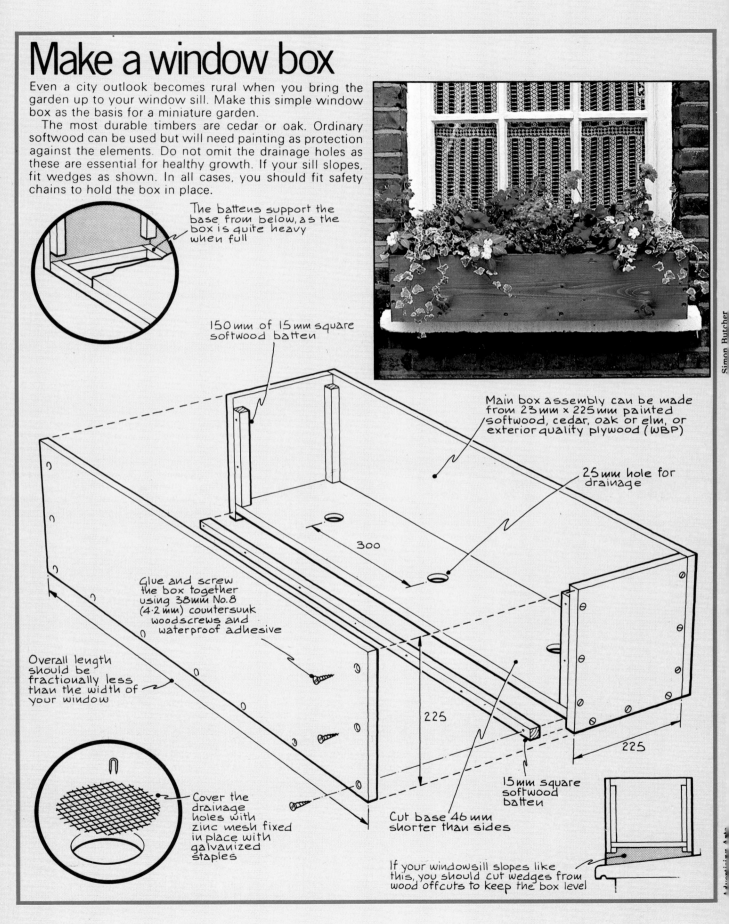

The battens support the base from below, as the box is quite heavy when full

150 mm of 15 mm square softwood batten

Main box assembly can be made from 23 mm x 225 mm painted softwood, cedar, oak or elm, or exterior quality plywood (WBP)

25 mm hole for drainage

300

Glue and screw the box together using 38 mm No.8 (4·2 mm) countersunk woodscrews and waterproof adhesive

Overall length should be fractionally less than the width of your window

225

225

15 mm square softwood batten

Cover the drainage holes with zinc mesh fixed in place with galvanized staples

Cut base 46 mm shorter than sides

If your windowsill slopes like this, you should cut wedges from wood offcuts to keep the box level

Simon Butcher

Building a greenhouse

● **The advantages of building a greenhouse from scratch** ● **Basic considerations to bear in mind** ● **Design and construction of basic lean-to assemblies—one clad with PVC corrugated roofing sheets, and one glazed**

John Ward

In temperate climates, the growing season for many plants in the open is short, and this is bound to restrict your choice of plants and flowers. But a greenhouse can alter the situation completely, enabling plants of many kinds to be grown all the year round. In colder climates, an even greater variety of plants can be propagated and grown if the greenhouse is heated, as this will allow you to grow exotic examples from warmer regions around the world.

A. Above: *A lean-to greenhouse is a pot planter's paradise and an asset to any home. In it you can be 'outside' and relax even when the weather is bad—and it is far cheaper than an extension*

Building your own greenhouse is not a very complicated job, and it permits you to design and tailor the building to suit your individual needs, the requirements of the site, and the plants that you wish to grow. It can also be surprisingly cheap.

Basic considerations

One of the first things to decide is the type of crop to be grown, noting any special requirements; for example, indoor carnations grow best in tall greenhouses, and need more ventilation than most crops. If you are uncertain about the most suitable greenhouse for your needs consult a nursery or an experienced gardener. However, for average purposes, it is usually a matter of selecting a convenient and sunny spot, either making use of an existing wall to build a lean-to greenhouse, or alternatively siting it apart from other buildings as a free-standing unit.

The size and type of greenhouse best suited to your needs are partly governed by the space available, the site itself, the crops and the final cost.

The lean-to type, best sited on an east-west axis in the sun, is usually cheaper to make, to heat (because of its better insulation), and to maintain than a free-standing model of similar size and construction. The mini greenhouse variation can be either a lean-to or free-standing type (see below).

Available space may be further restricted by planning regulations. Structures in front of the building line between the house and the road are normally prohibited in the UK. On the other hand small greenhouses which are less than 3m high and which do not occupy more than half the garden area are not usually subject to planning consent. Unless you are absolutely certain of the planning regulations in your area, you should consult the local council before starting work.

Design and construction

All buildings have a number of important design and construction requirements, and in the case of a greenhouse there are six main considerations.

● **Appearance:** This is influenced by the design and also by the construction materials—usually wood and glass.

● **Strength and durability:** A greenhouse should be capable of withstanding the worst possible conditions of wind, sun, storms, frost and snow. Timber glazing bars, for example, should ideally not be less than 20mm deep for a 1m span, and the depth should be increased by 12mm for each additional 500mm of span.

● **Light:** Maximum light is of course necessary all the year round so avoid narrowly spaced glazing bars, aiming for intervals of between 450mm and 750mm.

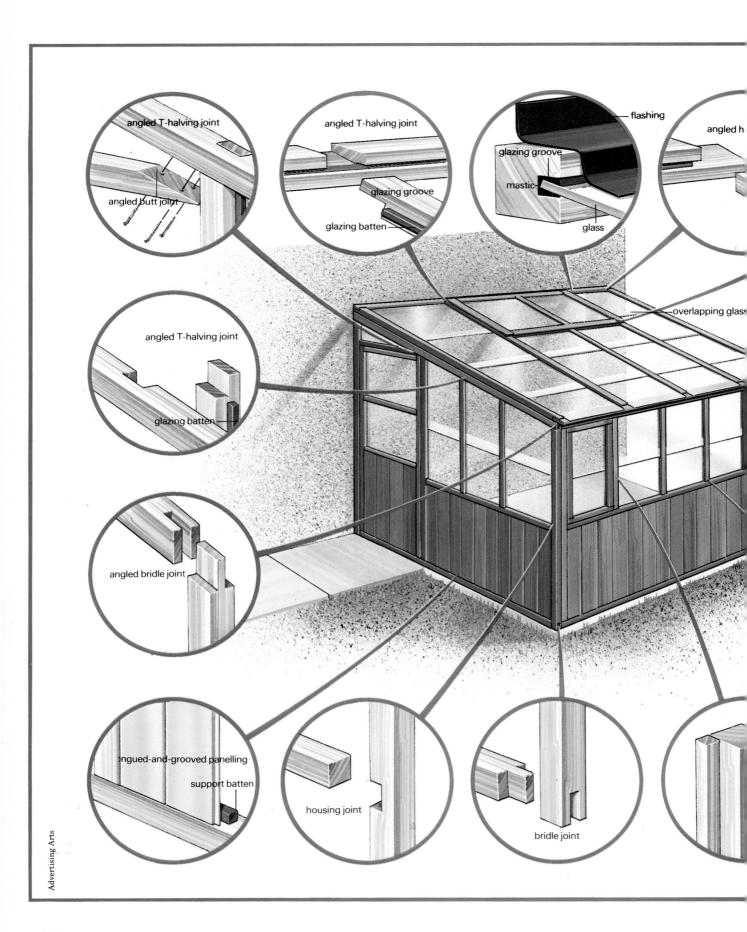

angled T-halving joint

angled butt joint

angled T-halving joint

glazing groove

glazing batten

flashing

glazing groove

mastic

glass

angled h

angled T-halving joint

glazing batten

overlapping glas

angled bridle joint

ongued-and-grooved panelling

support batten

housing joint

bridle joint

Alternative constructions

The glazed and boarded greenhouse **(left)** has been designed as simply as possible so that it can be constructed with a minimum of time and effort. The generous eaves height of 1520mm and a ridge height of 2130mm ensures adequate headroom, especially around the edges at bench or staging level where plants are sited. And the width of 2330mm allows considerable freedom of movement.

The timber section for the standard sized greenhouse should be at least 50mm × 50mm for all structural components and 75mm × 50mm for the door posts. The door battens should be 25mm × 25mm and the glazing beading should be 16mm × 16mm.

The measurements can be adapted according to your requirements, especially the length. If the design is extended in this way some extra reinforcing will be necessary mid-way along the roof and side. A glazing bar can be replaced by a 75mm × 50mm timber and a cross bar at the side would add rigidity and strength. A similar stout piece of timber should be inserted mid-way along the side section.

Throughout the design two main glass widths—460mm and 610mm—are used. The window and roof glass, it must be noted, is installed in 'modules' as nearly square as possible. This means in effect that the glass is panelled. For instance, on the roof each run of glass between timbers consists of four panes of overlapping glass.

In the case of a PVC sheet clad greenhouse (below) the timber section should be at least 50mm × 50mm. The hardwood corner posts should be 75mm × 75mm, but you can get away with 50mm × 25mm for the wall plate and vertical wall timbers.

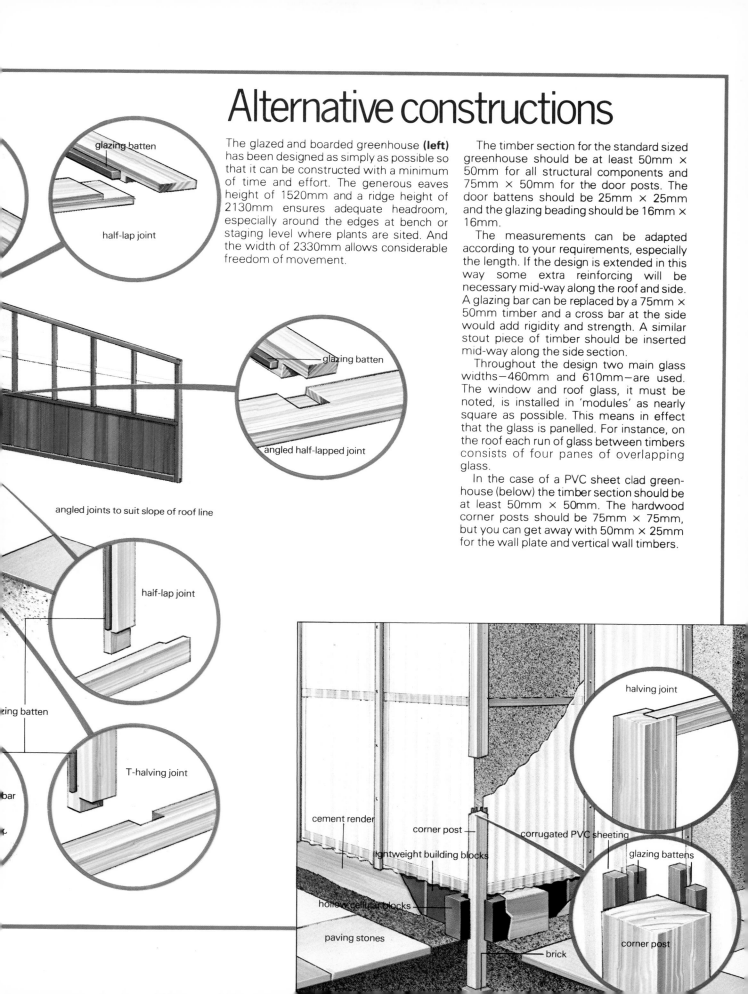

glazing batten

half-lap joint

glazing batten

angled half-lapped joint

angled joints to suit slope of roof line

half-lap joint

zing batten

T-halving joint

bar

halving joint

cement render

corner post

corrugated PVC sheeting

lightweight building blocks

glazing battens

hollow cellular blocks

paving stones

corner post

brick

● **Ventilation:** This is critical, and trials have shown that the total ventilator area should ideally not be less than 15 percent or one-sixth of the floor space.

● **Ease of construction:** It is very important that a greenhouse project does not demand great expense on tools and materials, and in this respect a timber frame is a good choice.

● **Low maintenance:** Costs need to be kept in mind, and simplicity of design, combined with sound construction techniques are of great importance.

Comparison with kits

When deciding whether to erect a proprietary kit greenhouse, or to build a home made unit, the acid test for most people boils down to cost; but to make a valid comparison you have to take into account many factors, including quality, design, construction and durability. Often the kit price excludes such items as the base, the glass and delivery, so the comparison must be made on the cost of the different greenhouses erected on site complete. This way you can make a fair assessment of relative costs.

The materials for a typical built-from-scratch greenhouse are no more than half of the price of a similar kit. And, given that you can take satisfaction from your own labour, making a greenhouse is still an economically worthwhile proposition.

Nature and scope of the models

Although this article describes how to build two lean-to types of greenhouse, a free-standing span or apex type with a high central ridge or a mini greenhouse can also be made with certain modifications.

Timber is excellent for the main structure because it is versatile and easy to work with, and presents few problems with either glazing or cladding. Also, less condensation forms on wooden frames than on metal ones because they retain a more even temperature. Given the occasional treatment with paint or preservative, timber structures can last 20 to 30 years and more.

Softwood should be treated with a horticultural grade of preservative containing copper napthanate (in the UK, a suitable choice would be Cuprinol). Special attention should be paid to joints and those parts of the building which are in contact with the ground. These should be soaked for a few hours in a container of the solution. Long timbers such as bottom plates can be laid on a long sheet of polyethylene gathered along the corners and edges to form a receptacle or bag into which preservative is poured.

Although it costs about 50 percent more, cedar wood is a timber which

requires little treatment or maintenance because it has a natural oil which resists decay and is ideal for outdoor use.

Both the lean-to greenhouse designs are made up of four sections – two ends, the front and the roof. The designs as shown are adequate for a greenhouse with an eaves height of 1.52m, a ridge height of 2.13m and a width of 2.33m. This should allow considerable freedom of movement, but the measurements can easily be adapted to your own requirements, especially the length. However, if and when altering sizes, keep in mind the standard sizes of cladding materials: this avoids needless cutting and subsequent waste. Also, when building larger structures, heavier timbers and bracing are necessary for extra strength.

The four frames of the greenhouse can be assembled in one or two ways. The

frames can be made up separately, then bolted together and screwed to the wall. Alternatively, the wall timbers or studs can be screwed to the wall first, and the framework then constructed in situ. The frame can later be glazed or clad with PVC corrugated roofing sheet (such as Novolux in the UK). Standard 4mm thick glass is adequate for glazing and this should be installed in 'modules' as nearly square as possible. This means in effect that the glass is panelled. For instance, on the roof, each run of glass between timbers consists of three panes of overlapping glass. This avoids the use of large panes of glass which are both vulnerable and difficult to instal.

When planning the greenhouse, remember to allow extra for the width of glass or PVC sheeting 'lost' in channelling grooves or housings.

1 First prepare the site, providing an even bed of hardcore which should be well tamped down, and paint the back wall with a weatherproof agent

2 Having cut the back horizontal and vertical timbers and applied a timber preservative, fix the horizontal wall plate with long coach bolts

3 Once the loadbearing wall plate has been fixed the vertical back frame can be secured to the wall using masonry nails

4 Lay a single course of lightweight building blocks then mortar treated posts into the hollow corner blocks. Make sure that the posts are vertical

5 *In order to save much wasteful trimming of the cladding material, it makes sense to use it as a guide when actually building the structure*

6 *The bottom plate of the front frame is a structural component and so it should be firmly fixed to the building blocks with wall anchors*

7 *At this stage apply a liberal amount of timber preservative to the bottom plate, making quite certain that you treat all cuts and end grain*

Making the four frames is very simple. The essence of the separate parts is that they are self-bracing, in other words they have an intrinsic strength in their un-assembled state. The following is only a guide however, and you should feel free to modify the construction if you want to change the dimensions.

End frame: Using planed softwood timber, cut the base, top, back and front to size then make half-lap angle joints at the ends using a tenon saw and chisel. Make T-halving joints to take the upright and horizontal timbers; these in turn are then cut to size with half-lap joints at the ends. The joints in the top rail must of course be cut to the appropriate angle.

In all cases, paint the prepared cuts with preservative before putting them together. Drill and countersink two screw holes at each joint to take the appropriate screws. Do, however, avoid drilling too deep or the screws will have an insufficient grip. Finally assemble the timber sections and screw them together, making sure that the bottom corners are perfectly square.

End frame with door: Preparation and assembly of the parts is the same as for the first end frame, but with three differences. The lower horizontal timber cross rail from the front stops at the centre upright instead of running through to the back. This allows for the door. Also necessary is a projecting vertical door stop fixed behind the centre upright and aligned with the door.

The door itself is made from two uprights, fixed to three cross pieces with half-lap joints at the ends and T-halving joints in the centre. Drill and countersink the appropriate screws as before. Then fix three 150mm 'T' hinges to the cross members of the door. The door should not actually be hung until the end frames are

8 *Once the preservative is dry, set the bottom plate on the building blocks. Make sure that it is flat then render the building block course*

fastened to the wall, but check that the door fits the frame before erecting the structure and adjust as necessary.

Front frame: Cut the four upright timbers to the correct length, making T-halving joints in the centres. Then cut the top, centre and base members, with half-lap end joints, plus two evenly spaced T-halving joints on each. Paint all joints with preservative and allow this to dry before drilling and countersinking to take two screws at each joint. Finally, assemble and screw the timbers together, making sure that the corners are square and that the bottom plate is laid flat side down like those of the end frames. If you decide to put a door in the front frame, follow the instructions given above. As before, do not hang the door until the structure is complete, but do make sure that it fits the frame before moving on to assemble the greenhouse.

9 *The PVC roofing sheets can be secured to the structure either with battens or in grooves – the latter being easy to make with a circular saw*

10 *The essence of the greenhouse structure is that the frame is self-bracing. The front top plate is thus nailed to the front corner posts*

Roof: Repeat as for the front frame, with the addition of a ventilator seating. Cut the ventilator seating timber with half-lap joints at each end and screw this securely into the extended half-lap joints of the two centre timbers. Because of the sloping roof it is necessary to chamfer the back timber by about 7°, just sufficiently to allow it to butt squarely against the wall when fixed to the wall plate. Make the ventilator frame in the same way as the door, with the necessary size adjustments. Fix two 150mm strap hinges to the roof frame for the ventilator and make sure that it is a good weatherproof fit.

Foundations
The base of the greenhouse must be raised above the ground level, to keep it clear of surface water.

11 *Where thin section timbers are butt or halving jointed it is best to secure them with a screw. Always drill holes to avoid splitting the wood*

12 *Housing joints are normally skew-nailed, but a galvanized steel angle bracket screwed under the joint provides added strength*

If you are building on soil then you will have to dig a foundation to provide a base, the top of which should be at least 25mm above ground level.

It may be that there will be an existing foundation of sorts, in the form of a driveway, path or patio. Providing this consists of paving slabs or concrete laid over a hardcore base it will be adequate, although the level will still have to be raised to the proper height.

One way of doing this is to fit a form-work of 25mm × 25mm battening around the base and fill it with concrete. If you use this method, you must ensure that the new concrete bonds well to the existing surface by coating the latter with a solution of PVA bonding agent.

An alternative is to 'build' the base by laying paving slabs or a layer of bricks—with mortared joints in between them—on the top of the existing surface.

Whichever method you choose, the finished surface must be painted with a proprietary waterproof sealing compound (such as Aquaseal 40 Heavy Duty) to damp-proof it.

The base must be absolutely level when finished otherwise the wooden frames of the greenhouse will be at staggered heights when you come to assemble them and therefore they will not fit.

A far simpler method of isolating the timber frame from the ground is to build a single course of lightweight building blocks on top of a shallow 150mm concrete foundation, then lay the bottom plates on the frames. Using this method, the two front corner posts, suitably preserved, may be anchored into hollow blocks, and the rest of the structure constructed about these (fig. 4). If the course is continued around the floor area, there will be a step at the base of the door.

13 *Alternatively, screw through joints after drilling and plugging the end grain of the longitudinal timber to avoid splitting it with the screw*

If you feel that this is a disadvantage, the blocks and bottom plate can be constructed with a cutout for the door. However, without the step it will be very difficult to both keep the door away from the rot-inducing soil, and to make the greenhouse draughtproof.

The receiving wall
The wall to which the greenhouse is attached should, ideally, be absolutely vertical. Unfortunately few walls are. If the wall is less than 12mm out of plumb, the gap can be filled with a bricklaying mortar. But, if it is over 12mm or you do not want a wedge-shaped mortar gap, then you will have to shape three lengths of 50mm × 50mm timber (two vertical battens support the two end frames, and the horizontal batten—the wall plate—supports the roof) so that they form a vertical surface to which the greenhouse frame will be attached. Carefully use the scribing technique then, having laid a thick layer of sealing mastic or compound along the wall and the timber where the surfaces will meet, screw the timber firmly to the wall with wall plugs or large bolts.

Construction
All the joints should be both glued and screwed, using a waterproof adhesive such as urea formaldehyde and either brass, galvanized or japanned screws. The glass or PVC sheeting can be housed either between narrow wooden battens or in glazing grooves cut with a plough plane, router or power saw.

Assembly
Drill the back plate of one end frame and fix it to the vertical timber attached to the wall, then do the same at the other end frame. Move the front frame into place, drilling and fixing the base to the bolts (which are set in concrete). Drill and screw the ends of the front frame to the respective front timbers of the end frames. The shell of the greenhouse is then ready to receive the roof frame. This should be drilled and fixed to the end and front frames as well as to the wall plate, and when fitting it, you should make quite sure that the frame is flush with the wall to avoid distortion.

PVC
To clad the frame first lay one sheet of PVC roofing on the ventilator (if fitted), bedding it down on foam eaves filler and fixing it with nails and washers. Then fix the casement stay and hinges. Carefully position and secure the remainder of the PVC sheets to the roof, using eaves filler, and securing them with screws and washers.

14 The PVC sheet can be cut using an abrasive disc fitted to a circular saw or saw attachment. Use a stout length of timber as a fence

15 When fixing the PVC cladding, support the sheets from below and from behind then drill through them and into the supporting timber

16 Use pre-formed polystyrene eaves filler strips when fitting the roof to provide rigidity and also to draughtproof the greenhouse

Fix PVC sheeting to the door frame in the same way as to the ventilator, then fix the door in place, making sure that it opens and closes freely. When covering the ends, it is necessary to measure carefully then cut the PVC sheet to shape using a fine toothed saw.

Glazing

The method of overlapping glass panes is quite simple. First press a bed of putty along the glazing beading shelf, then press the bottom pane of glass into the putty. Now hold the next higher pane where it will be fixed, and mark the sides of the structure where the bottom of the pane will be located.

Put the pane aside for the time being and drive a 25mm nail into each side of the woodwork immediately next to the lower pane, level with the marks, until just about 6mm of the head is still protruding. You now have two metal stops on which the next pane can rest while it is puttied in position. The process is repeated for successive panes. There are several types of proprietary clips that are made for joining overlapping glass sheets, but they all suffer from the same disadvantage – the final pane often has to be cut to fit. The nail method, on the other hand, allows you as little or as much overlap as you need.

Where a structure abuts against a wall you must provide a run-off for rain water at the junction point. This flash could be zinc, lead or copper chased into the mortar, but a simpler alternative is to use self-adhesive flashing.

Door catches, handles and the ventilator stay add the finishing touches, along with weatherboarding, which should be nailed over the roof ends and treated with preservative.

17 The window sill is fixed above the bottom cladding to provide a weather seal. All metal fittings must be of a type suitable for outdoor use

Variations on the basic theme

Mini greenhouse: A smaller version of the lean-to greenhouse, this is tended from the outside and has one or more opening doors at the front. Usually, this type of greenhouse is essentially a modified lean-to in which similar methods of construction to the basic design are used, with twin doors placed centrally and no end door.

The internal height should be at least 1500mm so that shelving can be fitted to double the effective area, allowing 700mm headroom for plants on each level.

Apex or span: This is a free-standing model which rises to a central ridge and it can be constructed along the lines of two lean-tos placed back to back.

The necessary modifications include a central ridge with capping, a central door in one end, and side and end bracing to provide rigidity.

18 One great advantage of cladding the greenhouse with PVC roof sheeting is that it can be stretched or squashed to take up minor adjustments

19 With the end of the roof butted against the backing wall, the joint can be made weathertight with a timber batten, mastic and self-adhesive flashing

Building a garden shed

● **The advantages of building your own garden shed** ● **Designing the shed** ● **Siting the foundations** ● **Constructing the floor** ● **Making the wall frames** ● **Adding the roof** ● **Cladding** ● **Doors and windows**

Simon Butcher

A garden shed is a versatile supplement to any home, serving the multiple purposes of storeroom, planthouse and garden feature. As a storeroom, it is ideal for bulky items such as bicycles, deckchairs, lawnmowers, and decorating equipment—things that would be out of place inside the house. As a workroom, it offers a space to store poisonous chemicals and dangerous tools—though in this case the door should have a secure lock—and an area where messy or noisy projects can be undertaken without disturbing the rest of the household.

Whatever your requirements, there are two ways to acquire a shed that will meet them. You can either build one from your

A. Above: *A garden shed is a highly practical and attractive addition to any house. This design, although not cheap, is extremely flexible*

own design and to suit your pocket, or else purchase a prefabricated kit which can be fitted together on a prepared site.

Prefabricated kits are available at prices that are competitive with the price you would pay for the raw materials, and in a wide range of sizes and styles. Designs vary but—despite their obvious advantages—these types of shed will not offer you the versatility, or the satisfaction, that would come from designing and building your own.

However, they are light and easy to assemble and are supplied with all the fittings—such as bolts, hinges, brackets and roofing felt—as well as suggestions for the type of foundation to use. If your time is limited, it is well worth examining this possibility. Even if you decide against it, studying prefabricated kits will suggest features you may not have previously considered.

Designing your own

Designing your own shed is a way of ensuring that you get what you want, and you can adapt it to the purposes for which you intend to use it. If you need it only for storage, consider the size and amount of equipment, and how best to arrange it. If you want a work area, consider the nature and position of the window. Bear in mind that a work bench would benefit from direct light but that the window should be at least 150mm above the work surface to avoid damage. For germinating or growing more sensitive plants, such as tomatoes or peppers, large windows which face the sun or a roof light would be an advantage.

The shed shown in fig. A is a good working model to base your design upon. It is a functional but sturdy and attractive shed intended for storage and general DIY projects. It is constructed in six sections: the floor on to which the four walls are screwed; the four wall frames which bolt together at the corners; and the roof. The size and position of its 50mm × 50mm vertical and horizontal members make them ideal for bearing shelves or as lateral supports for a work surface.

Additional horizontal members on the walls at appropriate heights provide support for tool-holders made from dowelling. These are simple and handy fixtures for supporting long handled tools such as rakes, hoes and brushes. Incorporate them in positions which will not interfere with work surfaces or shelves. When the shed is completed, use a 9mm wood bit to drill holes 25mm deep at 75mm centres on the horizontal member. Cut a length of 9mm dowelling into 75mm or 100mm lengths and smear a small amount of PVA woodworking adhesive on the end of each of them. Insert these into the holes, tapping them into position with a mallet. To avoid wastage, use a tenon saw to cut 12mm down the diameter of the dowel before you apply the adhesive. This will retain the adhesive rather than squeezing it out of the hole.

1 *Having levelled the ground below the shed, lay the completed base frame in position and check that it is square by measuring both diagonals*

2 *The joists must be well preserved, preferably by soaking them in bags of preservative. Use chocks to ensure that the frame is in fact level*

3 *Next screw the sheets of flooring grade chipboard to the frame, countersinking all the screws and overlapping the sheets over the joists*

4 *The walls are constructed using only halving joints and stopped housing joints. First assemble the frame 'dry' and check that it is properly square*

5 *Then glue and screw each of the outside corners, using two screws at each to prevent the frame from moving diagonally and distorting*

6 *The angle of the roof slope in this design is 13° from the vertical. To start with set this angle on a sliding bevel using a protractor*

The door is the only prefabricated element in the design. This is a 1.8m × 750mm boarded framed door, wide enough to allow a heavy lawn mower to be moved easily in and out of the shed. Though you could make a matching door by nailing shiplap cladding to ledges and braces, reasonably priced standard components are readily available. Use these to cut down the amount of work wherever it is feasible to do so. A further possibility is to purchase prefabricated windows. This would eliminate the really time consuming work, especially if you decide that you need openable windows.

Buy all these ready-made components before you begin work so that you can design and build the walls with openings of the correct dimensions.

When deciding on the size of a shed, consider the headroom you will need. Bear in mind that a ridged roof entails more work and careful thought, but will provide more headroom. A simpler alternative would be a single pitch roof sloping away from the wall in which the window is fitted.

Siting the foundations
Prepare a site for the shed in a position that is unobtrusive yet accessible. Corners are ideal because they are the least used part of the garden. Try to minimize the amount of space that the shed encroaches upon by siting it in an otherwise dead area.

Prepare the site by levelling the ground and clearing obstructions. Excavate the topsoil to a depth of 150mm over an area 200mm larger than the area of the shed. Insert shuttering boards so that you can lay a concrete raft in the normal way but so that the edges extend 50mm beyond the area that the shed will occupy. Lay 75mm of hardcore in the trench, leaving a gap around the edges. Pack this down and cover it with a polyethylene sheet which will act as a damp proof course. Lay 75mm of concrete membrane on top of this in the normal way and thoroughly tamp down the surface, especially at the edges. This will provide a raft foundation that is thicker at the edges (where it supports the walls) than it is in the centre.

A different method for providing a base is to lay normal paving slabs in the same way as you would for a patio or path. Make sure the surface is truly level so that it gives as much support to the floor joists as possible. Alternatively, lay 200mm deep concrete foundations at the two short ends of the shed and one at its centre. Make these appropriate to the width of the shed and at least 200mm wide. When it has set, lay a damp proof

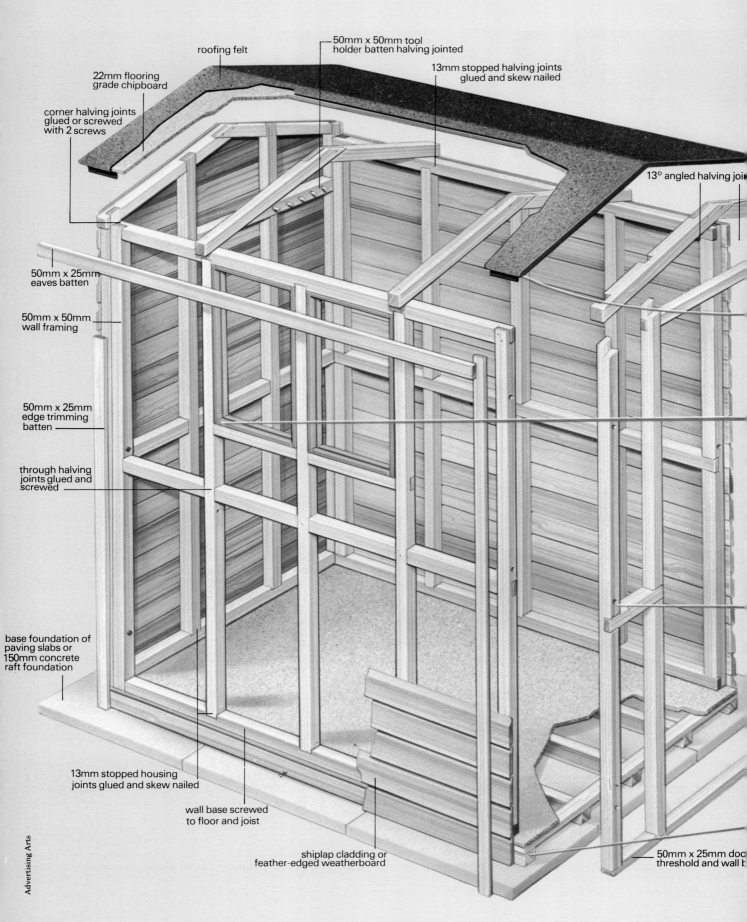

roofing felt

50mm x 50mm tool holder batten halving jointed

13mm stopped halving joints glued and skew nailed

22mm flooring grade chipboard

corner halving joints glued or screwed with 2 screws

13° angled halving join

50mm x 25mm eaves batten

50mm x 50mm wall framing

50mm x 25mm edge trimming batten

through halving joints glued and screwed

base foundation of paving slabs or 150mm concrete raft foundation

13mm stopped housing joints glued and skew nailed

wall base screwed to floor and joist

shiplap cladding or feather-edged weatherboard

50mm x 25mm doo threshold and wall b

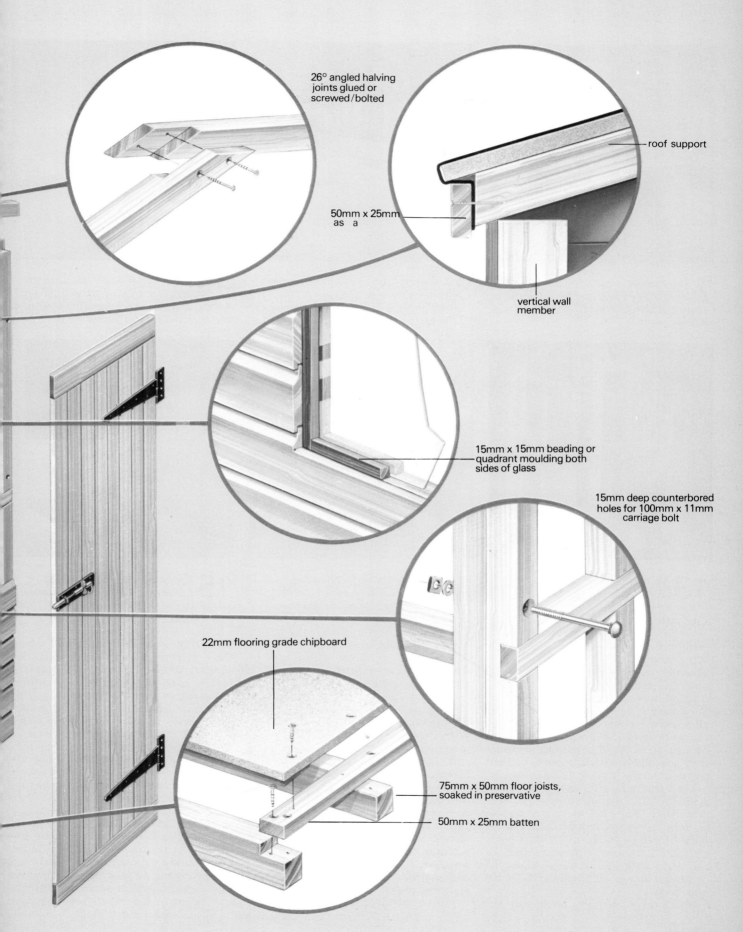

26° angled halving joints glued or screwed/bolted

roof support

50mm x 25mm as a

vertical wall member

15mm x 15mm beading or quadrant moulding both sides of glass

15mm deep counterbored holes for 100mm x 11mm carriage bolt

22mm flooring grade chipboard

75mm x 50mm floor joists, soaked in preservative

50mm x 25mm batten

7 *Mark the vertical wall members with the sliding bevel and cut all of them out at the same time. Then trim the joints with a chisel*

8 *The gable end roof supports are joined with a halving joint. The correct angle is 26° and all should be cut at the same time with an overlap*

9 *Glue the joint then fix the support timbers together with three screws, having drilled and countersunk the holes and then cut off the horns*

Simon Butcher

13 *Make absolutely sure that the walls follow the floor exactly then insert a carriage bolt, secure it loosely, then repeat this at each corner*

14 *Once all corners have been bolted loosely, insert the rest of the bolts and tighten up. Screw the walls to the floor frame with 90mm screws*

15 *Position the edge trimming batten accurately, using a piece of the shiplap cladding as a guide, then nail it securely in place*

membrane over the concrete and screw or bolt 75mm by 50mm timber bearers— liberally soaked in preservative—to the concrete, using wall plugs to hold it in position. Rag bolts or steel strips set into the concrete before it dries provide an alternative method of securing the timber bearers. However, you must make careful calculations if you are to ensure that the bolts will correspond to their positions on the bearers.

Yet another alternative—one also supplied by manufacturers of pre-fabricated kits—is to use concrete bearers, either on independent foundations like those above, or on brick piers. This is a particularly useful method for installing a shed on very uneven ground because it allows you to extend above the unevenness.

In all three methods, make sure the

base is flat and level. Ensure that the bearers are correctly positioned by checking them with a spirit level, if necessary using a long length of straight batten to stretch from one pier to the next.

The floor

With the foundation or base for the shed prepared, construct the floor, making sure that the size corresponds to the external dimensions of the wall frames.

Use 50mm × 75mm timber for the floor joists. Cut these to length and notch each end of the joists to accept a 50mm × 25mm batten. This will help to keep the floor square and the joists in their correct position while you position the floor covering. It also offers a support to the edges of the end floorboards where they span the joists.

Aim to provide joists at 300mm centres

to ensure that the floor will be able to bear the weight of any heavy garden equipment. Before joining the joists to the batten, soak all the timbers in a strong preservative such as creosote, paying particular attention to the end grains. Try to soak as much as possible of the timber in the preservative for at least 24 hours.

With the timber prepared, screw the batten in position on the joists, checking the diagonal measurements to make sure that the frame is square and true. Place the frame on to the foundations using a spirit level to ensure that it lies level on its supports. If necessary, pack up low sections with spare pieces of timber, again soaked in preservative.

When using piers or strip foundations that contain bearers, screw the joists to the bearers. L-brackets at the four

10 *It is most important that the joints are finished smooth and flush to allow the roofing sheets to fit flush, so trim them with a smoothing plane*

11 *Mark the position of the vertical members directly on to the roof support, then cut out the through halving joints and dry assemble*

12 *Hold two adjacent frames exactly in position with clamps, then drill and countersink holes for the fixing bolts*

16 *Next thread a length of twine tautly between the two gable ends to guide the positioning of the intermediate roof supports*

17 *With the roof supports in place fix the chipboard covering, allowing eaves and ends to overlap. Mitre the abutting edges to fit*

18 *Next position the first sheet of roofing felt over the chipboard, allowing a 180mm edge overlap, and fix it with galvanized flat heads*

corners will be sufficient to prevent any possible movement.

Use 100mm × 19mm tongued-and-grooved floorboards to cover the joists, or the cheaper and quicker flooring grade sheets of chipboard. If you use tongued-and-grooved floorboards, nail the first board in position, then cramp the subsequent boards – in threes or fours – tightly together against the first. Use two 50mm oval or floorboard nails to secure each board to each floor joist.

To cramp the boards tight, use sash cramps (bar clamps) or folding wedges. To use wedges for this purpose, nail the first board in position then place three subsequent boards alongside it. Cut four wedges from some spare 50mm × 50mm timber and nail a length of scrap timber alongside the loose floorboards, parallel to them but less than 100mm away from

the last one. Insert the two pairs of wedges between the scrap timber and the loose floorboards, tapping them with a hammer or mallet. The wedges will cramp the floorboards together against the first one. Use 50mm oval nails or floor brads to secure the floorboards before you remove the folding wedges, then remove the wedges and the scrap timber. Continue in this way – cramping three boards at a time – until the floor is complete. Punch the nail heads below the surface of the boards.

When using chipboard as a surface drill and countersink the holes at 200mm intervals along each joist. Use 33mm or 50mm countersunk screws to secure the chipboard to the joists. Bear in mind that only standard size sheets are available and that you may have to cut the sheets to size in order to cover the floor completely.

If this is the case, butt joint the sheets above a joist so that each sheet is adequately supported.

The wall frames

With the floor complete and in position, construct the wall frames. Make each frame separately using 50mm × 50mm timber throughout, and halving joists or stopped housing joists rather than butt joints; this allows you to dry assemble the structure as you proceed, and in this way you can keep a continuing check on the sizes and dimensions.

When each frame is complete, dry assemble it, checking it along the length of its diagonal measurements to make sure that it is square. Both diagonal measurements should be equal.

To ensure that the frame maintains its shape while you assemble the rest of the structure, glue and screw the corner joints first, using two screws for each corner. Tap home the intermediate vertical members, gluing and skew nailing (toe nailing) them to the top and base plates of the walls. Aim to provide vertical members at 400mm centres but adjust the positions to suit the dimensions of your shed.

A horizontal member at a point 900mm from the floor may seem unnecessary, but it will provide a very positive lateral support to the vertical members as well as offering a support for a work surface or bench. Incorporate such a timber into all four walls as you assemble them, again using halving joints.

Similar horizontal members for supporting shelves or tool-holders should also be incorporated at this stage. If you mark up all the joints at once, using a marking gauge and try square, chopping them out systematically with a chisel and mallet will save a great deal of time.

The shed shown in fig. A is designed so that the two short walls have integral gable ends. All four of the roof bearers—the two gable ends and the two intermediate roof bearers—are constructed at the same time to ensure a uniformity of angle. Each joist contains a 26° angled halving joint at the ridge, while the vertical bearers which support the roof are cut with 13° angled halving joints.

An alternative is to make all four walls rectangular, adding the ridge and gable ends separately. If you choose to adopt this method make all four walls the same height and add roof braces and the roof itself after all the walls are in position.

With all four wall frames complete, including openings for the door and windows, place two adjoining walls in position with the help of an assistant. Adjust them until they correspond to the edges of the floor, then use a G-cramp (C-clamp) to hold them temporarily.

Join the frames at each corner with three 100mm M9 coach bolts and countersink the heads (fig. 12). Do the same at all four corners then, with the frame erect, use 75mm or 100mm screws to screw the base plates of each wall to the floor. This will complete the shell of the shed on to which the cladding can be nailed.

Alternatively, nail the cladding—feather-edged weatherboard or shiplap cladding—to the frames before you erect them. Bear in mind, though, that each wall section will be much heavier and that you will need to bolt through the cladding as well as through the corner sections. In most cases, this will mean using longer bolts. In addition, temporarily clamping the clad sections together will demand the attention of at least two people whereas the skeletal

19 Secure the second sheet of roofing felt as before, nailing at 150mm centres, then fit a smaller capping piece across the apex of the roof

Simon Butcher

23 Similarly, having cut the gable end trimming pieces to size, nail them in place, sandwiching the felt behind to create a waterproof join

frames can be easily manipulated by one person. With either method, you will be able to dismantle each wall section as a complete unit simply by unscrewing the coach bolts from the inside.

The roof

The shed shown in fig. A is designed so that the end walls determine the pitch of the roof. The gable ends are integral to the end walls, with two corresponding intermediate roof bearers screwed to the top of the long walls. If you use this method, use a string line stretched between the end walls to determine the correct position of the intermediate bearers (fig. 16). Flooring grade chipboard, cut to size with an allowance for a 50mm overlap at the eaves and gables, then covered with roofing felt, completes the roof.

20 Having clad the framework with the shiplap panelling, cut the length below the roof to the correct size and cut it to fit the supports

24 Nail the window beading in place around the frame then glaze the windows using a putty bed and fixing the glass in place with beading

If you construct rectangular walls of equal height you will need to erect a ridge with a roof bearing framework to support the roofing material.

A single-pitch roof presents fewer problems but has the disadvantage of a much less attractive appearance and, generally, less head room. Simply build one side wall—preferably a wall containing a window—higher than its opposite counterpart. Run roof joists from one wall to the other, either screwing through them into the tops of the wall, or cutting birdsmouth joints. Alternatively, use simple steel twist brackets screwed to the joist and to the wall frame.

Whichever roof you choose, use chipboard as a covering, leaving an overlap of 50mm beyond the ends of the roof supports. This 50mm overlap can accommodate a 50mm × 25mm fascia which

21 *Cut the felt at the corners and fold and tack both pieces around the roofing sheets in order to prevent water from running over the timber*

22 *Having cut the eaves board to size nail it to the ends of the roof support timbers, sandwiching the roof felt against the cladding*

25 *Screw the sliding door bolt in place on the door, then, having determined the position of the receiving part, screw it in position on the frame*

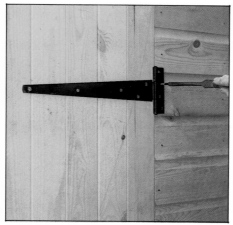

26 *Attach the T-hinges to the door then screw the hinge to the shed, making sure that the screws are long enough to penetrate the frame*

gives an attractive finish to both gutter and eave level as well as protecting the edge of the roofing felt (fig. 22). Screw the chipboard to the roof frame with 33mm countersunk screws at 200mm centres and cover the whole with at least two layers of roofing felt. Use flat-headed galvanized nails to secure the felt to the chipboard and give added protection to the ridge of the roof by adding a narrow strip of felt as a capping section.

Cladding

Certain grades of exterior hardboard sheets can be used as a cladding for a garden shed but this is not the most attractive material for this purpose. A far more common choice is either feather-edged weatherboard (wedge-shaped in section), or interlocking shiplap cladding.

Weatherboard is popular in shed con-struction because it weathers well and has a sturdy rustic appearance. When in position, each board overlaps the one beneath it by 25mm to 35mm to form a sheltered joint free from capillary action. Secure each board to the frame separately so that each board can expand and contract without cracking. Use 33mm or 50mm oval nails.

The corners – and the end grains of the boards are protected by edge trimming battens which are nailed into position before the boards are nailed to the frames. The edge trimming battens should be thicker than the boards and positioned so that they extend beyond the face of both boards (fig. 15). Shiplap cladding is protected at the corners in a similar way. However, methods for fixing these two types of boards differ. Shiplap cladding comprises softwood boards

milled and rebated to interlock. They provide a weatherproof and attractive exterior that can be treated with varnish, preservative or paint to create the desired effect. With edge trimming battens in position, fitting them to the framework is simply a matter of cutting them to length and slotting them together. Use galvanized nails to secure each board separately to the 50mm × 50mm wall frames, placing the nails 12mm above the joint between boards.

Doors and windows

If you use prefabricated door and window frames, screw the frames to the walls before you fit the cladding. The frames themselves can then act as trims against which you can butt the cladding, obviating the need for edge trimming battens at these points. If you do not use prefabricated units, nail 75mm × 25mm linings to the door and window openings to frame them and to act as edge trimmers for the cladding.

Use two or three gate hinges for the outward-opening door of the shed, incorporating a thin batten on the closing side of the frame as a door stop. Quadrant moulding pinned to the reveals of the window openings is adequate as a rebate for the window panes. Bed the panes on a thin bed of putty to prevent them from rattling and use quadrant moulding on the external side of the pane too, again bedding the glass on a thin layer of putty.

Openable windows demand more care when you come to fit them You will need to build a casement for the panes, but you can hinge this at the top, bottom or sides according to your tastes.

Weatherproofing

The floor and lower parts of the frame are the most susceptible to damp and the weather, so make sure that you apply a liberal coat of preservative to the floor. The joists should also be soaked.

The most versatile and effective wood preservative is pentachlorophenol. You can paint or varnish over it whereas creosote stains the wood much darker and does not permit painting. Use an old paint brush to apply it to all the exposed surfaces of the wood, adding another coat 24 hours later. Pay particular attention to joints and endgrains making sure that the preservative coats as much and as liberally as possible. Be very careful when using any kind of preservative and make sure that you read the manu-facturers advice – especially on safety.

If you decide to paint the shed, apply at least two coats of waterproof paint after priming and undercoating the timber. Spread the paint liberally along all the joints in the shed.

Patios

A patio is a bridge between the inside and the outside of a house. Garden furniture, plants and flowers, ornamental fences, unusual statues and barbecues can all help to make a patio an extension of your living space

A patio adds charm and character to both your home and your garden. And as well as being one of the most attractive exterior home improvement features it adds greatly to the value of your house.

A large expanse of lawn needs a great deal of care and attention to keep it looking tidy and attractive. All too often it is either too wet or too soft to take tables and chairs—just when you want to do some outdoor entertaining.

Giving over part of your garden to a patio is a practical and reasonably in-expensive answer to such problems. A lot of traditional gardening chores are cut out and you will find the hard, level surface of the patio much easier to maintain.

Siting the patio

Ideally a patio should be approachable from the living room or dining room and also have access to the kitchen or conservatory to avoid bringing muddy shoes into your living areas.

If you are planning a barbecue on the patio, easy access to the kitchen is even more important because you will need to transport food and equipment. It might even be worth installing a door which opens directly on to the patio if one does not already exist.

The aspect of the patio needs to be considered in relation to privacy, out-look and, of course, sunshine. As you are most likely to sit outdoors during the afternoon, look for the area which gets most sunshine during this time. A sunny aspect is more important than a pleasing outlook—the latter can always be improved.

Right: *This wooden deck verandah patio has been given an air of sophistication by furnishing it with elegant wicker chairs and loungers. A profusion of exotic plants completes the effect*

Below: *A planter full of soft green plants provides a stunning focal point in this covered patio. Planters of this size are almost gardens in their own right*

Below: *A novel idea for the modern patio. The large picture window divides the indoor/outdoor pond, creating continuity between the inside and the outside of the house*

Right: *Sunken patios let more light into basement rooms and create areas which can be used for outdoor dining or a play space for the children where you can keep an eye on them*

Elizabeth Whiting

Michel Nahmias/Brigitte Baert

For example, if your house has a room jutting out which forms a sheltered L-shape and a natural corner, it might look like the ideal area in which to focus your activities. But if there is somewhere else which is sunnier for longer during the day, this would obviously be a more suitable spot for the patio.

So before you embark on constructing a new patio—or extending an existing one—observe the sunniest and least windy positions during the day. You may need to build a screen wall to give the area more privacy or even re-site a flower bed, but in the long term it is well worth the extra effort.

Size and shape

The size of your patio will depend to a large extent on the size of your garden, your family's needs and the activities you share. If you have a small town garden or suburban backyard, you might consider paving it over completely.

The most important thing is to keep the patio in balance with the house and the rest of the garden. A large patio in a small garden looks totally out of proportion—it would probably be better if the whole garden were paved over.

Plan the shape of your patio on a piece of graph paper, as you would an interior room and start by choosing a focal point around which to build. Consider the outlook from your living room window—maybe there is a tree worth retaining, or a banked-up rockery to lead the eye down to the main garden area.

Whatever you choose as a feature will affect the overall shape of the patio, so aim at balance and simplicity in relation to the proportions of your house. It is so easy to start out with ideas which are too fussy and then to include too many features. You may fancy a barbecue, fountain, a free-standing sculpture and an apple tree but if there is only room for one of these, choose the feature which is best suited to the practical use of the patio.

And when making your scale drawing bear in mind the size of the slabs or bricks you are going to lay. By designing your patio in multiples of whatever materials are to be used you will save a lot of difficulty cutting later on.

Style and design

Family life usually dictates the form of a patio. Different age groups have different needs, all of which you must bear in mind at the planning stage.

Tiny tots need to be safely enclosed and should have a play area which is visible from the house—preferably in a sheltered corner. A rectangular cavity inset into the patio could initially hold a playpen and later be made into a sandpit. Later still you might even consider turning it into a paddling pool. This would be easy to include in the initial plan, and need be no more than about 1.5m square.

Older children might appreciate the addition of a swing or slide or even a simple climbing apparatus. But if you plan to let your children play ball-games or ride tricycles on the patio, ensure there are no flower borders nearby which could get damaged.

Older people look more for privacy and shelter on their patio; somewhere to eat out of doors or enjoy a coffee or glass of wine. Even on dull days, a well-sheltered patio with plenty of colourful foliage or points of interest, offers you pleasant surroundings for a bit of relaxation in the fresh air.

Remember though that toys, cycles, gardening tools and furniture all need to be stored somewhere, in easy reach for day-to-day use. Lift-up bunker-style units are a better choice than a garden shed and can be easily incorporated into the initial patio layout.

Convert that narrow passageway into an excellent storage area. Simply pave or tile the passageway in the same material as the patio, and cover it with a reinforced glass roof. Use the corridor as a workshop and potting shed as well as a store for outdoor equipment.

Choosing materials

When you come to choose a flooring material for the patio, try to find one which blends in with the exterior of the house. Precast concrete slabs—which have a non-slip, durable surface—are a popular material because they are comparatively cheap and easy to lay. Available in various sizes and thicknesses, they come in shapes which range from rectangular to hexagonal and circular. Coloured slabs are also available, though they can look rather garish; cream or stone grey looks more natural.

Bear in mind that concrete slabs look quite different when they are wet so it is a good idea, when buying them, to ask to see them wet as well as dry.

You can lay the slabs in a variety of ways to create different patterns and textures—such as square, using slabs all of the same size, for instance, or a random effect, using different-sized rectangles. A rectangular shape, with infils of another material, such as brick or granite setts, can also look very effective.

Jointing is important, as it contributes to the overall look of the finished paving. A butt-joint, with the slabs placed as closely together as possible and infilled with mortar, is less likely to allow weeds and water to penetrate. But if you want to give the paving stones a more defined look, infil with either liquid grouting or a dry mix of sand and cement.

Cutting precast paving stones into any kind of curve can be costly and is not always possible. If curved areas are called for, say around a tree or flower bed, you would be better to use granite setts or bricks.

A mixture of bricks and pre-cast paving slabs is very appealing, particularly in a small area. But as bricks are expensive, you will probably only want to use a few of them in your design. Make sure the bricks you choose are hard enough to withstand damp and frost, and have a textured surface to prevent slipping.

Bricks are not strong enough for a driveway, but are ideal for a rear patio-cum-courtyard and can be laid in various patterns.

Granite setts are a similar shape to bricks, and useful for defining large

areas of paving. Like bricks, they can be set at an angle and in curves.

Cobble stones, egg-shaped in size, are ideal for decoration or for filling in awkward corners. But they are unpleasant to walk on so avoid laying them in a main thoroughfare. The stones are normally set close together in a dry bed of concrete or mortar over a prepared base, though you could also use them combined with water plants and loose-laid in a recess.

If the patio is designed to be an extension of your living area, try laying ceramic or quarry tiles. A wide range of floor tiles is now available and you could continue your choice through from indoors. However, although many ceramic floor tiles are frost-proof, it is not a good idea to lay them in an area which is entirely open to the elements.

Patio decor

A small patio needs a focus of attention. It may be a tree which you have carefully preserved in the centre, and encircled with a pattern of bricks or granite setts. Or you may choose to focus attention on a side or rear wall:

a green-painted trelliswork decorated with roses or clematis looks really outstanding against a wall of white-painted bricks or concrete.

Larger patios-cum-terraces often need the addition of a screen wall either to give more privacy, act as a windbreak or simply to obscure an ugly view. Pierced screen walling is ideal for these purposes, though it needs to be used in moderation or it will become overbearing. Otherwise, there is a wide variety of wooden screen panels available from garden centres.

A pergola with trailing vines and greenery makes an excellent decorative feature which also provides partial shelter for dining outside. You can slant wooden struts of the pergola to follow the roofline of the house or square them up into a rectangle.

Much of the fun in planning a patio comes when you introduce elements of surprise. For example a stone sculpture of a small child or animal lit from behind at night; or a tree hung with fairy lights, as if for a constant party.

Consider using unusual objects for display—an old wooden wheelbarrow painted in bright colours to match the

Above: *Enclosing a patio with a pergola or series of climbing frames allows you to scatter hanging plants around and creates cool, shady spots on hot days. Painted white they bring a fresh, cool feel to your patio and provide an excellent lounging area*
Right: *This paved-brick patio has been livened up by a dramatic fence sculpture and massive climbing screens. Plants provide colourful decoration and help to disguise ugly pipes. Even the most boring patios will benefit from such imaginative treatments of fences and accessories*

Elizabeth Whiting

flowers perhaps. Or maybe a circle of round beer barrels, cut down into different heights and painted green. You could plant a laurel tree at the highest level in the rear, softer plants in the middle sections and perhaps some herbs and lettuces nearest the ground level.

Use wooden tubs to hold bay trees or hanging baskets for ferns and ivies. Or use even more unusual containers like old chimney pots, disused hay racks, a shapely Victorian hip bath or an old-fashioned pram. Remember that the more ordinary the space, the more you can liven it up in this way.

Dining out of doors
If you plan to do a lot of outdoor cooking and entertaining, a barbecue is a must and can easily be incorporated into the patio layout.

Commercial barbecues range from the simplest of constructions to the highly elaborate canopied types or wheel-around trollies which come equipped like a portable kitchen. But you might prefer to build your own barbecue from brick—perhaps a simple H-shape inset with a rectangular metal grid for cooking. Remember to allow plenty of horizontal space for plates, foodstuff and cooking utensils to keep everything tidy and in one spot.

Furniture for a patio is available in all shapes and sizes and in materials ranging from cast-iron and aluminium to wood, PVC and canvas. You can also buy fully upholstered sun loungers, though these can be rather expensive.

Decorative paving

Pathways are often left until last in the overall design of a garden. They end up as functional elements of the design rather than the decorative accents they could so easily become—with a little thought and planning

Alan R. Smith

Barnaby's Picture Library

Your garden path need not be a simple strip of concrete. By using unusual materials which blend in naturally with the surroundings, you can create a pathway which is an attractive feature of the garden and is not purely a functional necessity.

Using bricks

Bricks are a natural alternative to concrete, being both easy to lay and very durable.

Available as special paving bricks (**see picture left**) or simply as regular building site material—such as the hard engineering bricks **above**—bricks come in so many colours and textures that they can blend in with any type of garden.

For instance, the patterned red paving bricks **left,** provide a subtle contrast to the predominantly green and woody shrubs and plants. Just imagine what a simple concrete path would have looked like. The natural texture and warmth of the red bricks adds significantly to the overall atmosphere of the garden. They are by no means

240

Elizabeth Whiting

way of breaking up what might otherwise be a cold expanse of grey across the width of the patio.

The path across the lush grass lawn **below** could have been laid simply as a straight line with parallel sides; but how much better to stagger the pattern in semi-geometric steps, giving the effect of a winding pathway without elaborate curves.

Wooden paths

Usually, the first choice for paving material is some kind of stone, or other hard, rock-like covering. It is not generally realized that deep wooden beams can be just as effective. They are even simpler to lay than bricks—the best kind of wood to use being scrap or driftwood, which is cheap and easily obtainable.

As long as the wooden beams are thoroughly soaked in preservative before they are laid, a properly designed wooden pathway can take many years of wear.

But the ideal bedding material for a wooden walkway is a spread of gravel or small pebbles as in the picture, **top centre, overleaf.**

Well seasoned old wooden beams can be embedded in such material either by digging deep grooves in an existing sweep of stones or by laying the wood on the bare ground and then infilling with carefully graded pebbles to pack down the beams tightly against each other. Vary the lengths of each slat to get a ragged edge to the

a material for just another path!

Similarly the path **above left** has been laid with neutral coloured bricks to set off and enhance the bright flowers which line its length.

In this case bright red bricks would have been distracting. These bricks have been laid in mortar but most paving bricks can be laid simply on a bed of sand that has been well tamped down and compressed.

Full techniques of laying bricks and paving stones to make a pathway can be easily acquired.

Paving stones

Unlike brick, paving stones are usually fairly neutral or pastel coloured and to make the most of their special appeal they should be laid in interesting patterns.

They are the ideal paving materials for small gardens and patios and if they are laid as in the picture **above** they can allow quite a bit of greenery to spill over into any confined space. Using grass as a filler between staggered slabs is a particularly effective

Michael Warren

path and add that characteristically rustic, weathered look.

The pathway **below** has a bed of stones on one side, a lawn on the other and provides a natural link between two different areas of activity in the garden.

The beams have been laid lengthways to create a tidier effect than those in the picture **right** and a series of wooden steps links this section of the path to a conventional concrete type around the edge of the lawn.

Wooden paths age very differently from the brick or concrete varieties, developing a thin covering of moss and lichen. Although this can often add to their charm, such growths should be cleared from the actual trodden part of the path as they can be slippery in wet weather. Mossy borders, on the other hand, look delightful.

Pebbles, stones and mosaics

Beds of pebbles such as those in the pictures **left** and **above** are an easy way to cover large areas of ground where plants will not grow, because the ground is shady or otherwise unsuitable. Pebbles graded according to size and colour can be bought from specialist garden centres and sometimes from builders' suppliers. If you have the patience, a mosaic path made from finely graded pebbles can look very attractive, and almost Mediterranean in style (**above right**).

The small pebbles should be embedded in a screed of wet concrete and it is important to choose each stone carefully—setting it against its neighbours so that an even surface is produced overall.

A rough stone path such as that in the picture **right** is not as easy to lay

as it might at first appear. The stones are readily available from quarries and suppliers of rubble and hardcore, but you must choose each stone very carefully, looking for a flat surface which can be laid uppermost.

When they are laid, each slab must butt as closely as possible with the stones around it and the whole surface must be as level as possible. Properly laid, however, rough stone paths look very attractive and are particularly suited for gardens full of bushes and trees. They have an old-fashioned, country feel and lend an air of age and maturity to any garden, however small. Part of their charm is the weeds and plants that sprout up in the cracks but again, such growths are best cut back every so often or they will engulf the whole path and become a safety hazard in damp and wet weather.

Choosing your paving

If you are thinking of relaying one of your garden paths or even laying a completely new one, consider the various areas of the garden through which it will run.

There is no strict rule that says the nature of the path must be the same along its whole length. You can use one or more of the ideas discussed here to blend in the path with the surrounding aspects of the garden.

Photographs: Elizabeth Whiting

Dig a garden pond

Making a garden pond is not the daunting task it might at first seem. If you can dig a hole you can build a pond using an inexpensive stretch rubber liner

A simple garden pond is very easy to build—all you need is a hole in the ground dug to your chosen shape and lined with butyl rubber sheet, a tough durable material easily obtainable from specialist water garden centres.

Location is important. A pond looks best when sited at the lowest part of your garden, where water would collect naturally. But it is important to site the pond in full sunlight to maintain healthy plant growth, so you should avoid areas which are in the shade of walls or trees. Remember, a pond sited under or near trees will quickly clog with leaves in the autumn. If you plan to include a cascade feature, you will also need a waterproof electricity supply for the pump.

Dig the hole any shape you like provided you keep the basic dimensions of the butyl rubber liner (in Britain, 4m x 3m). You should follow the stepped profile of the sides as shown overleaf, including the planting shelf, which provides a suitable environment for plants which thrive in shallower water. The overall depth of the pond is to some extent optional, but should not be less than about 350mm. A good average is about 500mm.

When the pond has been lined and filled, paving stones are used to conceal the edges of the liner and to provide a firm surround. If you want a simpler pond, it can be left at this stage, but the design overleaf also incorporates a rockery and cascade.

The rockery is formed by the spoil from the excavation, covered with boulders. The cascade is easily arranged using a special waterproof pump and a small preformed fibreglass pool.

You should leave the filled pond for about one week before installing plants or stocking with fish. Water plants prefer still or slow-moving water, so you should plant them in the calmer areas of the pond. Line the bottom of the pond with 200mm of plain fibreless loam. Do not use leaf mould or manure, as these give off gases which are poisonous to fish. Alternatively, you can plant in special containers available from garden shops. These have a thin layer of gravel on top to prevent the plants from floating.

Different plants thrive at different depths. Marginals, like irises and arrowheads should be planted on the shelf. Lilies and other deep water aquatics go in the deeper part of the pond. Floating aquatic plants can just be placed on the surface of the water. Plant sparingly—remember that the plants will spread.

If you are stocking the pond with fish, such as goldfish or golden orfe, spread a thin layer of gravel in the bottom of the pond. Feed the fish sparingly and do not overstock a small pond. In winter prevent icing over with a couple of layers of rush matting—fish suffocate without air.

Allow the water a few weeks to clear and achieve its natural balance. A healthy pond should be clear and clean. Rockery plants will add interest to the border, but make sure that soil does not wash into the pond. Make sure, too, that no other forms of garden debris contaminate the water.

Right: *A water feature adds interest to any garden, particularly when it is well stocked with water plants, as this one is*

Design your own pond

It is easy to adapt the basic pond building technique to suit your own design. These three alternatives all use the same basic method of lining the excavation with a butyl rubber sheet to retain water. If the overall dimensions are similar, you can use the same sized sheet. A larger pond will need a larger sheet in proportion, but other constructional details are the same.

The first alternative, in a contemporary style, combines the pond with a large paved area. This is easy to build, as no pump is needed.

In a formal style, the second design uses a fountain which is obtainable from garden centres.

The last design is a very large version built on a mound or bank.

Workplan

Materials needed for basic pond:
4m x 3m butyl rubber sheet in black or a stone colour
Crazy paving slabs to cover 7m²
Sandstone boulders for rockery
Bricks for surround (approx 50)
Sand and cement as required
For pond with cascade feature:
Submersible pump
Plastic hose
Weatherproof electrical connector
Small preformed fibreglass pool
Weatherproof armoured cable to reach domestic electrical supply. This should be connected via a fused spur connector or wired into the consumer unit (main fuse box) at a spare way. It can be disguised in the undergrowth

Use the designs on this page to build this delightful pond with paved surround a rockery and double water cascade

Pumps and special waterproof cables are available from specialist water garden centres. Fit a submersible pump in the lower pool with a concealed pipe running to the upper pool. Use a special waterproof cable sealed into the pump under the water with a waterproof connector near the pool. This should be permanently wired into the house electricity supply with a special outdoor waterproof armoured cable. Bury this out of reach of digging, cultivators, etc (at least 500mm deep) or route it along a fence

Use the excavated earth and boulders to form a rockery, leaving a hole for a small pre-formed glassfibre pool. The hole should be slightly larger than the pool itself. Install the pool and pack earth all round the sides, making sure that the pool is level. Use boulders to conceal the edges.

Sandstone is particularly suitable for rockeries. Use as large stones as possible and place them close together. Rock plants thrive on small cracks and crevices

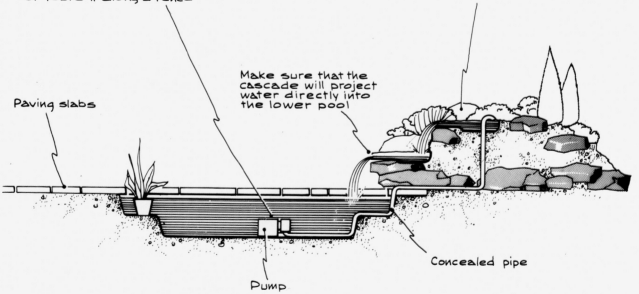

Paving slabs

Make sure that the cascade will project water directly into the lower pool

Concealed pipe

Pump

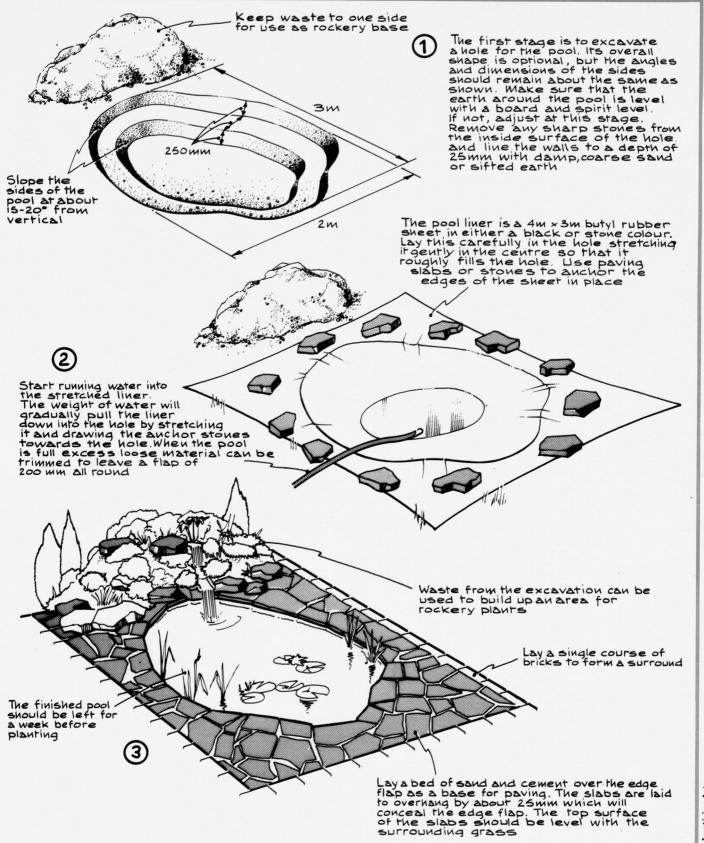

Keep waste to one side for use as rockery base

1 The first stage is to excavate a hole for the pool. Its overall shape is optional, but the angles and dimensions of the sides should remain about the same as shown. Make sure that the earth around the pool is level with a board and spirit level. If not, adjust at this stage. Remove any sharp stones from the inside surface of the hole, and line the walls to a depth of 25mm with damp, coarse sand or sifted earth

3m

250mm

Slope the sides of the pool at about 15-20° from vertical

2m

The pool liner is a 4m × 3m butyl rubber sheet in either a black or stone colour. Lay this carefully in the hole stretching it gently in the centre so that it roughly fills the hole. Use paving slabs or stones to anchor the edges of the sheet in place

2 Start running water into the stretched liner. The weight of water will gradually pull the liner down into the hole by stretching it and drawing the anchor stones towards the hole. When the pool is full excess loose material can be trimmed to leave a flap of 200 mm all round

Waste from the excavation can be used to build up an area for rockery plants

Lay a single course of bricks to form a surround

The finished pool should be left for a week before planting

3

Lay a bed of sand and cement over the edge flap as a base for paving. The slabs are laid to overhang by about 25mm which will conceal the edge flap. The top surface of the slabs should be level with the surrounding grass

Index